TRANSNATIONAL FILM REMAKES

Traditions in World Cinema

General Editors
Linda Badley (Middle Tennessee State
    University)
R. Barton Palmer (Clemson University)

Founding Editor
Steven Jay Schneider (New York
    University)

Titles in the series include:

Traditions in World Cinema
by Linda Badley, R. Barton Palmer and
    Steven Jay Schneider (eds)

Japanese Horror Cinema
by Jay McRoy (ed.)

New Punk Cinema
by Nicholas Rombes (ed.)

African Filmmaking
by Roy Armes

Palestinian Cinema
by Nurith Gertz and George Khleifi

Czech and Slovak Cinema
by Peter Hames

The New Neapolitan Cinema
by Alex Marlow-Mann

American Smart Cinema
by Claire Perkins

The International Film Musical
by Corey Creekmur and Linda Mokdad
    (eds)

Italian Neorealist Cinema
by Torunn Haaland

*Magic Realist Cinema in East Central
    Europe*
by Aga Skrodzka

Italian Post-Neorealist Cinema
by Luca Barattoni

Spanish Horror Film
by Antonio Lázaro-Reboll

Post-beur Cinema
by Will Higbee

New Taiwanese Cinema in Focus
by Flannery Wilson

International Noir
by Homer B. Pettey and R. Barton Palmer
    (eds)

Films on Ice
by Scott MacKenzie and Anna Westerståhl
    Stenport (eds)

Nordic Genre Film
by Tommy Gustafsson and Pietari Kääpä
    (eds)

*Contemporary Japanese Cinema Since
    Hana-Bi*
by Adam Bingham

Chinese Martial Arts Cinema 2nd edn
by Stephen Teo

Expressionism in Cinema
by Olaf Brill and Gary D. Rhodes (eds)

*French-language Road Cinema: Borders,
    Diasporas, Migration and 'New
    Europe'*
by Michael Gott

Slow Cinema
by Tiago de Luca and Nuno Barradas
    Jorge (eds)

Transnational Film Remakes
by Iain Robert Smith and Constantine
    Verevis (eds)

www.edinburghuniversitypress.com/series/tiwc

TRANSNATIONAL FILM REMAKES

Edited by Iain Robert Smith
and Constantine Verevis

EDINBURGH
University Press

For mum, who let me stay up late and watch Godzilla films at an
impressionable age
IRS

For Mia, my SCMS buddy
CV

We publish academic books and journals in our selected subject areas across the
humanities and social sciences, combining cutting-edge scholarship with high editorial
and production values to produce academic works of lasting importance. For more
information visit our website: edinburghuniversitypress.com

Edinburgh University Press Ltd
The Tun – Holyrood Road
12 (2f) Jackson's Entry
Edinburgh EH8 8PJ

Typeset in 10/12.5 pt Sabon by
Servis Filmsetting Ltd, Stockport, Cheshire
and printed and bound in Great Britain by
CPI Group (UK) Ltd, Croydon CR0 4YY

A CIP record for this book is available from the British Library

ISBN 978 1 4744 0723 6 (hardback)
ISBN 978 1 4744 0724 3 (paperback)
ISBN 978 1 4744 0725 0 (webready PDF)
ISBN 978 1 4744 0726 7 (epub)

CONTENTS

ILLUSTRATIONS

TRADITIONS IN WORLD CINEMA

General editors: **Linda Badley and R. Barton Palmer**
Founding editor: **Steven Jay Schneider**

Traditions in World Cinema is a series of textbooks and monographs devoted to the analysis of currently popular and previously underexamined or under-valued film movements from around the globe. Also intended for general inter-est readers, the textbooks in this series offer undergraduate- and graduate-level film students accessible and comprehensive introductions to diverse traditions in world cinema. The monographs open up for advanced academic study more specialised groups of films, including those that require theoretically oriented approaches. Both textbooks and monographs provide thorough examinations of the industrial, cultural, and socio-historical conditions of production and reception.

The flagship textbook for the series includes chapters by noted scholars on traditions of acknowledged importance (the French New Wave, German Expressionism), recent and emergent traditions (New Iranian, post-Cinema Novo), and those whose rightful claim to recognition has yet to be established (the Israeli persecution film, global found footage cinema). Other volumes concentrate on individual national, regional or global cinema traditions. As the introductory chapter to each volume makes clear, the films under discussion form a coherent group on the basis of substantive and relatively transparent, if not always obvious, commonalities. These commonalities may be formal, sty-listic or thematic, and the groupings may, although they need not, be popularly identified as genres, cycles or movements (Japanese horror, Chinese martial arts cinema, Italian Neorealism). Indeed, in cases in which a group of films is not already commonly identified as a tradition, one purpose of the volume is to establish its claim to importance and make it visible (East Central European Magical Realist cinema, Palestinian cinema).

Textbooks and monographs include:

- An introduction that clarifies the rationale for the grouping of films under examination
- A concise history of the regional, national, or transnational cinema in question
- A summary of previous published work on the tradition
- Contextual analysis of industrial, cultural and socio-historical conditions of production and reception
- Textual analysis of specific and notable films, with clear and judicious application of relevant film theoretical approaches
- Bibliograph(ies)/filmograph(ies)

Monographs may additionally include:

- Discussion of the dynamics of cross-cultural exchange in light of current research and thinking about cultural imperialism and globalisation, as well as issues of regional/national cinema or political/ aesthetic movements (such as new waves, postmodernism, or identity politics)
- Interview(s) with key filmmakers working within the tradition.

INTRODUCTION:
TRANSNATIONAL FILM REMAKES

Iain Robert Smith and Constantine Verevis

On 14 April 2016, Paramount Pictures released the first image of actress Scarlett Johansson in the lead role of the science-fiction film *Ghost in the Shell* (2017). This promotional image generated a great deal of controversy online, with much of the attention focused upon the decision to cast a white actress in the central role of cyborg Major Motoko Kusanagi. This criticism was part of a wider critique of 'whitewashing' within Hollywood where white actors are cast in non-white roles – other notable examples include Mickey Rooney in *Breakfast at Tiffany's* (1961) and Emma Stone in *Aloha* (2015) – yet this particular instance was especially controversial as *Ghost in the Shell* is a Hollywood remake of a 1995 Japanese anime (and manga) and therefore raised further issues surrounding planned changes to the source text. In fact, many of the initial reports on the controversy (Abad-Santos 2016; Child 2016; Loughrey 2016) cited a series of tweets by comic-book writer Jon Tsuei in which he expressed concern that the Hollywood remake would lose the cultural resonance that the source text's themes have with Japan's post-World War II history. Central to Tsuei's argument was the notion that *Ghost in the Shell* is a text deeply rooted in a specific era of Japanese technological development, and that it should therefore be understood as 'inherently a Japanese story, not a universal one' (Tsuei 2016a). Consequently, Tsuei's objection was not only to the casting of a white actress in the lead role but also to the very decision to produce a Hollywood remake, arguing that 'You can "Westernize" the story if you want, but at that point it is no longer Ghost in The Shell because the story is simply not Western' (Tsuei 2016b). This intervention generated a substantial amount of online debate, and was soon followed by an influential article on *Nerds of Color* that argued that 'the relevance *Ghost in the Shell* has to Japanese culture is something that should be honoured in any live-action production' and that, by producing this kind of remake, 'Hollywood is destroying what makes properties like these special and valuable' (Jones 2016).

There were a number of commentators, however, who felt that the notion of an inherently Japanese text as posited by Tsuei and Jones was itself problematic and somewhat essentialist. Ryu Spaeth in *New Republic*, for example, drew attention to the lengthy history of transnational influences and exchanges that helped shape the development of Japanese anime and manga, and he argued that this process complicates ideas of a 'quintessentially Japanese story' (Spaeth 2016). Similarly, producer Steven Paul responded to the controversy by defending the choices of the Hollywood studio, stating, 'I don't think [the source text] was just a Japanese story. *Ghost in the Shell* was a very international story' (quoted in Cheng 2016). Indeed, it is notable that Masamune Shirow's original manga and Mamoru Oshii's 1995 anime adaptation exhibit the influence of numerous globally circulating intertexts including Arthur Koestler's *The Ghost in the Machine* (1967), Ridley Scott's *Blade Runner* (1982) and William Gibson's *Neuromancer* (1984). It may be a Japanese text that is embedded in local anxieties regarding post-war Japanese society, yet it is also a multivalent cultural text that incorporates numerous cross-cultural influences from around the world. Furthermore, it is evident that *Ghost in the Shell* has had a considerable transnational influence beyond Japan, with Hollywood films such as the Wachowski's *The Matrix* (1999) and James Cameron's *Avatar* (2009) owing a significant debt to Oshii's film. This tension, between an understanding of *Ghost in the Shell* as an 'inherently' Japanese text that needs to be situated and understood primarily within its Japanese context and a reading that points to its place within a global history of cultural exchange, is indicative of the complexity of the transnational film remake and the broader cultural issues that are raised by this form of cinematic repetition. Remakes are often dismissed within critical discourse as unoriginal, derivative and inferior to their source texts, yet this mode of critique takes on additional layers of meaning when films are remade transnationally as this process raises further issues surrounding national and/or ethnic identity and questions of cultural power.

In order to investigate these kinds of complexities, this collection of original essays focuses its attention on the phenomenon of transnational film remakes and the wider social and cultural issues that they raise. What happens when a film is remade in another national context? To what extent can a film embedded within one cultural context be adapted for another? How might a transnational perspective offer us a deeper understanding of a specific socio-political context, and of the politics underpinning film remaking more generally? Given the increasing emphasis on reworking existing material within global film (and screen) culture, there is a pressing need for scholarship to address this phenomenon in a rigorous and systematic way. While there have been a number of recent monographs and edited collections that have studied film remakes (for example, Mazdon 2000; Verevis 2006; Zanger 2007; Loock and Verevis 2012), this is the first book to focus specifically on transnational film remakes and to engage with case studies drawn from across the globe. Of course, this is not to say that scholars have been ignoring transnational film remakes – indeed, there is already a growing body of literature on the topic – but that these interventions have tended to be within publications devoted to individual national cinemas or to the phenomenon of film remakes more generally. With much contemporary scholarship shifting away from considerations of the national in order to investigate the transnational dimensions of cinema, this book is therefore designed to bring together these myriad perspectives in order to provide a more inclusive account of transnational film remaking across the globe.

Before outlining the various ways in which the chapters in this collection make an intervention, it is important that we first address the existing scholarship and the debates that have been taking place over the last couple of decades. Given the Hollywood-centrism of film remake scholarship, and film studies more broadly, it is perhaps no surprise that the majority of publications dealing with transnational film remakes have focused on Hollywood remakes of films from other national contexts. Indeed, given the ways in which the relationship between Hollywood and Europe has traditionally been framed, it should also come as no surprise that the cinematic exchanges that have attracted the most critical attention have been Hollywood remakes of European cinema, and especially those derived from French source texts. In *European Cinema: Face to Face with Hollywood*, Thomas Elsaesser discusses the oppositions that often structure comparisons between Europe and America, in which 'Europe stands for art, and the US for pop; Europe for high culture, America for mass entertainment; Europe for artisanal craft, America for industrial mass production' (2005: 300), and it is clear that much of the initial wave of scholarship on remakes was designed to challenge exactly these kinds of simplistic binaries. Lucy Mazdon's *Encore Hollywood: Remaking French Cinema*, for example, proposes a decisive shift away from criticism that frames Hollywood remakes as a 'one-way, vertical trajectory from the high art of the French "original" to the popular commercialism of the American "copy"' (2000: 5), and replaces this instead with a model based around 'intertextuality and hybridity' (27). Mazdon's work, alongside Carolyn A. Durham's *Double Takes: Culture and Gender in French Films and Their American Remakes* (1998) and David I. Grossvogel's *Didn't You Used to Be Depardieu?: Film as Cultural Marker in France and Hollywood* (2002), also helped establish many of the key case studies used to explore cross-cultural relationships, including such examples as *À bout de souffle* (1960) / *Breathless* (1983), *La Cage aux folles* (1978) / *The Birdcage* (1996), *Trois Hommes et un couffin* (1985) / *Three Men and a Baby* (1987), and *La Femme Nikita* (1990) / *The Assassin* (1993). *Breathless* is perhaps the most discussed example (see also Gripsrud 1992; Wills 1998; and Evans 2014a), although there has been further scholarship on the remake of *La Femme Nikita* (Grindstaff 2002) and *La Cage aux folles* (Hanet 2012) in addition to more recent case studies such as *L'Appartement* (1996) / *Wicker Park* (2004) (Hanet, 2010). A broad range of methodological approaches have also been used in order to interrogate the topic of Hollywood remakes of French cinema. For example, Harney (2002) discusses the relationship between economics and aesthetics in the critical dismissal of such films; Welsch (2000) focuses upon the different uses of film sound in Jean Renoir's *La Chienne* (1931) and Fritz Lang's *Scarlett Street* (1945); Park (2009) emphasises the role that copyright plays within remakes of French and Japanese cinema; Williams (2002) uses the remakes of *Le voile bleu* (1942) and *Le Corbeau* (1943) to discuss the 'benefits and pitfalls of transcultural bricolage' (2002: 152); and Verevis (2012) employs the self-reflexive, faux-documentary strategy of *H Story* (2000) – a film about a (failed) Japanese remake of *Hiroshima mon amour* (1959) – to make an ontological point about the potential multiplicity of remakes and cinema in general. Despite the diversity of these approaches, however, there has nevertheless been a consistent attempt within the academic scholarship on Hollywood remakes of French cinema to challenge the ways in which such texts have traditionally been maligned and dismissed within critical discourse.

While much of the initial work on the phenomenon of the transnational film remake has centred on French cinema, there has also been a substantial amount of scholarship on Hollywood remakes derived from other European cinemas, although it should be noted that the coverage has tended to be less comprehensive. For example, despite provision of the source texts for a considerable number of Hollywood remakes, there has been relatively little written about Hollywood remakes of German cinema. There are some exceptions, such as Jones (2005) on *Der Himmel über Berlin* (1987) / *City of Angels* (1998) and a number of articles discussing Michael Haneke's auto-remake of *Funny Games* (1997) / *Funny Games* (2007) (see Monk 2010, Hantke 2010, and Messier 2014), yet there has been relatively little to date on further examples such as *Viktor und Viktoria* (1933) / *Victor Victoria* (1982), *Bella Martha* (2001) / *No Reservations* (2007) and *Das Experiment* (2001) / *The Experiment* (2010). Coverage of remakes from other major European countries has also been rather sparse, with Carolan (2014) on Hollywood remakes of Italian cinema being one of the few works to deal with that process, while the scholarship on remakes of Spanish cinema tends to focus on *Abre los ojos*

(1997) / *Vanilla Sky* (2001) (see White 2003 and Smith 2004) and scholarship on remakes of Dutch cinema tends to focus on *Spoorloos* (1988) / *The Vanishing* (1993) (see Schneider 2002 and Varndell 2014) with few attempts to discuss wider trends within those particular national cinemas. Nevertheless, the aforementioned piece from Schneider also discusses the remake of the Danish film *Nightwatch* (1994) and is therefore part of a growing body of work on Hollywood remakes of Nordic cinema. Stenport (2016), for example, provides an overview of numerous recent remakes of Nordic cinema from *Insomnia* (1997) / *Insomnia* (2002) through to *Let the Right One In* (2008) / *Let Me In* (2010), while Gemzøe (2013) focuses specifically on *Brødre* (2004) / *Brothers* (2009), and Archer (2012/13) and Mazdon (2015) discuss *The Girl with the Dragon Tattoo* (2009) / *The Girl with the Dragon Tattoo* (2011). Much of this scholarship centres on recent examples, reflecting the current trend within Hollywood for reworking Nordic texts, although there has also been scholarship that looks at earlier examples of this phenomenon such as Brashinsky (1998) discussing Wes Craven's *Last House on the Left* (1972) as a loose remake of Ingmar Bergman's *Virgin Spring* (1960).

Before the recent trend for Nordic remakes, however, it was East Asian cinema that was to provide the source for numerous Hollywood remakes, and this has been the subject of an already substantial body of scholarship. Much of the attention has been on Japanese cinema, with *Ringu* (1998) / *The Ring* (2002) acting as the primary case study for numerous articles discussing this trend (see Balmain 2004, Hills 2005, Stringer 2007, Rawle 2010 and Wee 2011). The most comprehensive study of this phenomenon is Wee's subsequent book on *Japanese Horror Films and Their American Remakes* (2014), which supplemented her analysis of *The Ring* with further case studies such as those on *Dark Water* (2002) / *Dark Water* (2005), *Ju-On: The Grudge* (2002) / *The Grudge* (2004), and *Kairo* (2001) / *Pulse* (2006). Meanwhile, Wierzbicki has been examining the sonic content of Hollywood remakes of Japanese horror in order to demonstrate that while the remakes may look quite similar they often sound remarkably different (2010, 2015), and Crawford has used a philosophical framework in order to highlight the 'valuable cultural overlapping' (2016: 113) that these remakes represent. The focus within this body of work has tended to be on the late 1990s and early 2000s crop of J-Horror remakes, although David Desser's (2008) chapter on remakes of *Seven Samurai* (1954) puts this phenomenon into a historical perspective, tracing the transnational influence of the Japanese classic within American texts such as *The Magnificent Seven* (1960) and *Battle Beyond the Stars* (1980), and also within other national contexts such as Hong Kong (*Seven Swords*, 2005) and India (*China Gate*, 1998). Similarly, Rachael Hutchinson's work on Kurosawa remakes complicates the model of a unidirectional transnational film remake, framing *Yojimbo* (1961) / *A Fistful of Dollars* (1964) in relation to the

American Western genre and providing a model for rethinking these kinds of remakes as part of a 'dialogue within a wider film genre' (2007: 172).

While Hollywood remakes of Japanese cinema have received more attention, the rise of China's film industry and its increasing interactions with Hollywood are the subject of a number of recent publications. Kenneth Chan's *Remade in Hollywood: The Global Chinese Presence in Transnational Cinemas* (2009), for example, discusses Hollywood remakes of Chinese cinemas in relation to the broader post-1997 surge in Chinese visibility in Hollywood. Similarly, Jinhua Li's *Transnational Remakes: Gender and Politics in Chinese Cinemas and Hollywood* (2011) and Yiman Wang's *Remaking Chinese Cinema: Through the Prism of Shanghai, Hong Kong, and Hollywood* (2013) use the subject of transnational film remakes in order to interrogate the larger political dynamics underpinning these processes. In addition, there have been a number of articles interrogating specific remakes of Chinese-language films such as *Infernal Affairs* (2002) / *The Departed* (2006) (Li 2014, Lüthe 2015) and *Eat Drink Man Woman* (1994) / *Tortilla Soup* (2001) (Li 2016). It is important to note, however, that the scholarship on East Asian remakes has not been limited to case studies drawn from Japan and China. Leung (2013), for example, discusses the South Korean case study *A Tale of Two Sisters* (2003) / *The Uninvited* (2009), while Lim (2007), Xu (2008), Wang (2010) and Klein (2010) discuss the broader phenomenon of Hollywood remakes of East Asian cinema across a range of national contexts. Moreover, while France and Japan, and by extension Europe and East Asia, have been the focus of the majority of remake scholarship, there has been some limited work on Hollywood remakes from other regions such as Russia in *Solaris* (1972) / *Solaris* (2002) (Verevis 2009) and Brazil in *Doña Flor and Her Two Husbands* (1966) / *Kiss Me Goodbye* (1982) (Edinger 1991). The body of work on Hollywood remakes of world cinema is continuing to grow and develop although, as this account indicates, there has been a tendency for the phenomenon to be discussed in relation to specific national or regional cinemas. One of the few scholars to attempt a more comprehensive account of Hollywood remakes of world cinema has been Daniel Herbert in his Ph.D. dissertation *Transnational Film Remakes: Time, Space, Identity* (2008) and his published articles derived from that research (2006, 2009, 2010). In addition to theorising the transnational film remake, Herbert provides a detailed historical account of Hollywood remakes of European and East Asian cinemas, and one of his key interventions is in investigating the struggle for power that these texts represent. In his own words, 'As privileged articulations of globalization, transnational film remakes speak to vast interconnections among cultural spheres, yet simultaneously efface alternate paths and disavow those connections that do no serve dominant interests' (2008: 455). Interrogating the politics of these globalising processes, Herbert's work helps draw attention to the dominant position of Hollywood in shaping these practices of transnational film remaking and teases out the implications that this has in terms of global power dynamics.

When we turn our attention to remakes produced in the opposite trajectory, where Hollywood functions as the source text for films produced in other national industries, these political issues become even more acute. Given the ways in which Hollywood's influence throughout the globe is often framed as a form of cultural imperialism and/or Americanisation, scholars have been exploring the diverse ways in which these globally circulating Hollywood texts have been adapted and transformed in other national contexts. Smith (2016), for example, proposes the metaphor of the 'Hollywood meme' as a way to investigate the global spread of Hollywood and focuses on remakes produced within the film industries of Turkey, India and the Philippines. This is one of the few attempts at a comparative transnational account of the phenomenon, however, as the majority of the scholarship in this area focuses on reworkings of Hollywood within a single national context. The most complete account of the remakes produced in Turkey, for example, appears in Savas Arslan's *Cinema in Turkey* (2011), while individual articles have focused on specific case studies such as *Dünyayı Kurtaran Adam* (1982) / *Star Wars* (1977) (Erdoğan 2003), *Turist Ömer Uzay Yolunda* (1973) / *Star Trek* (1966–) (Smith 2008a), and *Şeytan* (1974) / *The Exorcist* (1973) (Özkaracalar 2003, Smith 2008b). There have also been overview articles discussing the broader phenomenon of Turkish remakes from Gürata (2006) and Raw (2016) that help situate these examples in relation to the traditions of Yeşilçam, the popular cinema of Turkey.

This cycle of Turkish remakes was largely confined to the 1960s to 1980s, so it is notable that Indian cinema, and especially the Mumbai-based Bollywood industry, has a long tradition of remaking Hollywood cinema that continues to the present day. Much of the scholarship discussing Indian remakes has focused on the post-1990s context, unsurprising perhaps given that the trend towards remaking became so prevalent in that period that 'ninety percent of the Hindi movies in production in August of 1993 were remakes' (Nayar 1997: 74). As Rosie Thomas has noted, popular Indian cinema has often been perceived as 'nightmarishly lengthy, second-rate copies of Hollywood trash' (1985: 117), and there is a marked attempt within the scholarship on Indian remakes (for example, Nayar 1997, 2003; Alessio and Langer 2007; Wright 2009; Krämer 2015a, 2015b) to challenge these kinds of dismissals and to draw attention to the numerous ways in which texts have been adapted for the Indian cultural context. This is often framed as a process of Indianisation in which 'the Bollywood remake becomes a simple act of translating a Hollywood film into Hindi by reconstructing its narrative to conform to Indian cultural practices' (Richards 2011: 342). The majority of these studies are text-based and comparative, as indeed are the majority of studies of transnational film remakes more generally, although it is notable that the anthropologist Tejaswini Ganti offers an alternative model in her research by drawing on first-hand observations of filmmakers as they prepare and produce transnational remakes, focusing on the ways in which Hindi filmmakers 'operate as cultural mediators, evaluating the appropriateness for their audiences of stories, characterizations and themes from certain Hollywood films' (2002: 283). Such an approach helps complicate the model of Indianisation as it draws attention to the role of filmmakers in mediating that process, and therefore helps challenge models of transnational film remaking that see this as a straightforward practice in which a text is reworked largely to conform with a different cultural context.

The bulk of scholarship in this area has focused on the contexts of Turkey and India, but it is important to note that these are not the only national traditions to produce remakes of Hollywood cinema. There has been a growing body of work on Chinese-language remakes of Hollywood such as *Cellular* (2004) / *Connected* (2008) and *Blood Simple* (1984) / *A Woman, a Gun and a Noodle Shop* (2009) (see Aufderheide 1998; He 2010; Evans 2014b). Meanwhile, Philippine remakes of Hollywood are discussed in Capino (2006); Korean remakes of Hollywood are analysed in Diffrient (2009) and Chung and Diffrient (2015); Brazilian reworkings of *High Noon* (1952) and *Jaws* (1975) are discussed in Vieira (1995); the Japanese remake of *Sideways* (2004) is discussed in Griffin (2014); while the Nigerian remake of *Titanic* (1997) is analysed in both Behrend (2009) and Krings (2015). This process of transnational film remaking is therefore far from being a practice restricted to specific national industries, but something that has occurred in the majority of established film industries around the globe.

Nevertheless, as this survey of scholarship on transnational film remakes suggests, even if we were to put to one side the substantial body of work on Hollywood remakes of Hollywood films, it is still notable just how Hollywood-centric this scholarship has been. While there have been some exceptions (for example, Shin (2012) on Japanese remakes of Korean cinema; Bergfelder and Cargnelli (2008) on British remakes of German cinema; Smith (2013) on Bollywood remakes of Korean cinema), it is nevertheless the case that the majority of scholarship on transnational film remakes deals to some extent with Hollywood. This partly reflects Hollywood's dominance within global processes of cultural dissemination, of course, but it may be time for scholarship to start addressing other remake trajectories. It is also evident that scholarship on the transnational film remake has tended to be published within books and journals focused on a specific national industry, and often with little discussion of parallel examples within other contexts. By investigating a variety of case studies of transnational film remakes and locating them within the current debates surrounding remake studies and cinematic transnationalism, the aim of this book is to engage with the fluid and dynamic ways in which texts are adapted and reworked across national borders, and to help bring together insights from across these myriad different traditions.

The chapters in this volume are organised in three parts, with the first – on 'Genres and Traditions' – taking a particular interest in some of the industrial and commercial questions posed by transnational film remakes. Lucy Mazdon begins with a high-profile European export, *The Girl with the Dragon Tattoo*, an example notable (in part) for the fact that Yellow Bird, the production company behind the Swedish-Danish film version (*Män som hatar kvinnor* 2009), bought the rights to Stieg Larsson's novel shortly after its publication (in 2005) and consequently earned a main production credit in the 2011 Hollywood version. The transatlantic collaboration yielded a much-anticipated remake (or 're-adaptation') directed by David Fincher and starring Daniel Craig and Rooney Mara. Although the remake performed financially below expectation, Fincher's authorial interests – established in psycho-thrillers such as *Se7en* (1995) and *Zodiac* (2007) – transformed the conservative *mise-en-scène* of the earlier version into cutting-edge genre film-making. For Mazdon, what is most interesting is the way that Fincher's authorial remake resists accusations of cultural imperialism, embracing instead the European character of its Nordic Noir sources (both novel and film) to disrupt 'the vertical trajectories [of original and copy] which have dominated accounts of the remake [and produce] instead a far more complex and fluid reworking'. Mazdon concludes that *The Girl with the Dragon Tattoo* along with other recent film and television remakes of Nordic Noir – notably, *Let Me In* (2010) / *Låt den rätte komma in* (*Let the Right One In*, 2008) and *Forbrydelsen* (2009–12) / *The Killing* (2011–14), which similarly foreground rather than disguise their Scandinavian origins – challenge past hierarchies and suggest 'a cultural landscape in which the dominance of Anglophone production has been disrupted and a new acceptance of the "other" is visible'.

In Chapter 2, R. Barton Palmer looks to an earlier period, that of American film noir, to consider two films by Fritz Lang – *Scarlet Street* (1945) and *Human Desire* (1954) – that are typically called up as transnational remakes of films directed by Jean Renoir in France: namely, *La Chienne* (*The Bitch*, 1931) and *La Bête Humaine* (*The Human Beast*, 1938). Palmer attends to the production histories of the films to argue that they were chosen for remaking not only because they perfectly suited the commercial trajectories of Lang's work of the period but also because they were re-adaptations of novels (by Georges de la Fouchardière and Émile Zola respectively) that showed profitable affinities with American hard-boiled fiction. In the following essay (Chapter 3), Andy Willis also comments upon the economic imperatives that underpin remakes of genre films, but in this instance focuses on the cultural politics of remaking Spanish horror films in the twenty-first century. Specifically, Willis considers two cases – *Quarantine* (2008), the US remake of *[REC]* (2007), and the *Come Out and Play* (2012) remake of *¿Quién puede matar a un niño?* (*Who Can Kill a Child?* 1976) – to argue that these North American remakes are divested of the most urgent political aspects of their Spanish counterparts in an endeavour to create globally marketable horror films.

The final essay in Part I (Chapter 4) also focuses on horror film remakes, but in this instance Iain Robert Smith casts a much wider net to consider the unlimited cultural production of Bram Stoker's Dracula, a figure who has appeared in various guises and settings in more than 300 feature films produced around the world: most notably, F. W. Murnau's *Nosferatu* (1922) and Tod Browning's 1931 adaptation for Universal. Given this massive body of work, Smith focuses his discussion on three films – the 1953 Turkish film *Drakula İstanbul'da* (*Dracula in Istanbul*), the 1957 Mexican film *El Vampiro* (*The Vampire*) and the 1967 Pakistani film *Zinda Laash* (*The Living Corpse*) – to set out a *methodology* through which to track these 'quasi-independent' repetitions of the *Dracula* story across a variety of national contexts and historical periods. Building upon an approach outlined in his recent book, *The Hollywood Meme* (Smith 2016), and extending existing scholarship devoted to canonical (Hollywood and Western European) versions of *Dracula*, Smith traces the specifically transnational afterlives of Dracula, 'using the structuring metaphor of the "meme" [an individual unit of culture that spreads, adapts and mutates] in order to interrogate the dynamic interplay of global and local within these *Dracula* remakes'. As is evident from Smith's chapter title – 'For the Dead Travel Fast' – the figure of the traveller not only conjures the transnational movement and afterlives of Dracula – which says something 'unique about the sheer memetic vitality of Stoker's tale and the myriad ways in which it has been adapted all across the globe' – but also provides a model for case studies beyond that of the Count.

The volume's Part II – on 'Gender and Performance' – continues some of the questions of industry and genre investigated in the first section, but with a more deliberate emphasis on issues of representation, and especially the politics of gender and sexuality. In the first of these (Chapter 5), Kenneth Chan focuses on a recent trend of East Asian directors and production companies for remaking American films into Asian versions, paying particular attention to Zhang Yimou's 2009 *A Woman, a Gun and a Noodle Shop* remake of the Coen Brothers' neo-noir, *Blood Simple* (1984). Chan makes a number of important points about the economic and cultural imperatives that inform this tendency, as well as several observations around the 'cinematic pragmatism' that lends Zhang's authorial body of work (economic and cultural) currency in a global marketplace. Specifically, Chan argues that in foregrounding the 'woman' (of the film's title), and her oppressed status, Zhang articulates a need to address women's issues in contemporary Chinese society, but at the same time panders to the liberal sensibilities of a contemporary (transnational) film-festival circuit. Like Chan, the next two contributors – Michael Lawrence and Rashna Wadia Richards – focus upon Eastern remakes of Western properties, in these cases from the Indian subcontinent, to underscore a point (also made by Chan) that major film industries, such as Hong Kong and Bollywood, have a long-standing tradition of unauthorised borrowings. In Chapter 6, Lawrence looks to the popular Hindi film *Khoon Bhari Maang* (*Blood-Smeared Forehead*, 1988), an unofficial remake of the Australian television mini-series *Return to Eden* (1983), to focus on how the remake fits with an 'avenging woman' cycle of Hindi film and – in its repurposing – challenges conventional family and gender roles. In Chapter 7, Richards turns to the example of Sanjay Gupta's *Kaante* (2002), an 'unabashed recreation' of Quentin Tarantino's *Reservoir Dogs* (1992), which itself is an uncredited remake of Ringo Lam's *City on Fire* (1987). Attending in particular to the performance of 'cool' across the three versions, Richards argues that the triadic exchange (between Hong Kong, Hollywood and Bollywood) reveals not a simple process of imitation but rather a level of engagement and critique. In the final chapter of Part II, Constantine Verevis discusses two versions of Erich Kästner's popular children's novel – *Das doppelte Lottchen* (1950) and *The Parent Trap* (1961) – to argue that Disney's teen dream of (family) togetherness is 'simultaneously reactionary and progressive, nostalgic and challenging' and that the exchange of twins – Susan and Sharon, in the 1961 Disney version – is more broadly symptomatic of that between originals and remakes.

The essays in Part III, 'Auteurs and Critics', pick up on some of the questions of authorial remaking and canonisation raised by examples such as Fincher's version of *The Girl with the Dragon Tattoo* and Zhang's *A Woman, a Gun and a Noodle Shop*. In the first of these (Chapter 9), David Scott Diffrient and Carl R. Burgchardt consider the case of Albert Lamorrise's *Le ballon rouge* (*The Red Balloon*, 1956), a short, but venerated, film that has generated a number of cultural associations and personal recollections, including Taiwanese director Hou Hsiao-hsien's *Le voyage du ballon rouge* (*Flight of the Red Balloon*, 2007). Diffrient and Burgchardt describe Hou's minimalist film not simply as a work of homage but one that, 'in keeping with its title, puts greater emphasis on the *movement* of the object, which metaphorically represents the intercultural transit of the border-crossing film itself'. While admitting that Hou's version does not exhibit the 'fantastical interludes' that have made Lamorrise's *Le ballon rouge* a favourite among audiences and critics alike, Diffrient and Burgchardt argue that Hou's feature-length work is 'no less compelling as a series of quotidian scenes concerning the interwoven themes of companionship, loneliness, memory, and the restorative power of art'. Even more pertinent, for this volume, is the way in which *Le voyage du ballon rouge* is figured as a point of intercultural contact and interplay, a cross-cultural remake that provides an opportunity to explore 'the relationship between *recollections*, *references*, and *reflections*, ultimately aiming to transnationalise (or "uproot") nostalgia and show how twenty-first-century cinephilia performs a similar cultural function to the remaking process'.

The next two essays in Part III extend the focus on authorship to examine the examples of 'self-remakes', David Desser arguing that while directors often (directly and indirectly) remake and recycle their own works, 'the transnational remake by the same director presents . . . the most radical shift in context and thus might be the most interesting test case for issues of remakes and remaking'. In Chapter 10, Desser looks specifically at the case of filmmaker Nakahira Ko, who made the influential and controversial *Kurutta Kajitsu* (*Crazed Fruit*, 1956) and later in his career, while under contract to the Shaw Brothers studio in Hong Kong, remade the film as *Kuang lian shi* (*Summer Heat*, 1968). Desser explains that the transformation of *Crazed Fruit* into the little-known *Summer Heat* is interesting not only because of the stature of the Japanese original, but also for its examination of post-war disaffected youth, an element of cultural engagement that finds only limited expression in the remake. In Chapter 11, Kathleen Loock examines another 'auto-remake' – Michael Haneke's 2007 version of his 1997 German-language film of the same title – arguing that Haneke resists adapting *Funny Games* to an American cultural context, and instead advances his own art-cinema reputation by dropping virtually the same film – a shot-by-shot, English-language remake – into American entertainment culture.

The final chapters of Part III further the discussion of authorship, but extend more deliberately into questions of reception and film criticism. In Chapter 12, Daniel Martin examines the ways in which Spike Lee – an auteur known for his interest in African-American cultural experience and race relations – undertook to remake Park Chan-wook's *Oldboy* (2003), the gruesomely violent tale from South Korea that had become a symbol of the East Asian 'extreme' cinema cycle. Martin outlines Lee's endeavour to brand the remake as an entry in his own auteurist canon, but takes a more deliberate interest in the film's critical reception, specifically 'the ways critics address the spectacle of violence, notions of taste, and the assumed cultural differences between American and South Korean audiences'. More broadly, the case of Lee's *Oldboy* provides an opportunity 'not only to examine the transformation of material from one director to another, but to interrogate broader debates over the intersection of the *auteur* as symbol/brand and the imagined (lack of) creative freedom afforded directors of remakes'. In the final chapter of the book, Daniel Herbert pushes further in this direction to note that critics typically engage in a discourse 'of quality, artistry, originality, and cultural specificity [which] assumes a hierarchy of critical taste that tends to nationalise and thereby simplify the transnational relations between [Hollywood films and their counterparts]'. While acknowledging that 'transnational film remakes require rigorous analysis that illuminates [their] complexities', Herbert additionally calls for closer attention to be paid to the function of (journalistic) film criticism in shaping an understanding of 'transnational film remakes'. Specifically, Herbert looks over US film reviews from the 1930s onward to demonstrate that while critics have typically denigrated Hollywood remakes, they have also created a rhetorical space for transnational cinema, associating both foreign sources and remakes with stars, auteurs, and/or genres, in lieu of (or in addition to) their nation of origin. As Herbert concludes, 'sorting through the ways in which "the remake" and "the transnational" operate within mainstream critical discourse [helps] us reflect on how and why we construct the very corpus of "transnational film remakes"'.

In summary, in and through its range of case studies and approaches – industrial, textual, critical and discursive – *Transnational Film Remakes* seeks to provide an analysis of cinematic remaking that moves beyond Hollywood-centric accounts and addresses the truly global nature of this phenomenon. From Hong Kong remakes of Japanese cinema, and Bollywood remakes of Australian television, and on to Turkish, Mexican and Pakistani versions of *Dracula*, this book explores the diversity of remaking practices around the world to draw attention to the prominence of remakes within global film culture, and mark out new directions in the study of transnational film remakes.

REFERENCES

Abad-Santos, Alex (2016), 'Why It Matters That *Ghost in the Shell* Is Japanese and Scarlett Johansson Isn't', *Vox*, 15 April, <http://www.vox.com/2016/4/15/11438080/ghost-in-the-shell-white-washing-johansson> (last accessed 30 June 2016).
Alessio, Dominic and Jessica Langer (2007), 'Nationalism and Postcolonialism in Indian Science Fiction: Bollywood's *Koi . . . Mil Gaya* (2003)', *New Cinemas*, 5: 3 (November), pp. 217–29.
Archer, Neil (2012/13), '*The Girl with the Dragon Tattoo* (2009/2011) and the New "European Cinema"'. *Film Criticism*, 37: 2, pp. 2–21.
Arslan, Savas (2011), *Cinema in Turkey: A New Critical History*. Oxford: Oxford University Press.
Aufderheide, Patricia (1998), 'Made in Hong Kong: Translation and Transmutation', in Andrew Horton and Stuart Y. McDougal (eds), *Play It Again, Sam: Retakes on Remakes*, Berkeley: University of California Press, pp. 191–9.
Balmain, Colette (2004), 'Lost in Translation: Otherness and Orientalism in *The Ring*', *Diegesis: Journal of the Association for Research into Popular Fictions*, 7 (Summer), pp. 69–77.
Behrend, Heike (2009), 'The Titanic in Northern Nigeria: Transnational Image Flows and Local Interventions', in Birgit Mersmann and Alexandra Schneider (eds), *Transmission Image: Visual Translation and Cultural Agency*, Newcastle Upon Tyne: Cambridge Scholars Publishing, pp. 224–39.
Bergfelder, Tim and Christian Cargnelli (2008) (eds), *Destination London: German-speaking Emigres and British Cinema, 1925–1950*, New York: Berghahn Books.
Brashinsky, Michael (1998), 'The Spring, Defiled: Ingmar Bergman's *Virgin Spring* and Wes Craven's *Last House on the Left*', in Andrew Horton and Stuart Y. McDougal

(eds), *Play It Again, Sam: Retakes on Remakes*, Berkeley: University of California Press, pp. 191–9.

Capino, Jose B. (2006), 'Philippines Cinema and Its Hybridity (or 'You're Nothing but a Second-Rate Trying Hard Copycat!')', in Anne Tereska Ciecko (ed.), *Contemporary Asian Cinema: Popular Culture in a Global Frame*, Oxford: Berg, pp. 32–44.

Carolan, Mary Ann McDonald (2014), 'Whither the Remake?', in Mary Ann McDonald Carolan, *The Transatlantic Gaze: Italian Cinema, American Film*, Albany, NY: State University of New York Press, pp. 109–30.

Chan, Kenneth (2009), *Remade in Hollywood: The Global Chinese Presence in Transnational Cinemas*, Hong Kong: Hong Kong University Press.

Cheng, Susan (2015), '"Ghost in the Shell" Producer Explains Why the Film's Approach Is "The Right Approach"', BuzzFeed, 30 June, <https://www.buzzfeed.com/susancheng/ghost-in-the-shell-producer-defends-scarlett-johanssons-role> (last accessed 30 June 2016).

Child, Ben (2016), '"Whitewashing" Row over Scarlett Johansson's Ghost in the Shell Role Reignites', *The Guardian*, 15 April, <https://www.theguardian.com/film/2016/apr/15/scarlett-johanssons-role-in-ghost-in-the-shell-ignites-twitter-storm> (last accessed 30 June 2016).

Chung, Hye Seung and David Scott Diffrient (2015), *Movie Migrations: Transnational Genre Flows and South Korean Cinema*, New Brunswick, NJ: Rutgers University Press.

Crawford, Chelsey (2016), 'Familiar Otherness: On the Contemporary Cross-Cultural Remake', in Amanda Ann Klein and R. Barton Palmer (eds), *Cycles, Sequels, Spin-offs, Remakes, and Reboots: Multiplicities in Film & Television*, Austin: University of Texas Press.

Desser, David (2008), 'Remaking *Seven Samurai* in World Cinema', in Leon Hunt and Wing-Fai Leung (eds), *East Asian Cinemas: Exploring Transnational Connections on Film*, London: I. B. Tauris, pp. 17–40.

Diffrient, David Scott (2009), '*Over That Hill*: Cinematic Adaptations and Cross-Cultural Remakes, from Depression-Era America to Post-War Korea', *Journal of Japanese and Korean Cinema* 1: 2, pp. 105–27.

Durham, Carolyn A. (1998), *Double Takes: Culture and Gender in French Films and Their American Remakes*. Dartmouth: University Press of New England.

Edinger, Catarina (1991), 'Doña Flor in Two Cultures', *Literature/Film Quarterly*, 19: 4 (October), pp. 235–41.

Elsaesser, Thomas (2005), *European Cinema: Face to Face with Hollywood*, Amsterdam: Amsterdam University Press.

Erdoğan, Nezih (2003), 'Powerless Signs: Hybridity and the Logic of Excess of Turkish Trash', in Karen Ross, Brenda Dervin and Deniz Derman (eds), *Mapping the Margins: Identity Politics and the Media*, Creskil: Hampton Press, pp. 163–76.

Evans, Jonathan (2014a), 'Film Remakes, the Black Sheep of Translation', *Translation Studies*, 7: 3, pp. 300–14.

Evans, Jonathan (2014b), 'Zhang Yimou's Blood Simple: Cannibalism, Remaking and Translation in World Cinema', *Journal of Adaptation in Film & Performance* 7: 3 (December), pp. 283–97.

Ganti, Tejaswini (2002), 'And Yet My Heart Is Still Indian: The Bombay Film Industry and the (H)Indianization of Hollywood', in Faye D. Ginsburg, Lila Abu-Lughod and Brian Larkin (eds), *Media Worlds: Anthropology on New Terrain*. Berkeley and Los Angeles: University of California Press, pp. 281–300.

Gemzøe, Lynge Agger (2013), '*Brødre* vs. *Brothers*: The Transatlantic Remake as Cultural Adaptation', *Akademisk Kvarter*, 7 (Fall), pp. 283–97.

Griffin, Jeffrey L. (2014), 'Turning Japanese: From *Sideways* to *Saidoweizu*: An

Examination of the Japanese Remake of a Hollywood Film', *Film International*, 12: 4 (December), pp. 84–98.

Grindstaff, Laura (2002), 'Pretty Woman with a Gun: *La Femme Nikita* and the Textual Politics of "The Remake"', in Jennifer Forrest and Leonard R. Koos (eds), *Dead Ringers: The Remake in Theory and Practice*, Albany, NY: State University of New York Press, pp. 273–308.

Gripsrud, Jostein (1992), 'French-American Connection: *À bout de souffle*, *Breathless* and the Melancholy Macho', in Michael Skovmand and Kim Christian Schrøder (eds), *Media Cultures: Reappraising Transnational Media*, London: Routledge, pp. 104–23.

Grossvogel, David I. (2002), *Didn't You Use to be Depardieu? Film as Cultural Marker in France and Hollywood*, New York: Lang.

Gürata, Ahmet (2006), 'Translating Modernity: Remakes in Turkish Cinema', in Dimitris Eleftheoritis and Gary Needham (eds), *Asian Cinemas: A Reader and Guide*, Edinburgh: Edinburgh University Press, pp. 242–54.

Hanet, Kari (2010), '*L'Appartement* and *Wicker Park*: Transculture and The Remake', *Literature & Aesthetics*, 20: 1 (July), pp. 52–68.

Hanet, Kari (2012), 'Fun with Fairies: Representation of Gender Identity in *La Cage aux folles* and *The Birdcage*', *Australian Journal of French Studies*, 49: 2 (May), pp. 167–82.

Hantke, Steffen (2010), 'The Aesthetic of Affect in the Shot-by-Shot Remakes of *Psycho* and *Funny Games*', *English Language Notes*, 48: 1 (Spring/Summer), pp. 113–27.

Harney, Michael (2002), 'Economy and Aesthetics in American Remakes of French Films', in Jennifer Forrest and Leonard R. Koos (eds), *Dead Ringers: The Remake in Theory and Practice*, Albany, NY: State University of New York Press, pp. 63–87.

He, Hilary Hongjin (2010), 'Connected Through Remakes: Intercultural Dialogue Between Hollywood and Chinese Cinema Industries', *Asian Cinema*, 21: 1 (Spring), pp. 179–92.

Herbert, Daniel (2006), 'Sky's the Limit: Transnationality and Identity in *Abre los ojos* and *Vanilla Sky*', *Film Quarterly*, 15: 1, pp. 28–38.

Herbert, Daniel (2008), *Transnational Film Remakes: Time, Space, Identity*, Ph.D. dissertation, University of Southern California.

Herbert, Daniel (2009), 'Trading Spaces: Transnational Dislocations in *Insomnia/Insomnia* and *Ju-on/The Grudge*', in Scott A. Lukas and John Marmysz (eds), *Fear, Cultural Anxiety, and Transformation: Horror, Science Fiction, and Fantasy Films Remade*, Lanham, MD: Lexington Books. pp. 143–64.

Herbert, Daniel (2010), 'Circulations: Technology and Discourse in *The Ring* Intertext', in Carolyn Jess-Cooke and Constantine Verevis (eds), *Second Takes: Critical Approaches to the Film Sequel*, Albany, NY: State University of New York Press, pp. 153–70.

Hills, Matt (2005), 'Ringing the changes: Cult Distinctions and Cultural Differences in US Fans' Readings of Japanese Horror Cinema', in Jay McRoy (ed.), *Japanese Horror Cinema*, Edinburgh: Edinburgh University Press, pp. 161–74.

Hutchinson, Rachael (2007), 'A Fistful of *Yojimbo*: Appropriation and Dialogue in Japanese Cinema', in Paul Cooke (ed.), *World Cinema's 'Dialogues' with Hollywood*. Basingstoke: Palgrave Macmillan, pp. 172–87.

Jones, Monique (2016), 'Jon Tsuei is Right: A #WhitewashedOUT Ghost in the Shell Misses the Cultural Mark', *The Nerds of Color*, 6 May, <https://thenerdsofcolor.org/2016/05/06/jon-tsuei-is-right-a-whitewashedout-ghost-in-the-shell-misses-the-cultural-mark/> (last accessed 30 June 2016).

Jones, Stan (2005), 'L.A. Transfer: From *Der Himmel Über Berlin* to the *City of Angels*', *Australasian Journal of American Studies*, 24: 2 (December), pp. 63–81.

Klein, Christina (2010), 'The American Horror Film?: Globalization and Transnational U.S.-Asian Genres', in Steffen Hantke (ed.), *American Horror Film: The Genre at the Turn of the Millennium*, Jackson: University Press of Mississippi, pp. 3–14.

Krämer, Lucia (2015), 'Hollywood Remade: New Approaches to Indian Remakes of Western Films', in Rüdiger Heinze and Lucia Krämer (eds), *Remakes and Remaking: Concepts – Media – Practices*, Bielefeld: Transcript Verlag, pp. 81–96.

Krämer, Lucia (2015b), 'The End of the Hollywood 'Rip-Off'? Changes in the Bollywood Politics of Copyright', in Dan Hassler-Forrest and Pascal Nicklas (eds), *The Politics of Adaptation*, Basingstoke: Palgrave Macmillan, pp. 143–57.

Krings, Matthias (2015), 'Black Titanic: Pirating the White Star Liner', in Matthias Krings, *African Appropriations: Cultural Difference, Mimesis, and Media*, Bloomington: Indiana University Press, pp. 84–119.

Leung Wing-Fai (2013), 'From *A Tale of Two Sisters* to *The Uninvited*: A Tale of Two Texts', in Alison Peirse and Daniel Martin (eds), *Korean Horror Cinema*, Edinburgh: Edinburgh University Press, pp. 173–86.

Li, Jinhua (2011), *Transnational Remakes: Gender and Politics in Chinese Cinemas and Hollywood*, Ph.D. dissertation, Purdue University.

Li, Jinhua (2014), 'From *Infernal Affairs* to *The Departed*', *CineAction*, 93 (Spring), pp. 29–35.

Li, Jinhua (2016), 'National Cuisine and International Sexuality: Cultural Politics and Gender Representation in the Transnational Remake from *Eat Drink Man Woman* to *Tortilla Soup*', *Transnational Cinemas*, forthcoming.

Lim, Bliss Cua (2007), 'Generic Ghosts: Remaking the New 'Asian Horror Film', in Gina Marchetti and See Kam Tan (eds), *Hong Kong Film, Hollywood, and the New Global Cinema: No Film Is an Island*, London: Routledge, pp. 109–25.

Loock, Kathleen and Constantine Verevis (2012) (eds), *Film Remakes, Adaptations and Fan Productions: Remake/Remodel*, Basingstoke: Palgrave Macmillan.

Loughrey, Clarisse (2016), 'Ghost in the Shell: Anger Mounting over Casting of Scarlett Johansson in What Is a 'fundamentally Japanese story'', *The Independent*, 19 April, <http://www.independent.co.uk/arts-entertainment/films/news/ghost-in-the-shell-anger-mounting-over-casting-of-scarlett-johansson-in-what-is-a-fundamen-tally-a6991436.html> (last accessed 30 June 2016).

Lüthe, Martin (2015), 'Hellish Departure? *The Departed*, *Infernal Affairs* and Globalized Film Cultures', in Rüdiger Heinze and Lucia Krämer (eds), *Remakes and Remaking: Concepts – Media – Practices*, Bielefeld: Transcript Verlag, pp. 97–112.

Mazdon, Lucy (2000), *Encore Hollywood: Remaking French Cinema*. London: BFI.

Mazdon, Lucy (2015), 'Hollywood and Europe: Remaking *The Girl with the Dragon Tattoo*', in Mary Harrod, Mariana Liz and Alissa Timoshkina (eds), *The Europeanness of European Cinema: Identity, Meaning, Globalization*, London: I. B. Tauris, pp. 199–213.

Messier, Vartan (2014), 'Game over? The (Re)play of Horror in Michael Haneke's *Funny Games U.S.*', *New Cinemas*, 12: 1–2, pp. 59–77.

Monk, Leland (2010), 'Hollywood Endgames', in Roy Grundmann (ed.), *A Companion to Michael Haneke*, Oxford: Wiley-Blackwell, pp. 420–37.

Nayar, Sheila J. (1997), 'The Values of Fantasy: Indian Popular Cinema through Western Scripts', *Journal of Popular Culture*, 31: 1, pp. 73–90.

Nayar, Sheila J. (2003), 'Dreams, Dharma and Mrs. Doubtfire: Exploring Hindi Popular Cinema via its 'Chutneyed' Western Scripts', *Journal of Popular Film and Television*, 31: 2, pp. 73–82.

Özkaracalar, Kaya (2003), 'Between Appropriation and Innovation: Turkish Horror Cinema', in Steven Jay Schneider (ed.), *Fear Without Frontiers: Horror Cinema Across the Globe*, Guildford: FAB Press, pp. 204–17.

Park, Myoungsook (2009), 'Hollywood's Remake Practices under the Copyright Regime: French Films and Japanese Horror Films', in Scott A. Lukas and John Marmysz (eds), *Fear, Cultural Anxiety, and Transformation: Horror, Science Fiction, and Fantasy Films Remade*, Lanham, MD: Lexington Books. pp. 107–28.

Raw, Laurence (2016), 'Jerome Bruner and the Transcultural Adaptation of 1970s Hollywood Classics in Turkey', in Andrea Esser, Iain Robert Smith and Miguel Á. Bernal-Merino (eds), *Media Across Borders: Localising TV, Film and Video Games*, London: Routledge, pp. 141–50.

Rawle, Steve (2010), 'Video Killed the Movie: Cultural Translation in *Ringu* and *The Ring*', in Kristen Lacefield (ed.), *The Scary Screen: Media Anxiety in The Ring*, Farnham: Ashgate, pp. 97–114.

Richards, Rashna Wadia (2011), '(Not) Kramer vs. Kumar: The Contemporary Bollywood Remake as Glocal Masala Film', *Quarterly Review of Film and Video*, 28: 4 (August), pp. 342–52.

Schneider, Stephen Jay (2002), 'Repackaging Rage: *The Vanishing* and *Nightwatch*', *Kinema*, 17 (Spring), pp. 47–66.

Shin, Chi-Yun (2012), "'Excessive' Remake: From The Quiet Family to The Happiness of the Katakuris', *Transnational Cinemas*, 3: 1, pp. 67–79.

Smith, Iain Robert (2008a), "'Beam Me Up Ömer': Transnational Media Flow and the Cultural Politics of the Turkish Star Trek Remake', *The Velvet Light Trap*, 61 (Spring), pp. 3–13.

Smith, Iain Robert (2008b), 'The Exorcist in Istanbul: Processes of Transcultural Appropriation Within Turkish Popular Cinema', *Portal: Journal of Multidisciplinary International Studies*, 5: 1 (Spring), pp. 1–12.

Smith, Iain Robert (2013), '*Oldboy* goes to Bollywood: *Zinda* (2006) and the Transnational Appropriation of South Korean Extreme Cinema', in Alison Peirse and Daniel Martin (eds), *Korean Horror Cinema*, Edinburgh: Edinburgh University Press, pp. 187–98.

Smith, Iain Robert (2016), *The Hollywood Meme: Transnational Adaptations in World Cinema*, Edinburgh: Edinburgh University Press.

Smith, Paul Julian (2004), 'High Anxiety: *Abre los ojos/Vanilla Sky*', *Journal of Romance Studies*, 4: 1 (Spring), pp. 91–102.

Spaeth, Rya (2016), 'Is Scarlett Johansson Too White for Anime?', *New Republic*, 18 April, <https://newrepublic.com/article/132763/scarlett-johansson-white-anime> (last accessed 30 June 2016).

Stenport, Anna Westerståhl (2016), 'Nordic Remakes in Hollywood: Reconfiguring Originals and Copies', in Mette Hjort and Ursula Lindqvist (eds), *A Companion to Nordic Cinema*, Boston: Wiley-Blackwell, pp. 436–56.

Stringer, Julian (2007), 'The Original and the Copy: Nakata Hideo's *Ring* (1998)', in Alastair Phillips and Julian Stringer (eds), *Japanese Cinema: Texts and Contexts*, London: Routledge, pp. 296–307.

Thomas, Rosie (1985), 'Indian Cinema: Pleasures and Popularity', *Screen*, 26: 3–4, pp. 116–31.

Tsuei, Jon (2016a), '*Ghost in the Shell* plays off all of these themes. It is inherently a Japanese story, not a universal one' [Twitter], 15 April, <https://twitter.com/jontsuei> (last accessed 30 June 2016).

Tsuei, Jon (2016b), 'You can "Westernize" the story if you want, but at that point it is no longer Ghost In The Shell because the story is simply not Western' [Twitter], 15 April, <https://twitter.com/jontsuei> (last accessed 30 June 2016).

Varndell, Daniel (2014), *Hollywood Remakes, Deleuze and the Grandfather Paradox*, Basingstoke: Palgrave Macmillan.

Verevis, Constantine (2006), *Film Remakes*, Edinburgh: Edinburgh University Press.

Verevis, Constantine (2009), 'Second Chance: Remaking *Solaris*', in Scott A. Lukas and John Marmysz (eds), *Fear, Cultural Anxiety, and Transformation: Horror, Science Fiction, and Fantasy Films Remade*, Lanham, MD: Lexington Books. pp. 167–80.

Verevis, Constantine (2012), 'A Personal Matter: *H Story*', in Kathleen Loock and Constantine Verevis (eds), *Film Remakes, Adaptations and Fan Productions: Remake/Remodel*, Basingstoke: Palgrave Macmillan, pp. 159–75.

Vieira, Joao Luiz (1995), 'From *High Noon* to *Jaws*: Carnival and Parody in Brazilian Cinema', in Robert Stam and Randal Johnson (eds), *Brazilian Cinema*, New York: Columbia University Press, pp. 256–69.

Wang, Shaojung Sharon (2010), 'Shall We Depart from Globalization Ring? Hollywood Remakes of East Asian Films and the Emergence of Cultural Reinvasion', *Asian Cinema*, 21: 1 (March), pp. 39–58.

Wang, Yiman (2013), *Remaking Chinese Cinema: Through the Prism of Shanghai, Hong Kong, and Hollywood*, Honolulu: University of Hawai'i Press.

Wee, Valerie (2011), 'Visual Aesthetics and Ways of Seeing: Comparing *Ringu* and *The Ring*', *Cinema Journal*, 50: 2 (Winter), pp. 41–60.

Wee, Valerie (2014), *Japanese Horror Films and Their American Remakes: Translating Fear, Adapting Culture*, New York: Routledge.

Welsch, Tricia (2000), 'Sound Strategies: Lang's Rearticulation of Renoir', *Cinema Journal*, 39: 3 (Spring), pp. 51–65.

White, Anne M. (2003), 'Seeing Double? The Remaking of Alejandro's Amenbar's *Abre los ojos* as Cameron Crowe's *Vanilla Sky*', *International Journal of Iberian Studies*, 15: 3 (November), pp. 187–96.

Wierzbicki, James (2010), 'Lost in Translation? Ghost Music in Recent Japanese Kaidan Films and Their Hollywood Remakes', *Horror Studies*, 1: 2 (November), pp. 193–205.

Wierzbicki, James (2015), 'Subtle Differences: Sonic Content in "Translation" Remakes', *Journal of Adaptation in Film & Performance*, 8: 2 (June), pp. 155–69.

Williams, Alan (2002), 'The Raven and the Nanny: The Remake as Crosscultural Encounter', in Jennifer Forrest and Leonard R. Koos (eds), *Dead Ringers: The Remake in Theory and Practice*, Albany, NY: State University of New York Press. pp. 151–68.

Wills, David (1998), 'The French Remark: *Breathless* and Cinematic Citationality', in Andrew Horton and Stuart Y. McDougal (eds), *Play It Again, Sam: Retakes on Remakes*, Berkeley: University of California Press, pp. 147–61.

Wright, Neelam Sidhar (2009), '"Tom Cruise? Tarantino? E.T.? ... Indian!": Innovation through Imitation in the Cross-cultural Bollywood Remake', in Iain Robert Smith (ed.), *Cultural Borrowings: Appropriation, Reworking Transformation* [Special issue/E-book], *Scope: An Online Journal of Film Studies*, 15 (October), pp. 194–210.

Xu, G. (2008), 'Remaking East Asia, Outsourcing Hollywood', in Leon Hunt and Wing-Fai Leung (eds), *East Asian Cinemas: Exploring Transnational Connections on Film*, London: I. B. Tauris, pp. 191–202.

Zanger, Anat (2007), *Film Remakes as Ritual and Disguise: From Carmen to Ripley*, Amsterdam: Amsterdam University Press.

PART I

GENRES AND TRADITIONS

1. DISRUPTING THE REMAKE: *THE GIRL WITH THE DRAGON TATTOO*

Lucy Mazdon

A key feature of the cultural landscape of the twenty-first century has been the global success of so-called 'Nordic Noir'. Indeed, it was this very global success which led both to the 'foreignising' remake which this chapter will discuss and to the controversy it provoked. In the words of the website which is devoted to and named after the genre and which organises London's annual 'Nordicana' festival, 'With its roots in the ground-breaking TV dramas *The Killing, Borgen, Wallander* and *The Bridge*, Nordic Noir has become a genre in its own right, influencing screenwriters far beyond the Scandinavian Peninsula' (Nordic Noir and Beyond n.d.). While to non-Scandinavian eyes this wealth of successful crime fiction might seem like a new phenomenon, this is far from true. As Kerstin Bergman illustrates in her overview of Swedish crime fiction (2014), the Scandinavian countries, in particular Sweden, have a long and fascinating tradition of crime literature. Crime novels have attracted large domestic readerships since the early twentieth century. However, it was the growing awareness of social injustice and political corruption in Sweden of the 1960s and the increasing politicisation of intellectual and public spheres which arguably led to a form of crime fiction (Bergman 2014: 21), the police procedural featuring a critique of wider social issues, which would dominate for years to come, notably in the form of the so-called 'Nordic Noir'. At the forefront of this sub-genre were the husband and wife writing pair, Maj Sjöwall and Per Wahlöö. From 1965 to 1975 Sjöwall and Wahlöö published a series of novels, beginning with *Roseanna* (1965) and ending with *Terroristerna* (1975), all featuring Inspector Martin Beck. Set in contemporary Stockholm, the novels feature both physical and psychological realism embodied in the thoughtful but flawed central figure of Beck. As Bergman points out, what really made these novels stand out from their predecessors, and what made them so influential in terms of the ongoing development of the genre, was their 'conscious inclusion of a critical perspective on Swedish society', their politicisation of the police procedural genre (22).

Despite this long and extremely rich history, it was not until Stieg Larsson's *Millennium* trilogy that Scandinavian, or more precisely Swedish, crime fiction achieved true global prominence. First published in Sweden between 2005 and 2007, the trilogy proved a global publishing phenomenon, selling over 65 million copies worldwide by 2011. While the USA typically represents a relatively limited market for literature in translation, Larsson's novels were to prove immensely popular and *The Girl Who Kicked the Hornet's Nest*, the third novel in the series, became the most sold book in the USA in 2010. Writing in a blog for the New York Public Library, Jeremy Megraw pithily captures this popularity:

> Maybe you've got the Nordic noir bug from reading Stieg Larsson's Millennium series (we've all seen those ubiquitous neon paperbacks on the subway) or were enthralled earlier by Peter Høeg's *Smilla's Sense of Snow* or the Detective Wallander series of books. However you encounter them, Scandicrime writers such as Henning Mankell, Larsson, or Jo Nesbø are like a good bag of chips, it's hard not to have another. (Megraw, 2013)

The huge international success of Larsson's novels, along with vast readerships for the works of Henning Mankell, Camilla Läckberg, Liza Marklund, Jo Nesbø and others, was extended by the ensuing proliferation of films and, in particular, television dramas adapted from or inspired by their literary predecessors. In Britain many of these dramas found a home on BBC Four. Following the success of the French police drama *Spiral* (2005–14) the channel developed a formula of screening double episodes of subtitled crime dramas on a Saturday night. The French series was followed by the Italian *Inspector Montalbano* (2008–12), and then, to particular acclaim, a series of Scandinavian dramas including: *Wallander* (2008–11); *The Killing* (2011–14); *Borgen* (2012–14); *The Bridge* (2012–15) and *Sebastian Bergman* (2012). The shows were to prove among BBC Four's most successful programmes in terms of audience. Average audience share for BBC Four stands at around 0.9 per cent, yet Series Two of *The Killing* (19 November 2011–17 December 2011) averaged 3.8 per cent, reaching 4.2 per cent for the final episode (see BARB n.d.). While this success story for BBC Four of course represents only a tiny fraction of the British viewing public, not entirely surprisingly given the dramas' subtitles and transmission on the somewhat highbrow channel, small audiences did not spell critical neglect. The dramas garnered extensive broadsheet column inches praising their complex and compelling plots, fascinating characters and gritty representation of the rain-drenched streets of Stockholm and Copenhagen. The critical success of *The Killing* was confirmed by the series' receipt of a BAFTA in 2011, a success matched by *Borgen* in 2012. In clear evidence of the perceived appeal of the Swedish stories upon which these dramas were based, BBC One aired an English-language version of *Wallander* (2008–10) starring Kenneth Branagh as the eponymous detective. As books flew off the shelves – by 2010 Larsson had sold over 2 million copies of his novels in the UK alone, making him the best-selling author in the country that year (Jones 2010) – and television dramas earned adoring audiences and critical praise, so the term 'Nordic Noir' was coined for this increasingly popular and recognisable cultural phenomenon. Anglophone audiences learned to associate the term, used as both critical definition and marketing strategy, with brooding crime dramas typically featuring dark storylines, flawed but intelligent police investigators, and depictions of the inequalities and evil lurking beneath the surface of Scandinavian society.

Given the tremendous international success of Larsson's *Millennium* trilogy a cinematic adaptation was surely inevitable, and in 2009 the Swedish/Danish co-production *Män som hatar kvinnor* / *The Girl with the Dragon Tattoo* (Niels Arden Oplev) was released. This was then followed by *Flickan som lekte med elden* / *The Girl Who Played with Fire* (Daniel Alfredson, 2009) and *Luftslottet som sprängdes* / *The Girl Who Kicked the Hornet's Nest* (Daniel Alfredson, 2009). The films, hugely successful at the Swedish box office, achieved creditable success on the international market, with *The Girl with the Dragon Tattoo* grossing over $10 million at the US box office and $2,342,433 in the UK. While it is indubitable that the success of the films' source novel contributed to their success, other factors were clearly at play. In their mobilisation of elements of the action/crime thriller genres the films are arguably far more 'American' than the slow-paced, broody dramas stereotypically associated with Scandinavian production by Anglophone audiences. The films were marketed in the English-speaking market so as to deliberately disguise their 'foreign' origins and position them as a Hollywood-style product. British distributors Momentum were very clear that they did not want *The Girl with the Dragon Tattoo* to be constrained by its foreignness. Its head of marketing, Jamie Schwartz, explained: 'Our approach was: what would we do if it was a blockbuster? If this was the *Da Vinci Code*?' (Gant 2010: 13). The film was treated as a major event, with poster campaigns both on the London Underground and on trains in the Southern commuter belt in a very deliberate attempt to target readers of the novel, and a front-page announcement on free newspaper *Metro* (widely read by Londoners) to announce the launch of the trailer online. In cinemas the film was promoted via a trailer which bore no trace whatsoever of the film's foreign language, effectively selling it as an English-language film to those not in the know. An initial release at 114 cinemas was an impressive opening weekend for a subtitled film from a little-known director. Interestingly, the dubbed print of the film was given a limited release in the UK market alongside the subtitled print. This is far from common practice in Britain and suggests the hope that here was a film which could break free from the typical market for 'foreign cinema' and achieve broader appeal.

Given the promotional strategies employed to market *The Girl with the Dragon Tattoo*, its borrowing of Hollywood-style genre traits and the efface-ment of 'foreignness' at the level of publicity and, to some extent, the film itself, one might expect it to escape the fate so often accorded to successful non-Eng-lish-language movies: the Hollywood remake. Yet for all its Hollywood-style action, the fact remained that the film was not in English. As I have argued elsewhere (Mazdon 2015: 209), the dubbed print of Oplev's film released in the UK proved unpopular with audiences while the subtitled print was faced with the usual resistance of the mainstream audience. So despite its attempts to avoid 'cultural discount' or reduced appeal in non-domestic (notably Anglophone) contexts owing to national or linguistic traits (Hoskins and Mirus 1988: 500), the audience for the film remained limited. With Larsson's novels riding high in the international bestseller charts, a Hollywood version was an extremely attractive prospect, and accordingly in 2011 *The Girl with the Dragon Tattoo* was remade in the US with director David Fincher at the helm.

Unsurprisingly, the decision to remake was not met entirely favourably. Particularly critical of the decision was the director of the Swedish/Danish version, Niels Arden Oplev:

> The director of the original Swedish version of *The Girl with the Dragon Tattoo* has questioned the need for the upcoming American remake, reigniting a long-running war of words over Hollywood raiding foreign language films to repackage them for a global audience. With an English-language version in the works, to be directed by *The Social Network*'s David Fincher, film-maker Niels Arden Oplev expressed anger at plans to cast an American actor in the lead role of Lisbeth Salander, drawing unflattering comparisons with the Hollywood adaptation of the French film *La Femme Nikita*, which was poorly received when remade as *The Assassin*, starring Bridget Fonda in the 1990s. He told the Word & Film website: 'Even in Hollywood there seems to be a kind of anger about the remake; like, "Why would they remake something when they can just go see the original?"' (Pulver 2010)

The remake, along with the sequel and other forms of cinematic 'rebooting', has been a staple of Hollywood production since the early days of cinema. Condemnation of this practice, alongside claims regarding its roots in financial uncertainty and/or paucity of original ideas, have an equally long history. Certainly the remake cannot be disentangled from the financial imperatives that drive the global film industry, notably Hollywood. As I have argued elsewhere for example, the rise, fall and re-emergence of American versions of French movies can be broadly mapped on to wider initiatives within the US industry and, to some degree, to corresponding developments in France (Mazdon 2000: 13–27). The remake is not simple proof of the inherent quality of the source material (an argument frequently advanced by critics of Hollywood remakes of European film) but rather the result of specific developments in industrial and indeed aesthetic practices within Hollywood. Moreover, the various factors which have influenced the decision to remake at specific junctures and the selection of source films are echoed in the diversity of remakes and remaking methods. The remake is not a homogeneous artefact and should be perceived in terms of diversity and difference: sound remakes of silent films, 'auto-remakes' or those films made twice by the same director, remakes based on sources from the indigenous cinematic culture (Hollywood remakes of earlier Hollywood films) and those based on foreign sources (Hollywood remakes of European films, for example).

Nevertheless, much critical discourse on the remake, and in particular on Hollywood remakes of foreign cinema, ignores this potential for diversity in favour of a blanket condemnation of the debasing impact of what is ultimately described as a straightforward attempt to make easy money. A one-way, vertical trajectory is established between the 'art' and 'value' of the non-English-language 'original' and the crass commercialism of the American 'copy'. This condemnation of the remake rests upon a number of pervasive and somewhat reductive binary oppositions: European high culture versus American popular entertainment; the value and tradition of European art versus Hollywood commerce; the authenticity of the European 'original' versus the superficiality of the American 'copy'. These oppositions and their retention of an 'original' and valuable source text are a common trope in much discussion of adaptation and translation of all kinds. Adaptation is seen to decentre the source text, to threaten its identity and that of the author/creator: the higher the perceived cultural status of the work to be adapted the greater this anxiety will tend to be. In the case of the cinematic remake, this anxiety is exacerbated. As Thomas Leitch explains, remakes compete directly with other products of the same aesthetic medium without necessarily providing adequate economic or legal compensation (2002: 38). Rather than creating new audiences for their source films, remakes typically seek to overshadow or even efface them. Leitch concludes somewhat pessimistically that if a remake does invoke its source it is simply to entice spectators into the movie theatre, only to deny this relationship once the film begins (2002: 43).

The hostility to the remake of *The Girl with the Dragon Tattoo* expressed by Oplev and others clearly followed a well-trodden path in terms of critical responses to the remake. However, it was perhaps exacerbated by the fact that the novel on which the film was based did seem to suggest a move away from the traditional market dominance of Anglo-American cultural artefacts. Discussing the prominence of Scandinavian crime fiction in Europe and North America, Andrew Nestingen and Paula Arvas remark:

> Its prominence stands in contrast to the diminutive size of the region. Roughly twenty-five million citizens inhabited the nation states of Scandinavia in 2009 – making it equivalent in population to the US state of Texas or slightly smaller than Saudi Arabia, Afghanistan or Malaysia. Yet crime writers from Scandinavia are comparatively well-known, having sold millions of books, having had their works translated into many languages and having also made an impact through influential reviews of their work and receipt of literary prizes. (2011: 1)

Anglophone cultures, the UK and the USA in particular, have historically read very little literature in translation. In the UK in 2014 for example, translated titles represented only 2.1 per cent of the top 5,000 bestsellers (Tivnan and Wood 2014). Nevertheless this figure did signify a notable increase on previous years: while there were 63 translated books in the top-selling 5,000 in May 2013, by the same point in 2014 there were 112. And these translated titles were dominated by crime fiction, much of it Scandinavian or 'Nordic Noir'. In 2014 Jo Nesbø alone had seventeen titles in the top 5,000, garnering 15 per cent of all translated revenue. In other words, the success of the Nordic crime novels had established new possibilities for translated fiction in the British and North American markets, creating an albeit small but nonetheless significant space for non-Anglophone literature which challenged the non-translated hegemony which had dominated for so many years. In the words of Jessica Bager, agent at Stockholm's Salomonssen Agency, whose clients include Nesbø, Anders de la Motte and Liza Marklund, 'Publishers are looking for great books, and today it doesn't really matter where the author comes from, as long as the book is good. Through the Scandicrime boom the publishers have opened their eyes for all kinds of literature from Scandinavia' (Tivnan and Wood 2014).

This growth in sales and readership for translated literatures suggests a 'foreignising' of Anglo-American literary culture, the burgeoning of a new openness to difference and diversity (Venuti 1995). While it is entirely possible, and I believe appropriate, to see the remake as a form of translation (Mazdon

2000), critical responses to it are typically very different from those afforded to literature in translation or films in translation. While translated literature and subtitled films are perceived to challenge cultural hegemony, introducing otherness and promoting diversity, the remake is condemned for doing the very opposite. So the announcement that the Swedish/Danish version of *The Girl with the Dragon Tattoo* was to be remade in Hollywood was not only faced with the usual hostility met by the remake: it also risked being perceived as a threat to the foreignising potential of the translated novels and their 'Nordic Noir' counterparts.

Yet I would argue that these fears were largely misplaced. Indeed the American version of Larsson's novel, rather than confirming the negative stereotypes which dominate accounts of the Europe to Hollywood remake exchange, can be seen to challenge them in a number of important ways. It is worth noting that David Fincher, the film's director, was adamant that his movie was not in fact a remake at all. He was of course well aware that his film would provoke controversy, stating:

> I know we are playing into the European, and certainly the Swedish, predisposition that this is a giant monetary land grab. You're co-opting a phenomenon. Now, there are plenty of reasons to believe we can make it equally entertaining a movie. But the resentment is already engendered, in a weird way. It's bizarre. (Hoad 2011)

The 'phenomenon' to which he refers here is the broader *Dragon Tattoo* franchise, novels and films. Nevertheless, by firmly positioning his own version as an adaptation of the source novel rather than a remake of Oplev's own adaptation he does set out to contain the hostility he clearly predicted. Of course, adaptations of novel to film are not spared controversy, as the persistence of the rather limiting discussions of 'fidelity' which have dominated readings of cinematic adaptations reveals. The historical proximity of Larsson's source novel and the two filmic versions complicates things further in this case as the sense of direct competition described by Leitch is heightened. Nevertheless, if we accept that Fincher's version is indeed a new adaptation of the novel rather than a remake of the film (notably, Steven Zaillian's screenplay is much more 'faithful' to Larsson's novel than was that for Oplev's film), then it does reduce those accusations of cinematic patricide outlined by Leitch. Rather than directly 'attack' the earlier film Fincher's version adapts the source novel. As my comments above suggest, this can be seen as a limiting gesture in itself as the Swedish source novel 'becomes' an American film. However, the very difference of medium and the expectation that readers of novels often choose to see the filmic versions of their favourite books while film spectators may seek out the books on which their favourite movies are based makes this a much less controversial process. Interestingly, the American film did not play down its relationship with the earlier texts. Promotional materials were emblazoned with the words 'From the international bestselling trilogy' in a clear attempt to entice the novels' fans into the movie theatres. It is also worth noting that prior to the film's release, American pay-per-view cable networks aired the television mini-series which had previously been shown on the subscription channel Canal+ in France and which comprised extended versions of the Swedish/Danish Millennium trilogy. While I have not been able to access more detailed information regarding these screenings or their audience, it does seem fair to say that this airing of the Scandinavian films just before the release of Fincher's adaptation would appear to give the lie to claims that the remake must inevitably 'destroy' or 'efface' its predecessor.

Crucial to this problematisation of the remake as an aggressively homogenising practice was Fincher's decision to make an American remake that in many ways appeared very un-American, a film that in many respects was less 'American' than its Scandinavian predecessor. His own role as director immediately overturned the art versus commerce dichotomy which typically underpins oppositions between European cinema and Hollywood. As I have argued elsewhere (Mazdon 2015), many critics read the film as a 'Fincher movie' with connections to his oeuvre prioritised over relationships with the source texts. Moreover:

> The 'author function' afforded by the direction of Fincher informed spectators and critics alike that, in contrast to so many remakes, this was a film which was not to be immediately consumed and forgotten, a film which was so much more than an attempt to make an easy buck. (Mazdon 2015: 210)

Stylistically and indeed thematically, the film certainly echoes much of Fincher's earlier work, notably *Se7en* (1995) and *Zodiac* (2007). The central narrative focus on a socially dysfunctional character (Lisbeth Salander), while evidently taken from Larsson's novel, is in fact a recurrent trope in Fincher's own work, further complicating the film's status as remake or adaptation. In contrast, Oplev was best known for his televisual work when he came to direct *Män som hatar kvinnor* (originally made for television of course) and had no such auteur status. The film itself is hugely indebted to classical Hollywood style with its predominance of studio sets, conventional three-point lighting and unambiguous continuity editing. As befits a movie originally made for television release, close-ups and medium close-ups predominate and there is none of the visual or indeed narrative ambiguity evident in Fincher's film. Here, then, we can see a reversal of the Europe/art to Hollywood/commercial mainstream trajectory which, as previously discussed, dominates accounts of the remake. Thanks to Fincher's privileged and respected status as an American 'auteur', his film cannot easily be reduced to simple remake or adaptation.

This complication of *The Girl with the Dragon Tattoo*'s American identity can be seen most strikingly at the level of the film itself. The film was largely shot in Sweden using a local crew, and initially Fincher worked with a Swedish cinematographer intending to create what he perceived as a Swedish, rather than an American, aesthetic. Fincher remarked:

> It was an aesthetic choice. We wanted it to look and feel like a Swedish film, and I think it does. We were already getting flak for doing a Hollywood version of the story, so we made a commitment to doing as much of the movie as possible in Sweden, with a Swedish crew. (Holben 2012: 32)

Although the cinematographer was eventually replaced with Fincher's long-time collaborator, Jeff Cronenweth, the film arguably retains the Swedish aesthetic Fincher describes. Notable is the emphasis put on location and the harshness of the weather. Both cinematic adaptations include a shot of a train travelling through the Swedish landscape carrying Mikael Blomkvist (Michael Nyqvist in the source film, Daniel Craig in the remake) to the Vanger family's island home. In the American version, and in contrast to its Swedish counterpart, the landscape is covered in thick snow and this depiction of extreme cold is emphasised repeatedly as Blomkvist spends time on the island. As cinematographer Jeff Cronenweth remarks:

> We set out to embrace the Swedish winter. It's a strong element in the story, almost a character of its own, and we spent a lot of time out in the snow with those very unique light tonalities. We embraced all of the idiosyncrasies of the locations. (Holben 2012: 36)

Upon Nyqvist's arrival at the island Fincher emphasises his inability to receive any mobile phone signal owing to his location. Here again the extremity of the geographical location is underlined, an extremity which Fincher described as singularly Scandinavian (Holben 2011: 34). While Fincher's search for authenticity is perhaps cliché-ridden, his stereotypes are almost certainly shared by much of the film's international audience and as such are an effective device in an attempt to make the film look and feel Swedish. This is furthered by Fincher's choice of cast, which for the most part features British actors speaking with slight Swedish accents (with the notable and rather odd exception of Daniel Craig) as well as Swedish actor Stellan Skårsgard in the key role of Martin Vanger. Both Fincher and Cronenweth reference Sven Nykvist, the Swedish cinematographer famous for his collaborations with Ingmar Bergman, in their discussion of the film (Holben 2011) and *The Girl with the Dragon Tattoo* (like the British *Wallander* before it) at times emulates the very particular soft light which typified Nykvist's work and which was largely inspired by that of his far northern home town.

In apparently embracing the 'Europeanness' of its cinematic and written sources, Fincher's remake disrupts the vertical trajectories which have dominated accounts of the remake, producing instead a far more complex and fluid reworking. As I have argued elsewhere (Mazdon 2015), it can be perceived as that rare thing, the 'foreignising' translation which makes no attempt to conceal its status as translation (Venuti 1995). When we place this 'foreignised' remake alongside a 'source' film which, as we have seen, borrows in a great number of ways from the style and tropes of Hollywood cinema, this disruption becomes even more apparent. Significantly, this disruption and 'blurring' of on-screen national characteristics can be seen at work in a number of other televisual and cinematic texts which emerge from, or connect to, 'Nordic Noir'. I have already mentioned the particular use of light in the British televisual adaptation of *Wallander* and this, combined with its Swedish locations and oddly stilted use of dialogue, make it feel, to British viewers at least, in some ways 'more Scandinavian' than its Swedish televisual predecessor. *Let Me In* (2010), Matt Reeves' American remake of Tomas Alfredson's Swedish vampire movie *Låt den rätte komma in/Let the Right One In* (2008), retains an aesthetic and a narrative ambiguity which also feels rather more European than Hollywood. Cinematography creates a look very similar to the Swedish film while suggestions of parental child abuse and the failure to flesh out supporting characters eschew the tendency to moral clarity which typifies so many Hollywood reworkings. Like Fincher's *The Girl with the Dragon Tattoo*, *Let Me In* was not accorded the blanket hostility which so often meets Hollywood remakes and this, I would suggest, is precisely because of this very process of foreignisation.

Both the Swedish *Wallander* and the Swedish/Danish *The Girl with the Dragon Tattoo* were co-produced by the highly successful Scandinavian production company, Yellow Bird. Yellow Bird is part of the Zodiac Media Group, which owns over forty-five 'brands' operating across fifteen territories in Europe, the Americas, Australasia and Asia. Alongside its Scandinavian projects, Yellow Bird claims to have 'an active slate of international projects in development' (Zodiak Media 2015). With this in mind it comes as no great surprise to learn that Yellow Bird also had co-production credits on both the UK *Wallander* and Fincher's US version of *The Girl with the Dragon Tattoo*. In other words, the Europeanisation that we can see at the level of narrative, cinematography and *mise-en-scène* is underpinned by a process of transnationalism at the level of production.

It seems to me that this goes to the heart of the remake pair discussed in this chapter and the 'foreignisation' of Fincher's film I have suggested. Fincher's attempts to blur the national traits of his film, to introduce characteristics more typically associated with Scandinavian or more broadly European cinema, do not happen in isolation but rather are part of a much wider process of globalisation in which the Nordic Noir 'genre' is a key player. We have already discussed the international success of the novels, notably Larsson's trilogy, which played such an important role in establishing the Nordic Noir phenomenon and creating a market for it beyond Scandinavia. If we look again at the successful television series which were also instrumental in establishing the international prominence of Nordic Noir, we can see that they were in fact part of a very deliberate attempt to establish international audiences for Scandinavian production. As Helen Vatsikopoulos remarks:

> The successes of Borgen and The Killing were no accident. The producers consciously sought to professionalise the way the [Danish] public broadcaster told Danish stories. Twenty years ago you couldn't find a Danish TV series that rated a mention overseas. Then DR staff decided to get serious – and went to Hollywood. They hung around the sets of American shows such as The West Wing, NYPD Blue and LA Law. They talked with writers and producers and studied the formulas of multi-episode dramas. (Vatsikopoulos 2013)

Like Yellow Bird in Sweden, Danish state broadcaster DR set out to create television drama which would appeal to an international audience, and they achieved this through dramas such as The Killing, which were undeniably 'Scandinavian' and yet which simultaneously and actively emulated the highly successful US dramas against which they would compete on the international market.

These attempts to create what we might term a 'global European' drama of course have their antecedents. We can recall the European co-productions of the 1950s and 1960s which set out to create a popular cinema which could compete with Hollywood at the European box office. More recently we have seen the work of Luc Besson, who as writer, director and producer has endeavoured to make films which break down the perceived Europe/Hollywood opposition and create new audience constituencies. What is particularly noteworthy about these more recent attempts is that they are always already part of a thoroughly globalised media environment in which concepts of the national become ever harder to define. They are moreover situated within a culture of media convergence. In the words of Aniko Imre they are 'part of an increasingly integrating entertainment industry in which media forms, platforms and technologies are intertwined' (Imre 2012: 2).

That Fincher's The Girl with the Dragon Tattoo, which, despite the director's protestations, is evidently both remake and adaptation, should evidence this blurring of national traits is perhaps surprising. The remake has typically been seen to consolidate national oppositions as it performs what Lawrence Venuti terms a 'fluent translation strategy' in which the 'difference' of the source text is replaced by a product entirely familiar to the target consumer:

> The aim of [fluent] translation is to bring back a cultural other as the same, the recognizable, even the familiar; and the aim always risks a wholesale domestication of the foreign text, often in highly self-conscious projects, where translation serves an appropriation of foreign cultures for domestic agendas, cultural, economic, political. Translation can be considered the communication of a foreign text, but it is always a communication limited by its address to a specific reading audience. (Venuti 1995: 15)

As we have seen, in marked contrast Fincher's film, along with a number of other remakes of 'Nordic' films and television series, eschews such fluency in favour of a 'translation' which very clearly bears the traces of its source. This 'foreignisation', unusual as it may be in the cinematic remake, is, I would suggest, far from abnormal in the context of Nordic Noir. As the success of the translated novels described above suggests, these texts now have a global readership and an appeal which lies both in their difference *and* their familiarity. As a genre these crime fictions are firmly rooted in their specific national cultures yet they are co-opted for an international readership as 'Nordic Noir': in other words they are both 'foreign' and part of a domestic appropriation which makes that very foreignness central to their appeal. The television shows and films which are adapted from or inspired by these fictions adopt similar strategies; the relative success of those series aired on BBC Four was surely partly due both to their rather exotic appeal, and the distinction afforded by their subtitles, and to the familiarity of their 'Nordic' genre and regular slot. In this context (and we should recall the huge success of the Larsson novels in the USA as well as the relative American success of a number of the filmic and televisual 'Nordic noirs') Fincher's decision to make a film which would look and feel 'like a Swedish film' (Holben 2012: 32) is, I think, much less surprising. As we have noted, he was very aware of the hostility his American remake would provoke and was keen to make a film which would avoid the accusations of Americanisation as cultural imperialism so often meted out to the Hollywood remake. When we consider that other remakes of Nordic Noir (*Let Me In*, *Wallander*) similarly appeared to reveal rather than disguise their Scandinavian origins we can begin to see the beginnings of a non-fluent remaking process which may have the potential to disrupt the dominant trajectories of the past. This optimistic interpretation is furthered when we consider the wider influence of Nordic Noir on Anglophone cultural production, notably television drama. The British series *Broadchurch* (2013–) and *The Fall* (2013–), along with the American *True Detective* (2014–), are hugely indebted to Scandinavian crime dramas such as *The Killing* both stylistically and at the level of plot and characterisation. The British psychological thriller *Fortitude* (2015–) makes its debt even more explicit, as it features a number of leading Scandinavian actors alongside its British and American stars, including Sofie Gråbøl, best known for her lead role as Sarah Lund in *The Killing*, and is set in the fictional town of Fortitude in Arctic Norway. Writing in *The Times* in 2013 Jack Malvern noted:

> After the snow-flecked landscapes and Faroese jumpers of Nordic television thrillers such as *Wallander* and *The Killing* comes an altogether more familiar squad of investigators. The latest batch of inquisitors with flawed private lives are equipped not with Scandinavian snow-boots and knitwear but waterproofs to repel the rain of Wales, Scotland and Ireland. (Malvern 2013)

Malvern is referring here to a series of crime dramas set in the Celtic fringes of the UK and including the Welsh/English *Y Gwyll / Hinterland* (2013–), the Scottish/Gaelic *Bannan / The Ties that Bind* (2014–) and the prime-time BBC drama *Shetland* (2013–). Again these series are hugely indebted to their Scandinavian predecessors in terms of style and narrative, a debt made visible by the coining of the term 'Celtic Noir' to describe them. Moreover, the decision to make a number of these dramas multilingual surely owes something to the space carved out by the likes of *The Killing*, and they in turn extend and enhance this opening up of a televisual space for the foreign: notably, *Hinterland* was part-financed by pre-sale to Denmark's national broadcaster DR, was shown in Norway, Belgium and Holland, and, via a Netflix deal, was subsequently introduced to the USA and Canada.

So should we, then, see David Fincher's *The Girl with the Dragon Tattoo* as a new kind of remake, a remake for which foreignness is in fact a crucial selling point (Hoad 2011)? The global circulation and influence of Scandinavian crime fiction, albeit via the homogenising concept of 'Nordic Noir', certainly gives cause for optimism as it suggests a cultural landscape in which the dominance of Anglophone production has been disrupted and a new acceptance of the 'other' is visible. Fincher's film allays the fears and expectations of Niels Arden Oplev and many others by eschewing the effacement and negation of the foreign 'other' which so often identifies the Hollywood remake. While it was perhaps somewhat disingenuous of Fincher to deny that his film was a remake at all, its dual identity as both adaptation and remake reminds us of the impossibility of defining clear points of origin, as all texts are part of a network of exchange and influence which can surely never be simply reduced to a straightforward linear trajectory. If this is kept in mind it is clear that the remake has enormous capacity for revealing the potential for diversity and plurality through adaptation, a gesture which Fincher's film does, I believe, admirably. As I write this chapter, the sequel to Stieg Larsson's trilogy is being widely advertised in the UK. *The Girl in the Spider's Web* (2015) was written by David Lagercrantz as Larsson himself had died suddenly in 2004. The release of the novel of course prolongs the afterlife of Larsson's books, negating any fears that this might have been threatened by the filmic versions. It also further problematises the relationship between source novel and films and between film and remake, as another text, and indeed another author, extend this particular network of exchange. If the novel proves successful, it is likely more films will be made. Given Fincher's status as influential cinematic auteur, will these films be influenced by his version of *The Girl with the Dragon Tattoo*? It is surely not impossible, and reminds us again of the limitations of a search for origins and linear trajectories from 'original' to 'copy'.

REFERENCES

BARB (n.d.), BBC Marketing and Audience Data, <http://www.barb.co.uk> (last accessed 29 June 2015).

Bergman, Kerstin (2014), *Swedish Crime Fiction: The Making of Nordic Noir*, Fano: Mimesis International.

Gant, Charles (2010), 'The Film That Broke Rules', *Sight and Sound*, 20: 5, p. 13.

Hoad, Phil (2011), 'The Girl with the Dragon Tattoo Rethinks the Hollywood Remake', *Guardian* Film Blog, 20 December, <http://www.guardian.co.uk/film/filmblog/2011/dec/20/girl-with-dragon-tattoo-remake> (last accessed 28 March 2013).

Holben, Jay (2012), 'Cold Case', *American Cinematographer*, XCIII: 1, pp. 32–47.

Hoskins, Colin and Rolf Mirus (1988), 'Reasons for US Dominance of the International Trade in Television Programmes', *Media, Culture and Society*, 10, pp. 499–515.

Imre, Anikó (2012), 'Eastern European Cinema from No End to the End (As We Know It)', in Anikó Imre (ed.), *A Companion to Eastern European Cinemas*. Malden, MA: Wiley Blackwell, pp. 1–24.

Jones, Philip (2010), 'Stieg Larsson's Sales Figures', <http://www.telegraph.co.uk/culture/books/7803084/Stieg-Larssons-sales-figures.html> (last accessed 29 July 2015).

Leitch, Thomas (2002), 'Twice-Told Tales: The Rhetoric of the Remake', in Jennifer Forrest and Leonard R. Koos (eds), *Dead Ringers: The Remake in Theory and Practice*. Albany, NY: State University of New York Press, pp. 37–62.

Malvern, Jack (2013), 'How Celtic Noir Is Set to Make a Killing', *The Times*, 3 November, <http://www.thetimes.co.uk/tto/arts/tv-radio/article4255585.ece> (last accessed 29 July 2015).

Mazdon, Lucy (2000), *Encore Hollywood: Remaking French Cinema*, London: BFI.

Mazdon, Lucy (2015), 'Hollywood and Europe: Remaking *The Girl with the Dragon Tattoo*', in Mary Harrod, Mariana Liz and Alissa Timoshkina (eds), *The Europeanness of European Cinema: Identity, Meaning, Globalization*, London: I. B. Tauris, pp. 199–212.

Megraw, Jeremy (2013), 'A Cold Night's Death: The Allure of Scandinavian Crime Fiction', <http://www.nypl.org/blog/2013/01/14/scandinavian-crime-fiction> (last accessed 29 July 2015).

Nestingen, Andrew and Paula Arvas (2011), 'Introduction: Contemporary Scandinavian Crime Fiction', in Andrew Nestingen and Paula Arvas (eds), *Scandinavian Crime Fiction*, Cardiff: University of Wales Press.

Nordic Noir and Beyond (n.d.), <http://nordicnoir.tv> (last accessed 29 July 2015).

Pulver, Andrew (2010), '*The Girl with the Dragon Tattoo* Director Lashes Out at American Remake', *The Guardian*, <http://www.theguardian.com/film/2010/nov/09/girl-dragon-tattoo-american-remake> (last accessed 29 June 2015).

Tivnan, Tom and Felicity Wood (2014), 'Sales of Translated Titles Surge in 2014', *The Bookseller*, 23 May, <http://www.thebookseller.com/news/sales-translated-titles-surge-2014> (last accessed 29 June 2015).

Vatsikopoulos, Helen (2013), 'Soft Power: How TV Shows Like *Borgen* Put Denmark on the Map', *The Conversation*, 13 November, <https://theconversation.com/soft-power-how-tv-shows-like-borgen-put-denmark-on-the-map-20064> (last accessed 29 June 2015).

Venuti, Lawrence (1995), *The Translator's Invisibility*, London: Routledge.

Zodiak Media (2015), <http://www.zodiakmedia.com/index.php> (last accessed 29 June 2015).

2. FRITZ LANG REMAKES JEAN RENOIR FOR HOLLYWOOD: FILM NOIR IN THREE NATIONAL VOICES

R. Barton Palmer

A commonplace of criticism devoted to the classic American film noir (*c.*1941–58) has been that this post-war series is essentially a transnational phenomenon, with its style, themes, and characteristic narrative patterns emerging from a complex interplay among several native and European traditions, both literary and cinematic (see Schrader 1972: 8–10 and Palmer 2016: chs 4–5). Acknowledged as the most significant of these are Weimar Expressionism and the Neue Sachlichkeit; French poetic realism and Surrealism; American post-war semi-documentarianism; and the different genres of popular literature that are usually, not without distortion, bundled together under the rubric of hard-boiled fiction, whose principal authors, including James M. Cain, Raymond Chandler, Dashiell Hammett and Cornell Woolrich, were associated directly or indirectly with *Black Mask* magazine, constituting something like an informal school (see Nolan 1987: Introduction).

Already amply demonstrated by scholars, of course, is that even more complex forms of transnationalism define post-classic noir, as well as its 'branches' in many other national cinemas; this filmic development, like classic noir itself, has a literary reflex, evidenced in the worldwide popularity of the English-language *roman noir* (successor to the hard-boiled tradition) and its imitations in other cultures such as Nordic Noir (for global noir, see Pettey and Palmer 2014; for Nordic Noir, both cinematic and literary, see Nestingen 2008). Understandably partial to explanations that emphasise strictly filmic developments, historians of classic noir have often tended to underestimate the importance of 'dark fiction' of various kinds and national origins for the development of the series, a blindness to which this essay offers a partial corrective.

In the aesthetic mixing that resulted in the emergence of classic noir, three national voices made for an interesting harmony that, as we shall see, cannot be reduced to a simple division between visual style/art design, where the French and German high art movements make their influence felt in motif and technique, and themes drawn from American popular culture that provide these films with character, setting, and narrative. Hollywood's absorption of noirish releases from 1930s French cinema speaks to the transauthorial creation of noirness as a repertoire of themes, characters, and narrative patterns upon which subsequent productions in the series continued to draw. Indicating a resonance across different cultures and artistic traditions, this deep transnationalism interestingly forecasts the emergence of noir traditions in other industries as the series went global in the second half of the twentieth century. In any case, though historians postulate classic noir's transnational hybridism, there has been little accounting for its emergence through the little histories of actual production, even though the considerable extent and breadth of the noir series provide some richly transnational examples, among which are the two Fritz Lang noirs that are the focus here. Both these films are conventionally, but somewhat misleadingly, understood as remakes of films directed by Jean Renoir in France during the 1930s: *Scarlet Street* (1945) and *Human Desire* (1954).

It seems true enough, as Richard Maltby has observed, that attempts to invoke the 'synchronic events' of the period, including those derived from cinema and literary practice, in order to explain the emergence and nature of classic film noir have remained 'essentially metaphorical' (1984: 51). To be sure, I have just done much the same by characterising the foundational transnationalism of the series as a harmony of three voices. But we don't get very far even if we understand this musical trope as figuring a synchronous blend of different elements whose individuality is submerged but not eliminated. This essay takes a different approach to transnational mixing through an examination of crucial elements of the production histories of the 'Renoir remakes', emphasising the neglected fact that they are also adaptations of fiction that showed profitable affinities with American hard-boiled narrative.

A focus on the remaking of these films must thus be complemented by due attention paid to their transmediality. An essential point is that remaking and adaptation are two sides of the same coin of reuse, describing formally different but essentially quite similar ways in which the cinema redeploys material whose popularity is already established. Thomas Leitch points out that 'remakes differ from other adaptations to a new medium because of the triangular relationship they establish among themselves, the original film they remake, and the property on which both films are based' (1990: 139). In fact, such remakes could just as accurately be termed re-adaptations, with the desirability of the original property, albeit filtered through an anterior screen version, often proving to be decisive in production calculations. To be sure, the re-adaptation process unfolds in the full light of that initial screen version, but that first film might actually prove more or less irrelevant to the 'remakers'. Leitch argues that 'the uniqueness of the film remake . . . is indicated by the word property', but, although legal rights are obviously involved in any project dependent upon a prior source, this seems too much of a reification, a reduction to the fact of textuality of those processes involved in what is usually called remaking; a focus on property and rights does little to address the relative ease with which such reuse can often be accomplished in a world cinema that has been essentially transnational (especially in terms of distribution and exhibition) since screen narrative first evolved and prospered (Leitch 1990: 138).

At least in regard to film remakes of adaptations, the key concept seems to be one more appropriate to the performance art that is the cinema: production. No one can remake a lyric poem, as Leitch observes, but that has everything to do with the fact that lyric poems are never 'produced', being, as it were, ontologically complete and needing no further artistic work in order to 'be'. Only through production, of course, can film and stage dramas can be realised, and this process is, or at least can be, more or less independent from their original conception. Just as plays generate different productions, so do literary properties purchased for screening. To be sure, the sale of rights from one producer to another is a financial transaction involving property, but more importantly, such transference permits the reuse of production materials, including the script as desirable, with, of course, no restriction on the changes that might be made in yet another adaptation of the source text, where copyright most heavily applies. The remake is often simply another version of an originary property, and there is no limit to how many times the process of re-production (or re-adaptation if you prefer) might be repeated. The first notable film noir, just to take a familiar example, is such a remade adapted text; John Huston's *The Maltese Falcon* (1941) is the third version of Hammett's 1928 novel produced by Warner Brothers; Huston's film is more often, and correctly so, regarded as a re-adaptation of a well-regarded novel (whose narrative it follows more or less faithfully) than as a remake of two somewhat inferior prior film versions.

A neo-romantic emphasis on authorship (even in the shared sense present in the remake) tends to slight the other forms of exchange between cinemas, including especially the transnational circulation of properties, movements characteristically engineered by producers or production companies. To say, then, as I have in the title to this essay, that Fritz Lang 'remade' Jean Renoir is to indulge in a complex figure of speech (equal parts metonymy and personification) that is as misleading as it is revelatory, emphasising authorial expressivity but neglecting industrial considerations, including the range of actions, and actors, involved in the redeployment of an already-used source.

The transnational remake emerges as particularly important since it provides direct, material links between cinemas. The remake, unfortunately, has suffered much the same calumny as has been heaped on the adaptation, where many critics and historians have been disposed to dismiss it as fatally flawed by its secondariness. It is possible, if distorting, to view the remake as only a pale reflection of the work that constitutes its origin and whose cultural life in some sense it extends and broadens (see Verevis 2006 for further discussion). Speaking of the sale of Marcel Carné's *Le Jour se lève* to Hollywood (subsequently remade by Anatole Litvak in 1947 as *The Long Night*), British critic Roger Manvell, for example, displayed a deep misunderstanding of the film industry when he despaired: 'This vandalism must stop before the cinema destroys more landmarks of its own greatness in the voracious search for new material' (quoted in Mazdon 2013: 557). *Pace* Manvell, the free and continuing circulation of properties, as well as the extension of successful productions through forms of seriality and cycling, constitutes the life blood of world cinema, which is not, despite the wishes of enthusiasts, organised around individual 'landmarks', but rather around multiplicities: units of more than one text, linked in various ways that are calculated to extract the maximum profit from the properties involved, taking advantage of exposed veins of popular taste in the process.

As film noir demonstrates, multiplicities take shape in the industry in response to various pressures and intentions, but they, of course, may also be fashioned by critics interested in canon-formation or evaluation. To approach, as does Lucy Mazdon, Hollywood's several Renoir remakes as a body of works that can be analysed with something like a revisionist auteurism has the considerable virtue of rescuing these films from critical oblivion, assigning them new forms of value by relocating their secondariness in a renewed sense of authorship. Thus she usefully calls attention to the collective presence of Renoir's French productions in Hollywood history and, in her earlier work, to the significant body of French remakes produced during the period (Mazdon 2013, 2000). Conceiving *Scarlet Street* and *Human Desire* as 'Renoir remakes', of course, prioritises the originary (if also secondary) texts and their much-celebrated director in much the same way as do adaptation studies devoted to the film versions of E. M. Forster novels or Tennessee Williams plays.

Produced at different times, under various conditions, and for distinct markets, the Hollywood 'Renoir' films in question often have little in common besides a shared originary cinematic author, a fact that in this case had little or nothing to do with how they came to be made and, more important perhaps, what exactly that making means for the history of the Hollywood cinema. Text-centred, Mazdon's discussion accounts expressively for their 'whatness' through a process of reading; to be sure, she broadens existing accounts of authorship by commenting on the differences in approach between Renoir and Lang. But assimilating them to a Renoir-centred category does not speak at all to what *Scarlet Street* and *Human Desire* tell us about the transnationalism of film noir: or, to put this a different way, why American producers were interested in remaking them at that particular moment. It might seem natural enough for a 'landmark' film in one national cinema to be selected for remaking in another, but that is to confuse a critical history of the cinema, in which taste and aesthetics matter deeply, with its material counterpart, where the bottom lines are re-usability and box-office potential.

More important, in pursuing an essentially auteurist line, Mazdon misses the irony that the Renoir films are themselves secondary, in the important sense that they are largely faithful adaptations of literary sources whose appeal in terms of story materials had already been amply demonstrated in the French and American marketplaces. And, of course, though it is of little significance, Renoir's film can be regarded as a remake of the original screen version of *Bête*, Ludwig Wolf's *Die Bestie im Menschen* (1920). Both the novels Renoir adapted had been published in English translation before the films made from them were exhibited, though neither possessed the 'legs' for this earlier approval, however useful for predicting box-office success, to be a marketing asset. And, as the record shows, it is not the considerable artistic excellence of the Renoir films that led American producers to remake them; nothing in the production history of the two films suggests that this was even remotely a consideration. Instead, the particular qualities of the original fictional sources that Renoir showcases proved to be the decisive factor. A necessary, but not sufficient, condition, for the remaking of these films was that their sources in a general way resonated deeply with the noir films then being turned out by Hollywood that were based on thematically similar American crime fiction. Decisive in their being selected, however, was the fact that they suited in each case micro production trends associated with Lang's authorship.

These two films, however, cannot be claimed confidently for a traditional auteurist account of Lang's Hollywood career in which intentionality and unconditioned expressivity are thought paramount. Instead the two projects suited his career in a very different way, as his colleagues involved recognised clearly, since they fit perfectly the commercial trajectories of his work for an industry in which profitable releases customarily generate entirely similar yet completely different sequels (in the general sense of repetitions or imitations). To put this another way, the cinema's foundational dialectic between newness and sameness plays out in artistic careers as well, fostering differentiated reconfigurations that have a claim to being considered as remakes in a general sense. Though not based on the recycling of a 'property', such following texts are remakes in the sense that key elements of production, especially casting, are repeated in the hope that the original film's popularity with viewers might be repeated as well. To be sure, auteurism of a more traditional kind does stake some valid claims here on behalf of both directors in terms of the connection established for them to the developing noir series (or the 'crime melodrama', as this film type was known at the time). After all, in the case of these two noirs we have a German émigré filmmaker, perhaps the most celebrated director of what has come to be known as the Expressionist cinema, remaking in Hollywood two of the most successful, and acclaimed, films by the period's most famous French director, who is often credited with revitalising a moribund national industry in the early sound period. Renoir did so by making films, including *La Chienne*, that, as Raymond Durgnat suggests, made for a more popular cinema à l'Américain by designing a narrative around 'psychological consistency in depth' that reflected a realist 'social context': as part of this movement away from the anti-realism previously dominant in a French cinema enthralled by Surrealist psychologism (1974: 74).

Bête is acclaimed as one of the central texts of the informal movement known as poetic realism, considered by some historians to be an important precursor of the American film noir. Edward Baron Turk distinguishes this brand of filmmaking from both the cinema fantasies popular in 1930s France and those politically engaged releases that addressed Popular Front issues, like Renoir's own *La Grande Illusion* (1937). Poetic realism, he suggests, 'blunts populism's social edge', focusing on 'social milieu' for 'the mood its representations might effect' (1989: 109). Hard-boiled fiction, and its screen versionings, do much the same, with its substantial if not complete disengagement from politics distinguishing these works from the then contemporary, and in many other ways quite similar, proletarian novel (see Foley 1993 and, for a contrary view, McCann 2000). Film noir also generally soft-pedalled the political, usually populist edge of the contemporary cultural discontents that supplied it with narratives and themes. Lang's authorship found itself very much in accord with this trend, as did Renoir's, and this is evident in the notable noir project he directed after relocating to Hollywood in 1940: *Woman on the Beach* (1947).

Even though they deal with the dissatisfactions of settled bourgeois life, defined by entrapment in loveless marriage and unrewarding routinised employment, both *Scarlet Street* and *Human Desire* likewise eschew the somewhat shrill social reformist strain that had dominated Lang's notable early Hollywood productions: *Fury* (1936) and *You Only Live Once* (1937). What links all these films, of course, is their concern with issues of violent crime, both collective and individual, and the inadequacies or, indeed, irrelevance of the official police and the justice system, issues that Lang had explored in his most famous German sound film, *M* (1931), remade as a film noir by Joseph Losey twenty years later. To be sure, Lang's formation as an artist in the German industry during the 1920s and 1930s conditions deeply his approach to the remaking process, with the treatment of the two Renoir properties reflecting in particular the distanced realism of the Neue Sachlichkeit movement, which, as art historian John Willett affirms, 'to a great extent was an offshoot of German Expressionism as well as a reaction against it' (1970: 192; see Prinzler 2012 for further detailed discussion of individual films). Though he left his artistic mark on them, Lang did not choose these projects. They chose him.

A crucial fact is that the Renoir 'originals' are self-consciously literary, if in quite different ways, and this is what the director, who also wrote the screenplays, intended. These are films that advertise themselves as adaptations of well-known works, and fidelity to the sources in each case was an important consideration, even as Renoir, like Lang, mounted these properties with a distinctive style and artistry appropriate to each. From the outset, his voice was subordinate to those of the sources. The screenplays for *Scarlet Street* and *Human Desire*, in contrast, make no reference to novels that in the USA carried no pre-sold cachet; the title for *Scarlet Street* is a complete fabrication, intended to be misleadingly titillating, suggesting, with some truth, a film about some 'red light' district, while *Human Desire* vaguely recalls the Zola and Renoir, but in a gesture surely understood or appreciated by few besides producer Jerry Wald, who was an enthusiast of the novelist and whose idea this new title was. As Lang famously pointed out, it makes no good sense; he is said to have asked what other kind of desire there is but 'human' (see McGilligan 1997: 408–9). Wald, however, was a sharp operator. He must have realised that titling the film *The Human Beast* (as the project was initially called), however faithful to Zola and Renoir, would have strongly suggested it was a horror pic; 'desire' suggested an agenda in keeping with how, in the previous three or four years, the illicit eroticism of film noir had been promoted over its concern with crime and its detection in such productions as *Out of the Past* (Jacques Tourneur, 1947) and *Criss Cross* (Robert Siodmak, 1949).

These late 1940s films feature, respectively, a hard-boiled detective investigation and an elaborate armoured car robbery, but their centres are the fatal and steamy romances between Robert Mitchum and Jane Greer in the one case, and Burt Lancaster and Yvonne de Carlo in the other. Influenced at least in part by the success of *Scarlet Street*, this tradition was well established by the time Lang was making *Human Desire*, and he emphasises the illicit eroticism of the scenes between stars Glenn Ford and Gloria Grahame, including an elaborate seduction sequence early on that has no counterpart in Renoir's version. As part of its calculated box-office appeal, *Scarlet Street* features a sexually intense, and also abusive, relationship between Joan Bennett and Dan Duryea that pushed the limits of what the Breen office would then permit since producer Walter Wanger and Lang wanted to retain provocative images of his star (who seems to be constantly in a negligée), as well as some fairly suggestive stagings in her bedroom, including a toenail-painting scene that raised disapproving eyebrows at the Legion of Decency (see Bernstein 1999 and McGilligan 1997: 322–5 for details). Intended to further Wald's profitable interest in lurid melodrama, *Human Desire* offers something similar, with a psychologically weak, yet brutal and self-hating husband in effect pimping his wife not just once, but twice, only then to turn violently on her in 'revenge' after she finally admits her disgust for him. As commentators have often observed, the film does offer a less misanthropic vision of human virtue than its source, but this material, as even a brief summary suggests, was still pushing the limits of what the socially conservative Production Code then sanctioned in terms of sexual themes. That the Breen office certificated both these films, however, suggests the shift in what the industry's watchdog had considered suitable during the last years of the war that did so much to make noir's relative transgressiveness acceptable (see Doherty 2007: 243–8). What was outré in Renoir's sources remains more or less so in both Hollywood re-versionings.

Motivated by the pre-soldness of these properties for a French viewership in the 1930s, the literariness of the Renoir originals naturally does not survive the recontextualisation required for a very different market. The advertising trailers in each case present *Scarlet Street* and *Human Desire* as stand-alone productions, of interest to audiences simply because of their limit-pushing story materials that bear more than a passing similarity to the plots of both Cain's *The Postman Always Rings Twice* and *Double Indemnity* (both published in 1936). These narratives had been banned from the outset by the Breen office from Hollywood adaptation, despite their popularity. But in 1944, *Double Indemnity* was suddenly approved for a Paramount production, directed by Billy Wilder, who was every bit as cynical about human virtue as Zola and de la Fouchardière (see Biesen 2005). Both the Lang/Renoir films recall that shocking, and quite profitable, production, which is probably one factor that argued for their production. That Jean Renoir was the director of the original versions would have meant nothing to American viewers, who would also have been equally indifferent to any sense in which *Scarlet Street* and *Human Desire* might be valued as Fritz Lang projects. However, it is easy enough to see in general why these narratives were selected for remaking as the film noir series developed and then prospered.

Scarlet Street is based on *La Chienne* (*The Bitch*, 1931), which is itself adapted from a contemporary (published in 1930) novel and play of the same name by Georges de la Fouchardière; and *La Bête Humaine* (*The Human Beast*, 1938) reverentially announces its source in the Émile Zola novel of the same name, published nearly half a century earlier in 1890, with the film's prologue offering an image of the author and a quotation from the text (upon which his signature appears) that speaks to the 'poisoned blood' of the main character, Jacques Lantier (Jean Gabin), a man desperate to enjoy the love of a woman despite his fear that he will suddenly turn on and murder her for no reason other than an inherited proclivity for violence, which is exactly what happens. Here too a romantic triangle figures as the central motif of the plot, which Renoir has considerably simplified, with Lantier drawn by accident into covering up an earlier crime to which he is an indirect witness: Roubaud (Fernand Ledoux) murders the man who had seduced his wife, the very rich Grandmorin (Jacques Berlioz), but this is only after the frightened husband begs Séverine (Simone Simon) to approach this influential man, who is her godfather, in an effort to preserve his job as a station master. As an adolescent, Séverine had been seduced by Grandmorin, and it is the revelation of their past relationship that encourages the jealous and resentful Roubaud to kill him. Now disgusted by and fearful of her husband, Séverine expects that Roubaud will kill her in turn and seeks out Lantier as a protector, but then she becomes the object of her lover's homicidal frenzy. After the murder, Lantier, appalled and remorseful, kills himself.

By the time Renoir made *Bête*, Zola had been celebrated for decades as one of the masters of French literature. Viewers would accept his cut-down version of the book, with an increased and flattering focus on heartthrob Jean Gabin (the producers intended the films as a star vehicle of sorts) that is compromised only slightly by his character's psychopathology and suicide. The film is no costume drama; in composing the screenplay, Renoir discards this historical framework and sets the narrative in contemporary France, which aided its Hollywood remaking. Character established by subtle, often enigmatic aspects of performance is the filmmaker's focus, but Zola's closely linked themes of erotic obsession and violence continue to dominate, though the story, pruned of minor characters and sub-plots, centres more clearly and movingly on the imposing figure of Lantier, a romantic hero *malgré lui*, as he fails to navigate a complex social landscape and keep his dark side in check. As André Bazin remarks, the abridgement of the novel, done at great speed (or so the screenwriter affirms), is a quite remarkable compositional accomplishment:

> On the whole, we can say that Renoir has in almost every way improved on the book. The sense of milieu in the film is not inferior to that of the book, and the explanation of the characters is much better. Renoir founds this explanation not on psychology, but on a metaphysics of actors. (1992: 69)

It is Renoir's screenplay that provided the basis for the rewrites done by Alfred Hayes and Lang, who were charged by Wald with making the protagonist, now called Jeff Warren (Glenn Ford), resistant to the pleas of his lover, Vicki (Gloria Grahame), who is desperate to have him save her by killing her violent husband Carl (Broderick Crawford). Jeff refuses to do the murder and he finds himself disgusted by her story of how she had revelled in the attentions of Owens (Grandon Rhodes), the former seducer killed by Carl in a jealous fit. Vicki tries to leave town and make a new life, but the film ends with Carl seeking her out and strangling her when she taunts him for his inadequacies.

As is the case in *Scarlet Street*, the murderer is not apprehended by the police, but is left with the wreckage he has made of his life. It was at Wald's insistence that the Lantier character was made more sympathetic, in the manner of other noir protagonists – such as Rip Murdock (Humphrey Bogart) in John Cromwell's *Dead Reckoning* (1947) – who fall for a dangerous woman, but then see through her lies, often, but not always, disentangling themselves before they are themselves destroyed. There was, of course, no pressure on Lang, as there had been on Renoir, to remain faithful to the novel's most shocking and notorious plot point; that Vicki is murdered by Carl is, on the one hand, poetically just, but, on the other, a brutal, shocking acknowledgement of his emotional weakness, which manifests itself in frustrated violence (forging a link, of course, with Chris's murder of Kitty in *Scarlet Street*).

Compared to Zola, de la Fouchardière was a much lesser figure, a well-known journalist who published a continuing stream of novels in the period, most of them in the vein of light social satire; *La Chienne* is his only work that has not faded from popular memory because of the Renoir and then the Lang screen versions. Many of de la Fouchardière's novels are social satire (directed against France's colonial subjects, the Catholic hierarchy, the officer corps, and *fonctionnaires* of every stripe). *La Chienne* is distinctive in offering a bitter vision of the quiet desperation of the life lived by a somewhat arrogant petit bourgeois, ironically named Legrand (Michel Simon), who is carped at by a dissatisfied wife, even as he longs for the love of a beautiful woman and for some kind of meaningful *métier* in which to explore unrealised talents. As the novelist portrays him, Legrand is 'a nice enough but timid guy, extraordinarily naïve even though no longer young . . . disposing of a refinement in terms of feelings and intellectual interests that, in the social milieu he moved, insured that he would be thought an imbecile' (de la Fouchardière 1930: 10, my translation).

In both film versions of the novel, his wishes come spectacularly, but disastrously, true; at one point, Legrand has installed himself in an *atelier*, turning out paintings, and accompanied by a beautiful woman, Lulu (Janie Marèze), who protests her love for him. He is blissfully unaware that his work is being marketed to gallery owners by Lulu's 'boyfriend' Dédé (Georges Flamant), who is revelling in the high style of living (including a fancy roadster) that these illicit gains are affording the two of them. The only apparent blight on Legrand's happiness is the demanding harridan he married, but, in a gesture of wish fulfilment right out of a fairy tale, her previous husband turns up; the man is not dead, as all had thought, but now returns, and foolishly, to blackmail his successor. Easily bamboozled, the errant spouse is forced to reunite with his ex, freeing Legrand to marry Lulu. This moment of resolution, however, is illusory since everything is founded on lies that Legrand has foolishly swallowed, including the rather obvious fact that Lulu is a prostitute working to support her pimp Dédé; forced finally to face the truth of her deception, Legrand murders her, an act so out of character that he never even falls under suspicion.

In the end, Legrand is reduced to roaming the streets in search of his next meal, tortured by regret and chagrin; his paintings become celebrated by the art world, but, as a result of a scam perpetrated upon him by Lulu and Dédé, he is not acknowledged as the artist. Instead, it is the scheming and untalented young woman whom the world acclaims as a wonderful new discovery, but then this is small comfort to either her, murdered by Legrand in a jealous rage, or the streetwise but foolish Dédé, who is quickly arrested for the crime. With circumstantial evidence against him, including his own bad character, he is swiftly convicted and executed with a justice of precisely the ironic sort that seems to have fascinated the cynical novelist. The despicable Dédé dies for a crime he might well have committed but did not commit, while Legrand, surely the most aggrieved party in this sordid business, survives only to suffer deeply the guilt that his sociopathic rival would certain have found untroubling had the shoe been on the other foot.

These Renoir films, as Durgnat, among others, has observed, can be seen as continental precursors of what has often been termed the noir sensibility, and this is why they were transferred to the American screen with very few changes beyond those made necessary by a change of setting in each case to America. It is particularly interesting that through the process of remaking they were eventually in a sense incorporated into the very series they probably in part inspired:

> If we define the *film noir* as a crime thriller with a pessimistic, cynical, sardonic approach and mood, then Renoir pioneers the French *film noir* of the '30s with *La Chienne*, while *La Bête Humaine* teaches the Americans that such a film needn't be an all-action, all-swaggering picture. (Durgnat 1974: 183)

By the early 1940s, when the first noir films were hitting American screens, hard-boiled fiction had already demonstrated an international appeal, especially in France, where the prestigious publishing house Gallimard in 1945 founded the *Série Noire* (still thriving in the twenty-first century) in order to commission and publish French translations of Chandler, Hammett and the others under the directorship of one of the country's leading literary figures, Marcel Duhamel (see Lhomeau 2000). More interesting for our discussion here, as Duhamel and others have noted, the hard-boiled trend resonated with established strains within modern French fiction writing (and, of course, in its cinema as well, which was like Hollywood very dependent on literary adaptation). The relentless search for useful material for what were then known in the industry as crime melodramas meant that *Black Mask* fiction would not be the only source of new productions. *La Chienne* and *Bête Humaine*, it is clear, were attractive to Hollywood *not* because they were Jean Renoir 'landmarks' that might be profitably recycled, but because they had demonstrated that the source material they showcased could readily be reconfigured for the current Hollywood series. To *Scarlet Street*'s screenwriter Dudley Nichols, the de la Fouchardière novel, published in the USA as *Poor Sap* in 1931, proved crucial, as McGilligan records. In putting together the screenplay, Nichols 'returned to the well-constructed de la Fouchardière novel . . . the through-line for the scenario would follow the novel almost scene by scene' (1997: 321).

It is a remarkable tribute to the novelist's sardonic view of an unredeemed human condition, with a turn towards violence a possibility even in the most skittish and naïve of men, that this grim story survives in all its essential details in not only the Renoir, but also the Lang versions. Some local censorship boards in the USA found it problematic that the pathetic protagonist, now named Chris Cross (Edward G. Robinson), is not arrested and convicted for the murder of Kitty (Joan Bennett), who, somewhat sympathetically, is portrayed as being just as erotically enslaved to her pimp Johnny (Dan Duryea) as Chris is to her. Lang, and his producer Wanger, claimed that the story offers a deep endorsement of conventional morality since Cross, failing to kill himself, turns into a homeless bum, a judgement with which the Catholic Legion of Decency concurred (see Bernstein 1999 and McGilligan 1997 for further details). Lang and his collaborators change the ending, but only slightly. In the original novel, Legrand suffers the final indignity of watching his self-portrait, sold for a huge sum to a private collector, then loaded into a delivery van, a scene that dramatises the final, humiliating severing of his person from the celebrity that only bears his image, and whose riches and fame he cannot share. In *Scarlet Street*, it is a portrait of his murdered beloved that Chris, wandering the streets of New York, spies in the window of a fancy gallery, yet another reminder of Kitty's perfidy, which includes passing herself off as the artist.

The American version emphasises the *amour fou* that is a characteristic noir theme, even as it provides a strong and unmistakable link to Lang's very successful previous film, *Woman in the Window* (1944). Lang and Wanger even emphasise the connection between the two productions with an intriguing gesture. *Scarlet Street* prominently features a portrait of sexy Joan Bennett displayed in the window of a midtown art gallery. There, a middle-aged man who had desperately wished for sexual adventure gazes upon the image he painted, in a recapitulation of one of the most memorable sequences from *Woman in*

Figure 2.1   Ruined and homeless at film's end, Chris Cross (Edward G. Robinson) sees the portrait he painted of his inamorata Kitty (Joan Bennett) carried out of the gallery where it has just been sold as one of 'her' best works, *Scarlet Street* (1945)

the Window. Once again, Robinson embodies a poignant longing that cannot be satisfied, even as attempts to do so – both real and imagined – must end in frustration and self-destruction of one form or another. Once again, Bennett finds herself aestheticised, idealised in artistic gestures that confirm the remoteness that makes her the ideal object of male fantasy. These parallels, however, should not be read as authorial in the traditional sense; they were selected and instantiated for quite another purpose entirely.

And, it should be clear at this point, the film's fidelity to *La Chienne* was incidental, of no significance to the filmmakers. The novel's concentration on three main characters, in whose different voices it is narrated, was important because *Scarlet Street* was meant to reunite the principal cast of *Window* in which Robinson, Duryea, and Bennett played roles almost identical to the ones they were assigned in the Renoir remake. Based on a popular novel by J. H. Wallis, *Once Off Guard*, to which producer Nunnally Johnson had purchased the rights, *Woman in the Window* tells the story of a bored academic named Wanley (Robinson), who is, as Wallis conceives him, 'fifty-six years old. Growing old, growing old. Not much fun left. Of course, no girl would look at

Figure 2.2   Professor Wanley (Edward G. Robinson) gazes dreamily at the portrait of a beautiful woman (Joan Bennett), who suddenly materialises to make his acquaintance, *Woman in the Window* (1944)

him now . . . he had had no sexual experience in his life except with his wife' (1942: 13). After an evening with colleagues at his club, he wanders the streets of midtown, not eager to return home because his wife and children have left the city for a summer vacation. Staring at the portrait of a beautiful woman that he and his companions had earlier found attractive, he suddenly finds the woman, Alice Reed (Bennett), by his side. His mild flirtation is met with some interest and an invitation to visit her apartment.

Barely inside, Wanley finds himself attacked by yet another middle-aged man, who is apparently her lover, a prominent businessman named Mazard (Arthur Loft), whom he kills with a pair of scissors handed to him by Alice. It's clearly self-defence, but Wanley fears professional ruin if the police are called. He loads the body into his car and dumps it in the woods off the West Side Parkway. Drawn into the investigation, which is conducted by one of his friends, Wanley finds it nearly impossible to avoid self-incrimination, but the real threat to the cover-up comes when a private detective (Duryea), who had been shadowing Mazard, shows up at Alice's apartment. Realising that the man's blackmail will never end, the erstwhile couple try to poison him, but fail. Fearing certain exposure, Wanley takes the poison himself just as the detective is tracked down by police, killed in a shoot-out, with evidence in his pocket that implicates him in Mazard's murder. Fearing such a conclusion might be too grim, Johnson added a surprise ending: bored by his reading of a romantic text (the Song of Songs), Wanley had fallen asleep at the club. He only imagined the adventure that ends so badly for him, confirming that life holds nothing for him but the dull routine in which he is thoroughly trapped.

Woman in the Window was a substantial box-office success, and when Lang formed Diana Productions, his new partner, Wanger, dug *La Chienne* out of the studio files hoping to repeat the popular aspects of the production (the property had been purchased by Ernst Lubitsch some years before, but, with the Breen office disapproving, had never been produced). *Scarlet Street* proved the ideal vehicle for a remake, with a strikingly similar plot and main characters providing the opportunity for substantial improvement on the original, as more scenes were written for Duryea and Bennett, who are now lovers rather than antagonists, and fewer of them feature Robinson in what is for the most part a passive role. He is now no longer trapped in a narrative devoted to the exposure of his character's wrongdoing, little more than a bystander providing one guilty reaction after another. Now his character, though yet that of another middle-aged man in search of erotic adventure, is rounder and more sympathetic, following the complexities sketched out by de la Fouchardière. Chris's desire for an artistic career poignantly expresses his dissatisfaction with a life of deadly routines, including a domestic arrangement in which his overbearing wife forces him to manage the kitchen. The entrapment from which he derives no happiness offers a telling contrast to the erotic, yet equally exploitative, relationship between Johnny and Kitty, in which she is his proper counterpart.

La Chienne thus offered the successful acting ensemble of *Woman in the Window* the opportunity to develop in more depth and complexity the more two-dimensional characters sketched out in the earlier production. Furthermore, this time Lang and Wanger did not retreat from the downbeat ending they found in their source, and the grim inconclusion, riddled with ironies, added considerably to the film's aura of realism, contesting – as many noirs would in the years to come – the industry emphasis on happy endings and the provision of 'compensating moral value', as the Production Code Administration termed it, to balance the presence of wrongdoing.

Another change, of course, is the reconfiguration of the acts of violence – one committed, the other only attempted – that are at the centre of the plot in *The Woman in the Window*. In both films the streetwise, scheming, and thoroughly unlikeable characters played by Duryea come to unmerited bad end at the hands of the law, but in *Scarlet Street* Cross kills Kitty in a fit of righteous and jealous rage after she humiliates him. It seems true enough, as Julie Grossman observes, that 'a large majority of the so-called bad women in noir are not demonized in the films in which they appear and are very often shown to be victims' (2009: 2). This is certainly true of Kitty, who is pushed by Johnny to lead Chris on, and then, once his interest is aroused, wheedle money from the poor man that he must steal from his employer. And it is true of Vicki in *Human Desire* as well. Lang was able to deliver interesting portraits of women who are victimised victimisers, and this talent was furthered in his work with producer Wald at Columbia, where he signed a one-year contract, with the possibility for extensions, in 1953.

Partnered with Norman Krasna, Wald had been the producer for one of Lang's most successful American films, *Clash by Night* (1952), based on a Clifford Odets play in which the main character, played by Barbara Stanwyck, is an independent woman profoundly dissatisfied by her life and her relationship with men, including an attractive misogynist (Robert Ryan), who mistreats her but whom she finds it difficult to resist. Columbia soon provided Lang with another project featuring a woman trapped in an abusive relationship. Despite the fact that its narrative is a tissue of clichés (crusading cop cracks mobster ring and delivers Mr Big to justice), *The Big Heat* (1953) offers a rich texture that pleased audiences; Debby Marsh (Gloria Grahame) is the moll of one of the gang's underlings, Vince (Lee Marvin), who, jealous of her apparent interest in the film's protagonist, Detective Dave Bannion (Glenn Ford), throws boiling coffee in her face, scarring half of it horribly. Debby is soon transformed into a righteous avenger, providing Bannion with the information he needs to arrest the gang boss and involving herself in the round-up of those involved. In a confrontation with Vince, she throws boiling water in his face, and in the resulting shoot-up the two kill each other, with Bannion by Debby's side in her poignant death scene.

Human Desire provides Gloria Grahame with the opportunity to repeat this performance, with Glenn Ford this time her lover, as the plot focuses on this relationship in a way that their previous pairing had not permitted. Furthermore, as did not happen in *The Big Heat*, the duo are now provided with a steamy encounter as Vicki, after the murder, seduces Jeff to ensure that he will not reveal her presence in the railroad car. In the Renoir original, this calculating move is underplayed, with Séverine only briefly chatting up an impassive Lantier, but it proves successful. In Lang's film, Jeff's falling under the spell of Vicki is more convincingly explained. Seduced as a young girl, an exploitation she in turns revels in and is repelled by, Vicki offers an instability that Jeff in the end cannot accept; the script offers up a number of scenes in which she speaks of her past to him, always telling the story a bit differently until she finally reveals her sense of empowerment by the abuse, and it is her sense of her own sexuality (just hinted at in the Renoir original) that causes him to recoil in disgust. She is, of course, proven right that only if Jeff murdered Carl could the two have found happiness together. Already exemplified by his murder of Owens, Carl's potential for jealous violence would have led him to murder her at some point sooner or later.

In Vicki, Lang offers up a fuller portrait of the dangerous but victimised woman than either Renoir or Zola, one that is in line with what Grossman (2009) identifies as one of the principal thematic concerns of the film noir. Like *Scarlet Street*, *Human Desire* not only remakes its official source, but also repeats crucial elements of previous Lang projects that had proven popular with audiences, as the filmmakers involved strove to coax further box-office success from a string of similar, yet entirely different properties, confirming the crucial role that multiplicities play in analysing production strategies, of which remaking is one of the most important. The hope of those involved was not to do artistic justice to two Renoir landmark films. It was, more humbly, that *Scarlet Street* would be as successful as *Woman in the Window*, and that *Human Desire* would please audiences as much as had *The Big Heat*.

References

Bazin, André (1992), *Jean Renoir*, ed. François Truffaut, trans. W. W. Halsey II and William H. Simon, New York: Da Capo Press.

Bernstein, Matthew (1999), 'A Tale of Three Cities: the Banning of *Scarlet Street*', in Matthew Bernstein (ed.), *Controlling Hollywood: Censorship and Regulation in the Studio Era*, New Brunswick, NJ: Rutgers University Press, 157–85.

Biesen, Sheri Chienen (2005), *Blackout: World War II and the Origins of Film Noir*, Baltimore: Johns Hopkins University Press.

De la Fouchardière, Georges (1930), *La Chienne*, Paris: Albin Michel.

Doherty, Thomas (2007), *Hollywood's Censor: Joseph I. Breen & the Production Code Administration*, New York: Columbia University Press.

Durgnat, Raymond (1974), *Jean Renoir*, Berkeley: University of California Press.

Foley, Barbara (1993), *Radical Representations: Politics and Form in U.S. Proletarian Fiction*, Durham, NC: Duke University Press.

Grossman, Julie (2009), *Re-Thinking the Femme Fatale in Film Noir: Ready for her Close-Up*, Basingstoke: Palgrave Macmillan.

Leitch, Thomas (1990), 'Twice-Told Tales: The Rhetoric of the Remake', *Literature/Film Quarterly*, 18: 3, pp. 138–49.

Lhomeau, Franck (2000), 'Le Véritable lancement de la série noire', *Temps noir*, Novembre, pp. 50–122.

McCann, Sean (2000), *Gumshoe America: Hard-Boiled Fiction and the Rise and Fall of New Deal America*, Durham, NC: Duke University Press.

McGilligan, Patrick (1997), *Fritz Lang: The Nature of the Beast*, New York: St Martin's.

Maltby, Richard (1984), '*Film Noir*: The Politics of the Maladjusted Text', *Journal of American Studies*, 18, pp. 49–71.

Mazdon, Lucy (2000), *Encore Hollywood: Remaking French Cinema*, London: British Film Institute.

Mazdon, Lucy (2013), 'Remaking Renoir in Hollywood', in Alastair Phillips and Ginette Vincendeau (eds), *A Companion to Jean Renoir*, Oxford: Wiley-Blackwell, pp. 555–71.

Nestingen, Andrew (2008), *Crime and Fantasy in Scandinavia: Fiction, Film, and Social Change*, Seattle: University of Washington Press.

Nolan, William F. (1987), *The Black Mask Boys: Masters in the Hard-Boiled School of Detective Fiction*, New York: Mysterious PR.

Palmer, R. Barton (2016), *Shot on Location: Postwar American Cinema and the Exploration of Real Place*, New Brunswick, NJ: Rutgers University Press.

Pettey, Homer M. and R. Barton Palmer (eds) (2014), *International Noir*, Edinburgh: Edinburgh University Press.

Prinzler, Hans Helmut (2012), *Licht und Schatten: Die grosse Stumm- und Tonfilme der Weimarer Republik*, Berlin: Schirmer-Mosel.

Schrader, Paul (1972), 'Notes on Film Noir', *Film Comment*, Spring, pp. 8–13.

Smith, Erin (2000), *Hard-Boiled: Working Class Readers and Pulp Magazines*, (Philadelphia: Temple University Press).

Turk, Edward Baron (1989), *Child of Paradise: Marcel Carné and the Golden Age of French Cinema*, Cambridge, MA: Harvard University Press.

Verevis, Constantine (2006), *Film Remakes*, Edinburgh: Edinburgh University Press.

Wallis, J. H. (1942), *Once Off Guard*, New York: E. P. Dutton.

Willett, John (1970), *Expressionism*, New York: McGraw-Hill.

3. THE CULTURAL POLITICS OF REMAKING SPANISH HORROR FILMS IN THE TWENTY-FIRST CENTURY: *QUARANTINE* AND *COME OUT AND PLAY*

Andy Willis

The financial potential of horror films has long been appreciated by producers and others in control of film finance. Many of the most successful horror films of recent decades, from *The Texas Chainsaw Massacre* (Tobe Hooper, 1974) to *Paranormal Activity* (Oren Peli, 2007), have been made on low budgets and have subsequently found large audiences that in turn ensured they provided high returns for those who had invested in them. Many of these successful horror films have also been part of cycles of production that have thrived on the reproduction of particularly familiar themes, settings, narrative structures and even visual styles and motifs. This reproduction of features that audiences are already accustomed to and familiar with highlights the horror genre's historical and continued reliance on the duplication of elements that filmmakers see as central to their appeal and which in turn contribute to their popular and financial success.

The slew of productions that appeared in the 1970s that centred on possession and exorcism are typical of such recycling and reworking of popular ingredients. In this case the cycle was driven by the popularity and global box-office success of *The Exorcist* (William Friedkin, 1973) and examples of productions influenced by it included a wide variety of international interpretations of that film's basic formula. These ranged from Turkey (*Seytan*, Metin Erksan, 1974) to Spain (*Exorcismo*, Juan Bosch, 1975) and Italy (*L'anticristo*, Alberto de Martino, 1974), with each instance offering similar stories of demonic possession in a number of different cultural contexts. In these cases the films were marketed in a fashion that clearly evoked Friedkin's hugely popular film in the hope of attracting local audiences who hoped that these more local titles would offer generic similar pleasures.

One way in which contemporary producers have attempted something similar is through remaking horror films that have already proved that their stories have box-office potential. Once again, the basics – plot, character, narrative organisation and even visual style – have demonstrated that they can be successful, so their reworking should prove less risky for financiers than a new product that may be more difficult to market and sell. As Ryan Lizardi has noted, the recent history of the horror film has seen a reappearance of various stories and figures from the 1970s and 1980s. According to him, this recent cycle of production 'has featured a rash of remakes – or "re-imaginings" in the parlance of the marketing campaigns – that have revived those same film texts and characters . . . This is a significant trend for a genre that has never been shy about making sequels to their franchises' (2010: 113). Lizardi goes on to argue that what is notable about these remakes is their 'cultural significance' (113). In addressing this issue he identifies a number of key concerns. These include assessing whether these horror remakes 'speak to current cultural issues', and asking if they have the same potential ideological significance as their originals (114). These questions about the cultural significance and ideological operation of horror remakes seem even more pertinent when the remakes involve a shift in geographical setting and a positioning in a very different cultural context. An example of such a shift would be the recent cycle of American remakes of horror films that originated in East Asia, particularly Japan and South Korea.

In these instances, the shift in global context often rather unceremoniously rips the story from the cultural context of its original incarnation as the architects of the remakes aspire to attract global audiences. This is clearly an economically driven as much as a wholly creative decision, and aspects that may seem to be overly culturally specific – and which have often been the reasons such films have worked for local audiences – are deemed something that needs to be shorn for global distribution and consumption. As Kevin Heffernan notes, for Hollywood productions this is part of an increased importance placed on its international markets and the creation of films that were 'globally marketable' (2014: 67). While the US remakes of East Asian horror films are perhaps the most high-profile examples of this in recent times, they have not been the only source for American companies looking for a good idea to rework and sell to the world.

In response to this wider explosion of international horror reworkings and remakes, this chapter will now focus on the very particular cultural politics of remaking Spanish horror films in the twenty-first century. At the centre of this will be a case study of the US feature *Quarantine* (John Erick Dowdle, 2008) a film that is both structurally and visually similar to its source material, the

2007 Spanish work *[REC]* (Jaume Balagueró and Paco Plaza). This will be followed by another case study, this time of the Mexican-set *Come Out and Play* (Makinov, 2012), a remake of the 1970s Spanish horror film *¿Quién puede matar a un niño? / Who Can Kill a Child?* (Narcisco Ibáñez Serrador, 1976). In both instances I will discuss the ways in which the remakes significantly omit key aspects of the originals and in doing so remove some of the most arresting political aspects of those works and, in their desire to create globally marketable films, render the new versions of these stories less socially engaged. Through the process of translation into another context, the USA and Mexico, the filmmakers behind both remakes choose not to use the model of a culturally engaged, and therefore more potentially political, cinema offered by the originals. It is my contention that it is not simply the process of remaking and translating location that renders these later versions less culturally engaged, but the omission of particular elements of the originals, elements that in both *[REC]* and *Who Can Kill a Child?* offer the audience a politicised rationale for the actions unfolding on screen.

QUARANTINE: REMAKING SPANISH HORROR IN THE TWENTY-FIRST CENTURY

Throughout the late 1980s and into the 1990s Spanish horror production had been in something of a lull since the boom in genre filmmaking that had taken place in the late 1960s and 1970s (see Lazaro Reboll 2012). That successful cycle of production had been facilitated by both international finance and a local appetite for horror films that allowed for the inclusion of elements, such as glimpses of naked flesh and physical violence, that were tightly controlled by the Spanish censors of the period. When censorship was abolished in 1977, following the death of the dictator General Franco two years earlier, the need for vehicles that could carry these elements lessened and the production of more directly sexually explicit soft-core films quickly replaced horror on Spanish cinema screens. The result was a rapid and severe reduction in the number of horror films produced in Spain. That reduction in production was accompanied by a subsequent critical high-handedness that rejected the genre productions of the 1970s in favour of the supposedly more clearly oppositional work of auteur directors, such as Carlos Saura, when the histories of this era of Spanish cinema were written (Willis 2003). For a generation this very particular combination of factors worked to marginalise both the production of horror films within the Spanish film industry and any acknowledgement of the genre's robust contribution to Spain's cinematic past. However, towards the mid-1990s this changed as a number of young directors such as Àlex de la Iglesia and Santiago Segura rediscovered and championed figures from this almost forgotten era of genre production such as Jess Franco and Paul Naschy, and in doing so began to legitimise horror's part in the history of Spanish cinema.

This in turn led to a twenty-first-century revival in Spanish horror film production which has seen both a resurgence of interest in the genre's Iberian past and a renewed popularity for local horror in Spain. Perhaps not surprisingly given the trends noted above, this has in turn led to an interest in remaking Spanish genre films for US and international audiences. While there have been reports of Hollywood reworkings of contemporary Spanish horror films such as *The Orphanage* (J. A. Bayona, 2007) in the film trade press, the most high-profile example of this trend to date is *Quarantine* (2008). As already noted, this is a US remake of *[REC]*, which was successfully released in Spain by Filmax in the autumn of 2007. As with the cycle of remakes of East Asian horror films mentioned earlier, *Quarantine* can be seen to serve the need of the American film industry to create something that is 'globally marketable' (Heffernan 2014: 67). To this end, while there is a credit for the writers of the original, 'based on the motion picture *[REC]* by Jaume Balagueró & Luis A. Berdejo & Paco Plaza', the promotion for the Screen Gems US and international releases of *Quarantine* makes little mention of it being a remake of another film. Indeed, on the commentary track by writer/director John Erick Dowdle and writer/producer Drew Dowdle for the DVD release of *Quarantine* there is no mention whatsoever of there having been an earlier version of the story. Indeed, the pair talk as if the whole thing sprang from their own imaginations and even at one point praise the art director for coming up with an interior design for the setting that resembles a 'Spanish-style' apartment block, as if this were an example of some kind of unparalleled creative inspiration rather than a reproduction of the look of the original Spanish set design. Indeed, even the most cursory comparison shows that the interiors used in *Quarantine* in fact are visually very similar to those utilised in *[REC]*. It seems likely that this seemingly conscious ignoring of *Quarantine*'s cinematic origins would have been at the behest of Screen Gems in their desire to maximise global audiences for their version of the story rather than open up the potential for inquisitive horror fans to seek out *[REC]*.

While Screen Gems may have wished to ignore that *Quarantine* was a remake of *[REC]* and hoped this fact would go unnoticed, genre observers writing on horror and fan websites commented on the similarity between the two films. For example, Bill Gibron's assessment of the similarities between the two films on the *popmatters.com* site is typical. For the most part he focuses on the films' story, characters, actors, direction and gimmicks to highlight the small differences and large similarities between the two. Ultimately, while acknowledging positives about both films, he states:

> Even though it's obvious that both films are trying to copy real life, only the original succeeds as a shocker. The set-ups work better, the over the shoulder reveals and diminished peripheral vision functioning better than

> say, random shocks and sudden looks in the lens. In fact, almost every set-piece sequence (the falling fireman, the textile factory attack, the little girl transformation, the last ditch escape to the penthouse, the discovery of what's inside) is handled better by *[REC]* than in *Quarantine*. (Gibron 2009)

Such an appraisal is typical. For many genre fans *[REC]* is unquestionably the better film. However, few of those commenting on the film consider the nuanced differences that are present that remove the remake from the original's cultural context, and in doing so depoliticise a potential reading of its content. In this case one of the most striking things is how far the remake reproduces the blueprint of the original's visual style but does not retain some of the other, more thematic, elements that resonate socially and politically in the context of Spanish, and even perhaps European, society. The most obvious of these is related to Spain's traditionally Catholic religious associations. At significant moments throughout *[REC]* the makers place Catholic iconography within the film's *mise-en-scène*, suggesting that there may be some links between the church and the virus that has been uncovered in the apartment block, or at the very least that the church might have some involvement in covering up its existence. In Spain, a country with such a strong history of politicised Catholicism, such references would potentially have great significance for certain members of the audience, who might be willing to believe in a potential Vatican-inspired conspiracy rather than simply accepting a supernatural rationale for the virus engulfing the characters. However, while that interpretation of the religious connotations of the original may potentially have been translated into the context of the USA, I would like to explore in more detail a second, more contemporary, political concern that appears in *[REC]*. This revolves around the issue of immigration, and through this I want to develop an argument that suggests the removal of such content, that comes from and speaks to a particular social context, can impact on the potential cultural politics of a story that contains such elements as this.

In the twenty-first century, Spain and much of Europe has seen a significant rise in concerns about migration. For example, within right-wing circles inside Spain there has developed a strong anti-East Asian feeling, and this attitude to immigrants is clearly, and importantly critically, incorporated into *[REC]* through the character of César (played by Carlos Lasarte), an older man who has lived in the apartment block for years. Significantly, while the character's own sexuality – something that could make him the victim of prejudice – is presented in an ambivalent way, particularly through Lasarte's preening and camp performance, César represents a familiar and highly reactionary strand of public opinion in contemporary Spain. The makers of *[REC]* are careful to signify this in their use of *mise-en-scène*, and it is through this aspect of their filmmaking that they suggest that such ideas and attitudes are firmly associated with Spain's more reactionary political past. For example, César wears clothes that seem sartorially conservative and that visually connect him to an older, more right-wing, political past linked to the conservatism and Catholicism of the Franco era. He is balding, with slicked-back, dyed-black hair; he sports a thin, almost pencil, moustache and wears an expensive looking dark sleeveless pullover with a light shirt, with the outfit finished with a striped cravat. For him Spain should be for the 'Spanish', and his idea of what constitutes that status seems drawn from the pre-1975 regime of General Franco, whose hair and moustache his own style evokes. While his slightly camp air, anchored by the way in which actor Lasarte waves his ring-laden hands around when he talks directly to the camera, suggests the potential of a repressed sexuality, the contradictory nature of his attitude to others who he sees as 'different' is not something the character seems ready or willing to acknowledge.

César is an important character, as he allows a reading of *[REC]* that positions the film in relation to contemporary politics in Spain. The character of César represents the attitudes of a bygone age and it is therefore significant that his fascistic scapegoating of the apartment block's East Asian residents gains no traction with many of the other inhabitants or the crew filming, who seem more than ready to mock him and his irrational ideas. His ignorance of others and unwillingness to accommodate any kind of difference is subtly underlined by the fact that he simply labels characters as Chinese, saying that they 'eat raw fish which smells ... They leave the doors open ... and run in and out shouting in Chinese, in Japanese, I don't know. Something I don't understand', while having no interest whatsoever in the actual facts of their origins. César just wants to simplistically blame these 'others' for the virus present in 'his' apartment block. The filmmakers' subtle critique of the character is further brought home by the fact that the film's credits list the characters he is referring to as Japanese rather than Chinese as he asserts when he is interviewed by the television crew.

[REC], particularly through its use of the character César, is a film that has social and political points to make, but does so in a manner that does not overwhelm the generic pleasures it offers its audiences. The manner in which *[REC]* represents César's views, drawing on discourses around race and migration that would be familiar to audiences in Spain, also makes this aspect of the film something that could easily be filleted out by those working to relocate the action to another continent. However, one might also argue that the USA faces similar issues and is engaged in comparable debates around migration. To this end, while the culturally specific politics of *[REC]* may not have been reproduced, as the story is removed from its original context, the more general social engagement of the original could easily have been retained in the remake. This aspect of *Quarantine*'s interpretation of *[REC]* raises an important question

regarding remaking horror films that have a clear social agenda: that is, how far can it be justified to simply cast those concerns aside when the action is relocated to another social and cultural context? Clearly, this process also offers the filmmakers involved in remaking the chance to engage with the issues raised by the original in their new context, reworking the social concerns to address their remake's new contexts. Alongside this, remaking and shifting location also offers other, new and different, opportunities to engage with other political issues, no less significant and maybe more culturally specific to the new setting. The decision not to take up that opportunity is one of the things that render *Quarantine* a less culturally engaged piece of work. This issue is also central to the next example I want to consider, *Come Out and Play* (2012), a Mexican remake of *Who Can Kill a Child?*.

COME OUT AND PLAY: THE POLITICS OF NOT REPEATING

The politics of remaking films with clear social concerns is even more of an issue when one is considering Spanish films from the 1970s, a particularly politicised moment in that country's recent history. *Who Can Kill a Child?* is one of the most striking genre films to come out of Spain in the immediate aftermath of the death of Franco in 1975. Its director, Narcisco Ibáñez Serrador, had previously directed the successful gothic horror film *La residencia / The Finishing School* (1969), which had been one of the cornerstones of the horror production boom in the late 1960s and early 1970s. However, Ibáñez Serrador had also enjoyed a fruitful career in television, and by 1976 was certainly more famous for his work within that medium in Spain than for his feature films. This television work included the influential horror series *Historias para no dormir / Stories to Keep you Awake* (1966–82) and the game show *Un, dos, tres . . . responda otra vez / One, Two, Three . . . Respond Again* (1972–2004). Both were enormously successful with Spanish audiences and made Ibáñez Serrador something of a household name (and face) owing to his personal appearances in them. As Antonio Lazaro Reboll has identified, Ibáñez Serrador's status as a familiar figure within popular culture was further enhanced by his links to a variety of publications, including book and comic tie-ins to his television work that carried both his name and on occasion his image (2012: 108–9).

Lázaro Reboll has investigated the critical response to *Who Can Kill a Child?* in Spain, and his research has unearthed a number of reactions that show that in that territory the film was promoted as something of a major genre release by an important figure within local popular culture (2012: 119–20). For example, the Spanish poster used to promote the film foregrounded its director's name ahead of anyone else's including the lead performers Lewis Fiander and Prunella Ransome. The film may therefore be seen as one driven by a seriously minded director who had something to say about the contemporary world. Having identified this, one might ask if Makinov, the filmmaker behind the remake, attempts in any way to renegotiate Ibáñez Serrador's cultural and political ideas, particularly about young people, alongside simply reproducing the earlier film's story? In remaking *Who Can Kill a Child?* in present-day Mexico, the makers of *Come Out and Play* remove the original's primary contextual power and fail to replace it with anything comparable that would enable it to be read as an equally forceful political comment.

As has already been argued in relation to the non-reappearance of a character carrying some of the social and political significance of César in *Quarantine*, when those behind a remake choose not to include or rework certain components it can work to depoliticise the newer version. In the case of *Come Out and Play* this can be seen from the very first frames of the film. In order to grasp the significance of the omissions in Makinov's version I want to look in some detail at the opening of Ibáñez Serrador's original film. In terms of their storylines both *Who Can Kill a Child?* and *Come Out and Play* focus on two tourists, a married couple who are expecting a child, who are on holiday and venture to a village on a small island. In utilising this set-up both films credit as their source the 1976 short novel *El juego de los niños* (Sala Editorial) by Juan José Plans. Its adaptation for *Who Can Kill a Child?* is credited to Luis Peñafiel, the pen name of Ibáñez Serrador, who has suggested that he basically took little more than the basic idea for the film from the source. In an interview contained on the Eureka 2011 DVD release of the film he states that in the novel what provokes the children's rebellion against the adults is a yellow powder that falls all over the village. However, he goes on to dismisses this idea as 'a little absurd and fantasy like', stating that '[the novel by] Plans gave me the idea for the story and that was enough for me to write the script . . . There are lots of differences between the novel and the script.' Interestingly, given his articulation of the differences between his film and the source novel, the remake does not credit Luis Peñafiel or *Who Can Kill a Child?*, only Plans' novel. Given the similarity between the two films' visual styles, particularly the use of bright sunlit locations, this seems a little disingenuous.

In *Who Can Kill a Child?* the central couple are Britons in Spain; in the remake they are Americans in Mexico. In the press reviews of the latter, critics acknowledged *Come Out and Play*'s status as a remake. In *The Hollywood Reporter* Frank Scheck described it as a 'nastily efficient remake of the little known 1976 Spanish cult item *Who Can Kill a Child?*' (2013), while Eric Hynes, writing for *Time Out*, stated that 'this remake of '70s Spanish horror film *Who Can Kill a Child?* is less a contemporary upgrade than an eagerly creaky exploitative throwback' (2013). Unlike the fans considering *[REC]* and *Quarantine*, and like most reviewers of the film, these writers, perhaps being unfamiliar with the earlier version, did not draw attention to any of the differences between the two versions of the same story. In particular they did not touch on one of the biggest dissimilarities between the two films – namely, their openings – as it is here that the remake diverges significantly from Ibáñez Serrador's original.

The opening sequence of *Who Can Kill a Child?* is a powerful overture to the themes of childhood and violence that will be explored throughout the film's main action. With the production's credits displayed over it, this introductory sequence is made up of a series of harrowing black-and-white archival and documentary images of children and young people in a variety of conflicts. A voice-over explains the context of each, emphasising the situations' impact on children. The first images are photographs from Nazi created ghettos and concentration camps. These include a montage of shots of malnourished people followed by images of dead bodies and medical experimentation. In all of these instances the focus of the pictures is on children and young people's suffering in these extreme situations. This emphasis on the anguish of the young continues when text appears on screen bluntly stating 'World War II, 14 million children dead'. This is followed a succession of more harrowing footage, this time of children's anguish during the India–Pakistan war. Over these shots the text proclaims, 'Indo-Pakistan war: total dead approx. 2 million, 1.2 million children.' Next on screen is footage from Korea; this includes shots of US forces undertaking military manoeuvres and disabled children on the streets, many of whom have clearly lost limbs. These shots are accompanied by the text 'Korean war, total dead approx. 1.2 million, 550,000 children'. The next part of the sequence uses images from the Vietnam War. Again these shots are accompanied by on-screen text, which this time states 'Vietnam war, total dead approx. 3 million, 1.8 million children'. What is worthy of note here is that this section includes footage of young people protesting against the war. The final part of the sequence shows footage from the war in Biafra. Once again text directs the viewer to the place of children in the conflict. It states, 'War in Biafra, total dead approx. 500,000, children 390 children.' After just over seven and a half minutes the sequence ends with a shot of a suffering child in Biafra which dissolves to one of a blond-haired child on a beach in Spain. On the surface the content could not be more different. By the end of the film we will have been asked to rethink this simple assumption as what will follow suggests something else.

To fully grasp the horror of *Who Can Kill a Child?* one might argue that the viewer has to have been positioned through the contextualising of the opening credits. The logic of the film seems to be that the horror that we witness in what follows in the main body of the story seems like a logical extension of the protests against violence glimpsed in the opening. The film

suggests that children cannot be continually treated like this without responding, and ultimately postulates that their actions in *Who Can Kill a Child?* may
be one horrific, yet unsettlingly coherent, possibility for action. Disquieting
though this sequence is, it is made all the more so by the occasional inter-
spersing of the sound of children giggling between the serious and informative
voice-over.

This opening sequence is powerful and distinguishes *Who Can Kill a Child?*
from many of the other horror films of the period. However, in some territories outside Spain the film was shorn of this sequence as distributors sought
to create a film that was closer to 100 minutes in duration and thus easier to
sell to theatres specialising in exploitation fare. This process also led to the
film acquiring a variety of alternative titles such as *Island of the Damned* and
Island of Death. However, whether this was done to depoliticise the film or
not, without its powerful opening preamble *Who Can Kill a Child?* lacks the
moral rationale for the carnage that follows. Significantly, the makers of *Come
Out and Play* do not include anything comparable with the original's shocking
opening. Without it the more recent film lacks the inventive anchor that makes
the original such a radical statement. So, even removed from the context Spain
in the 1970s, the cutting of the opening sequence takes away one of *Who Can
Kill a Child?*'s more universal statements: that is, that children will eventually respond to the horrors adults put them through. In an interview, again
included on the 2011 Eureka DVD release of his film, Ibáñez Serrador states,
'you can imagine if [children] were a different species they would defend themselves. Like ants would defend themselves.' Here, unsurprisingly, the director
is clearly aware of the potential meaning that the preamble suggested for the
rest of the film.

The thinking behind the inclusion of the images and voice-over in the credit
sequence also bleeds into the main body of the film. In particular, it informs the
decisions behind the visual style adopted throughout. Working with cinematographer José Luis Alcaine, who would go on to work regularly with Pedro
Almodóvar, Ibáñez Serrador has created a striking visual style for *Who Can
Kill a Child?*. This is centred on creating what might be termed an 'everyday'
atmosphere. The world of the film is very light and bright, with most of its
action taking place in blazing sunlight rather than the dark interiors of many
other horror films. This feeling is enhanced by the use of locations where the
streets have buildings that are covered in whitewash reinforcing the brightness
of the film's overall look. The island setting also allowed for the creation of
a sense of isolation but at the same time permitted the filmmakers to suggest
somewhere anyone could holiday, again enhancing the everyday feel of the
settings.

In another interview included on the Eureka DVD release of the film, cinematographer Alcaine states that, given the content, the setting, and the fact

that he saw the film as something that existed in the space between Alfred Hitchcock's *The Birds* (1963) and George A. Romero's *Night of the Living Dead* (1968), he tried to make the film look like an 'ordinary' film rather than a horror film. This idea of creating a world that looked like what Alcaine terms 'that of an everyday movie' certainly enhances the idea that the events that are shown, however extraordinary, could happen to anybody at any time. This approach to the visual style of the film clearly links to its major theme: that the extra-ordinariness of the events are made at the same time to have an everydayness that suggests they could happen to anyone. The children's actions are at once horrific, the use of shots of blood on their victims emphasising this, but via the film's visual style they are also rendered somehow ordinary, and by extension 'normal', particularly given the extremes we have seen children experience in the film's credit sequence. The isolation of the island also suggests a space where an almost Darwinian development in humans could take place, one that sees the next generation, the children we see on screen, responding to the type of violence seen in the credit sequence, and acting before they are acted upon.

Come Out and Play is able to reproduce the atmosphere and visual style of *Who Can Kill a Child?*. For example, it successfully utilises the original's brightness and island location. However, ultimately its makers choose not to anchor the horrific actions of its young children in any rationale or reason beyond simply an unexplained turn to the dark side. It does not even use the idea of a mysterious yellow powder that is present in Plans source novel. Because of this, *Come Out and Play*, like some of the international cuts of Ibáñez Serrador's work, lacks the potential of the original film's take on the story to suggest that the actions of the terrible children may be the result of humanity's ability to commit atrocity after atrocity without seemingly learning anything. It is significant then that *Come Out and Play* leaves out any allusion to a cause for the actions of its killer children. Here, once again it is clearly the act of omission that ultimately works to depoliticise a film remake.

I acknowledge that the approach to remaking Spanish horror films contained in this chapter may suggest that I am arguing that some kind of political authenticity exists or emanates from the 'original' versions. This, however, is far from the case. What I am suggesting is that focusing simply on the similarities and differences of remakes such as *Quarantine* and *Come Out and Play* often ignores the contexts within which the originals were conceived and produced and their particular engagement with social and political issues arising from these historical moments. What I have done here is move beyond such a simplistic approach and consider the contexts of production of, in this case, horror films, and suggest that this usefully reminds us of the political urgency of these particular originals, showing that they carry, in very particular historical moments, an earnestness that can be lost in different times in different ver sions. That is, unless a political engagement with the new cultural contexts is offered that is in some way comparable to that of the original.

REFERENCES

Gibron, Bill (2009), 'Anatomy of a Remake: *REC* vs. *Quarantine*', in *popmatters.com*, <http://www.popmatters.com/post/108115-anatomy-of-a-remake-rec-vs.-quarantine/> (last accessed 19 May 2016).
Heffernan, Kevin (2014), 'Risen from the Vaults: Recent Horror Film Remakes and the American Film Industry', in Richard Nowell (ed.), *Merchants of Menace: The Business of Horror Cinema*. London: Bloomsbury, pp. 61–73.
Hynes, Eric (2013), '*Come Out and Play*', in *Time Out*, <http://www.timeout.com/us/film/come-out-and-play-movie-review> (last accessed 19 May 2016).
Lazaro Reboll, Antonio (2012), *Spanish Horror Cinema*, Edinburgh: Edinburgh University Press.
Lizardi, Ryan (2010), '"Re-Imagining" Hegemony and Misogyny in the Contemporary Slasher Remake', in *Journal of Popular Film and Television*, 38: 3, pp. 113–21.
Scheck, Frank (2013), '*Come Out and Play*', in *The Hollywood Reporter* 20 March, 2013, <http://www.hollywoodreporter.com/review/come-play-film-review-429984> (last accessed 19 May 2016).
Willis, Andy (2003), 'Spanish Horror and the Flight from Art Cinema', in Mark Jancovich et al. (eds), *Defining Cult Movies: The Cultural Politics of Oppositional Taste*, Manchester: Manchester University Press, pp. 71–83.

4. 'FOR THE DEAD TRAVEL FAST': THE TRANSNATIONAL AFTERLIVES OF DRACULA

Iain Robert Smith

> As he spoke he smiled, and the lamplight fell on a hard-looking mouth, with very red lips and sharp-looking teeth, as white as ivory. One of my companions whispered to another the line from Burger's 'Lenore'.
> 'Denn die Todten reiten schnell'. ('For the dead travel fast'.)
>
> (Stoker 1997: 17)

In the opening chapter of Bram Stoker's *Dracula*, Jonathan Harker recounts his travels via Budapest and the northern Romanian town of Bistritz towards the castle of Count Dracula. He has been instructed to join a coach to the Borgo Pass where a driver and carriage will be waiting to take him on to the castle. In the scene quoted above, Harker meets the mysterious driver who he discovers has very red lips and sharp-looking teeth, and he overhears one of his travel companions whispering 'Denn die Todten reiten schnell' ('For the dead travel fast'). As Harker himself notes, these words reference the gothic poem 'Lenore' by the German author Gottfried August Bürger, in which the eponymous heroine rides swiftly through the night on horseback accompanied by a stranger who looks exactly like her recently dead fiancé William. This reference to that earlier gothic text is, of course, a hint at the vampiric status of the coach driver, but the quotation also resonates with the broader theme of travel and cultural encounter that runs throughout the novel. On the very first page, Harker reflects that 'The impression I had was that we were leaving the West and entering the East' (1997: 10), and that his travels were taking him 'among the traditions of Turkish rule' (1997: 10). The novel then repeatedly returns to this motif of travel in which Harker is venturing into an orientalised East, and it is notable that Dracula's later travels to London represent something of an inversion of this colonialist narrative, where it is now Dracula who is entering the West. The vampire figure, in Stoker's text and beyond, is positioned as a traveller – a threatening Other – who can transgress both physical and geographical borders, and it is important to note that this exploration of alterity was initially very much tied to its origins in late Victorian Britain.

Indeed, a number of scholars, including Elleke Boehmer (2004), Stephen Shapiro (2008) and Tabish Khair (2009, 2013), have discussed the postcolonial politics of Stoker's 1897 novel and the ways in which the text gives expression to a British 'imperialism that feels itself to be overstretched and insecure' (Boehmer 2004: 56). The Dracula figure in Bram Stoker's novel embodies many of the anxieties surrounding the British empire during that period – especially the notion that Britain might be under threat from a subsequent invasion from the East. As Khair has noted in his scholarship on postcolonialism and the gothic, depictions of vampirism throughout the nineteenth century tended to depend upon 'various discourses and fears that were most commonly employed to deal with colonial Otherness' (2013: 110). It is evident that the novel *Dracula* – written by an Irish novelist living in turn-of-the-century London and influenced by the Eastern European folklore surrounding historical figures like Countess Bathory and Vlad the Impaler – was engaging with the prevailing discourses and fears of otherness, and that these were very much anchored in their particular historical context.

However, despite the novel *Dracula*'s situatedness in relation to Victorian Britain and its imperial history, the character of Count Dracula has proven to be eminently adaptable, appearing in various guises in over 300 feature films produced all around the world. As with other iconic characters such as Sherlock Holmes and Batman, Dracula has been freed from his roots in a source text and has entered what Will Brooker describes as 'the realm of the icon' (1999: 185). Consequently, while the initial source text was very much rooted in the context of Victorian Britain, subsequent adaptations have transposed the character into innumerable different locations and periods. This rampant proliferation poses challenges for a study of Dracula films given that there have been so many incarnations of the character that it is near impossible to come up with a definitive list. While the Internet Movie Database (IMDb) lists 304 feature films that include a Dracula character in the credits, this doesn't include films like the Mexican *El Vampiro* (*The Vampire*, 1957) that renames the character Count Lavud, or films like the Ramsay Bros' *Bandh Darwaza* (*Closed Door*, 1990), which has a central character closely modelled on Count Dracula but placed within a wholly unrelated story. Nor does it include the numerous Indian films such as Bhoosan Lal's *Dracula* (1999) or

Harinam Singh's *Shaitani Dracula* (*Devilish Dracula*, 2006) that borrow the name Dracula but use it as a generic signifier of horror and have little to do with Bram Stoker's vampire tale. The extensive history of *Dracula* borrowings goes well beyond the legally sanctioned remaking of a specific source text, and this makes it a challenging, if nevertheless productive, text to consider within the framework of remake scholarship. As Constantine Verevis has argued:

> Film remaking can be regarded as a specific (institutionalised) aspect of the broader and more open-ended intertextuality . . . [that] can range from the limited repetition of a classic shot or scene . . . to the 'quasi-independent' repetitions of a single story or popular myth, for example, the successive versions of *Dracula*. (2006: 21)

This chapter is therefore partly an attempt to propose a methodology through which we might study these 'quasi-independent' repetitions of a single story such as *Dracula* – especially in cases where these repetitions take place across a variety of national contexts. While there has been a considerable amount of scholarship on the canonical versions of *Dracula* produced in Hollywood and Western Europe, very little has been written on the numerous versions of the Count Dracula character that have appeared in other film industries around the world, and it is my contention that this underexplored transnationalism has much to tell us about the role of remaking within popular filmmaking traditions more broadly. Existing scholarship on the global vampire has tended to frame this as a relatively recent phenomenon, with Martine Beugnet discussing contemporary French vampire cinema in relation to an era of 'intensified transnational circulation' (2007: 77) and Stacey Abbott concluding her history of vampire cinema with the observation that, in the twenty-first century, 'The modern vampire has gone global' (2007: 215). This chapter complicates this historical account by investigating the globalisation of the vampire figure through a number of Dracula films produced in the mid-twentieth century – focusing specifically on the 1953 Turkish film *Drakula İstanbul'da* (*Dracula in Istanbul*), the 1957 Mexican film *El Vampiro* (*The Vampire*), and the 1967 Pakistani film *Zinda Laash* (*The Living Corpse*).

Developing upon the methodology outlined in my monograph *The Hollywood Meme* (Smith 2016), this chapter uses a memetic model in order to trace the specifically transnational afterlives of Dracula. Building on the work of Franco Moretti (2000) and Dudley Andrew (2006) in mapping world literature and world cinema respectively, I am using the structuring metaphor of the 'meme' in order to interrogate the dynamic interplay of global and local within these *Dracula* remakes. Paying close attention to the variety of ways in which Stoker's source text has been adapted and reworked across these different cultural contexts, this chapter therefore complicates existing accounts of *Dracula*'s national specificity and investigates what these transnational remakes can tell us about the intertextual dynamics of global popular cinema. Centrally, what I am attempting here is not simply to analyse specific instances of transnational film remaking, but also to stand back and reflect at a meta-level upon what we are doing as scholars when we are studying transnational film remakes, and what possible ways forward there might be for this growing area of scholarship.

METHODS AND MODELS

It is notable that *Dracula* has become one of the key texts within the burgeoning field of remake studies. Andrew Horton and Stuart McDougal's edited collection *Play It Again, Sam: Retakes on Remakes* (1998), contains chapters on the topic from Lloyd Michaels and Ira Konigsberg, while Jennifer Forrest and Leonard Koos's *Dead Ringers: The Remake in Theory and Practice* (2002) contains numerous brief references to *Dracula* throughout. These two seminal texts focused primarily on the versions of *Dracula* produced in North America and Western Europe, but there have been a number of publications in recent years that have attempted to broaden the corpus by investigating the influence of Dracula beyond these contexts. Tabish Khair and Johan Höglund's edited collection *Transnational and Postcolonial Vampires*, for example, positions the 'vampire narrative as a global and transcultural phenomenon' (2013: 3); Dorothea Fischer-Hornung and Monika Mueller's *Vampires and Zombies: Transcultural Migrations and Transnational Interpretations* is based on the 'conviction that transcultural and transnational imaginaries have shaped and altered the zombie and vampire tropes' (2016: 8); and John Edgar Browning and Caroline Joan Picart's *Draculas, Vampires and Other Undead Forms* contains a section entitled 'Imperialism, Hybridity, and Cross-Cultural Fertilization in Asia' that includes chapters investigating vampires in Hong Kong, Japan, Pakistan and Malaysia (2009: 165–293). This shift towards cross-cultural approaches is, of course, part of a broader transnational turn within film studies scholarship in which scholars are increasingly attempting to investigate the cross-cultural interactions that underpin cinematic production and circulation.

The specific challenge for the study of *Dracula* remakes, however, is the sheer volume of texts from around the world that have borrowed and adapted the character. As Browning and Picart have noted, 'Foreign markets and nonmajor production studios [began] to outproduce "mainstream" cinematic depictions of Dracula by a ratio of at least 3:1 [from the 1960s onwards] . . . literally affording him an almost ravenous multiplicity in markets outside of England and America' (2009: x). Given this history, and the ways in which it complicates the established canon of *Dracula* remakes, we are then faced with the question: What are the most appropriate methods and models that we can utilise to get to grips with that ravenous multiplicity?

One option would be to take a primarily text-based approach and supplement the existing work on the so-called 'mainstream' depictions with close readings devoted to specific lesser-known works. This would certainly help broaden out the discussion, although the production of in-depth close readings of individual Dracula adaptations wouldn't necessarily help us grapple with the larger global processes at work that helped shape this multiplicity. There are factors that have influenced the spread of this source text into dozens of film industries around the world and we need an approach that not only focuses on individual examples but can also take account of that broader phenomenon. An alternative methodology would be to move away from a limited corpus and instead produce numerous close readings of a much wider range of examples. Lyndon L. Joslin's *Count Dracula Goes to the Movies: Stoker's Novel Adapted, 1922–2003* (2006), for example, functions as an encyclopaedia of Dracula cinema with a short summary and brief analysis of many examples from around the world. The issue, however, is that the analysis of individual texts never quite comes together into a broader overarching argument about the global phenomenon of Dracula remaking. There is a need to address the wider trends and cultural forces that have helped shape the repeated appearance of Dracula throughout world cinema. As Konigsberg has argued, 'We can certainly think of each filming as a reinterpretation to fit a changing time and culture, but we still wonder at the large number of remakes, at the popularity of the story, at the commitment of director after director to put the story, all over again, on film' (1998: 250). We need an approach that can accommodate the sheer scale of remakes that have been produced and can also interrogate the cultural and social implications of this phenomenon. Moreover, given that *Dracula* has appeared in films produced in industries all over the world, we need an approach that goes beyond the nationally specific in order to investigate the transnational dynamics of this process. I agree with Dale Hudson that the globalisation of the vampire figure means that we need to 'consider historiographic paradigms more complicated than the nationally or culturally discrete spaces of "national cinemas"' (2014: 465).

What I am attempting to do in this chapter, therefore, builds on Moretti's interventions in the study of world literature. In his influential essay 'Conjectures on World Literature', he argues that literature functions within a planetary system and that we need to develop a method for taking a macro-level perspective on these global dynamics. He suggests that simply producing more close readings of individual texts – even when we go beyond the Western canon to engage with other literary traditions – wouldn't really help us to interrogate the wider cultural processes at play. In Moretti's words:

World literature is not an object, it's a *problem*, and a problem that asks for a new critical method: and no one has ever found a method by just reading more texts. That's not how theories come into being; they need a leap, a wager – a hypothesis, to get started. (2000: 55)

In order to make such a leap, Moretti advocates a position of distant reading in which the scholar steps back from textual analysis entirely in order to map out global trends and phenomena. Moving away from a focus on individual texts and national traditions, Moretti proposes a model that attempts to comprehend the system of world literature in its entirety. While I find Moretti's model of distant reading immensely provocative and stimulating, I should make clear that I don't myself advocate dropping close reading entirely. Instead, I am working towards a methodology through which we can shift between the macro- and micro-level perspectives. This is building on Andrew's vision of an 'Atlas of World Cinema', in which scholars produce maps of cinema that provide a 'different orientation to unfamiliar terrain, bringing out different aspects, elements and dimensions' (2006: 19). Andrew envisages a shift away from nation-centric accounts of world cinema towards something more comparative that allows us to track influences and borrowings across a variety of national contexts. As he outlines:

For a long while the cognoscenti did little more than push coloured pins onto a map to locate the national origin of masterpieces ... Today's impulse – more ambitious because more dynamic and comparative – would track a process of cross-pollination that bypasses national directives. (2006: 19)

Building on Moretti's work, Andrew argues that national cinema studies have traditionally been framed as genealogical trees with one tree per country and that 'their elaborate root and branch structures are seldom shown as intermingled' (2006: 21). To combat this tendency, Andrew suggests the analogy of 'waves' which travel through adjacent cultures – the spread and influence of the various European 'New Waves' being a clear example of this phenomenon – and it is my contention that such an analogy is enormously useful when we turn our attention back to Dracula remakes.

What would the history of Dracula remakes look like as a series of waves rolling across the globe? Or, to use a more appropriately gothic analogy, what would the history of Dracula remakes look like as a series of plagues spreading around the world? Or, to use the term which I theorised in *The Hollywood Meme*, what would it look like as a series of memes? In that book, I proposed that we can use the structuring metaphor of the meme – a term coined by Richard Dawkins as a cultural equivalent of the biological gene (1989: 192)

– in order to investigate the numerous ways in which Hollywood cinema has been spread and adapted around the world. The term describes an individual unit of culture that spreads, adapts and mutates in a manner that is roughly analogous to biological evolution, and it allows us to study these processes of cross-pollination across a range of national contexts. What, therefore, would the history of Dracula remakes look like as a series of memes circulating around the globe, being adapted and reworked as they travel? To tackle this kind of comparative project, we need a model that is attentive to the different social and cultural contexts in which these borrowings take place. I am in agreement with Paul Willemen that a truly comparative form of film studies 'should be founded on the common experience but divergent histories of the development of a capitalist mode of production and the impact of its reformatting dynamics on social, including cultural, relations' (2005: 98). We need to move away from models of cinematic remaking that rely on unsophisticated notions of national and cultural fixity and instead engage with the complexities underpinning the various ways in which different socio-historical dynamics impact upon film production. Such a comparative memetic model therefore allows us to study how individual stories have been adapted across cultures, but it also allows us to interrogate the macro-level structures and forces that help shape the broader trends underpinning world cinema production.

To situate some of the subsequent close analysis, therefore, it is necessary to first map out some of the key clusters and cycles of Dracula films. The first appearance of Dracula on screen was in the 1921 Hungarian film *Drakula halála* (*Dracula's Death*), and this was soon followed by F. W. Murnau's *Nosferatu* (1922), but it wasn't until the 1931 Universal adaptations, directed by Tod Browning for the English-language market and George Melford for the Spanish language market, that the text began to show its memetic potential. Their success inspired the subsequent Universal horror films *Dracula's Daughter* (1936), *Son of Dracula* (1943), and *House of Dracula* (1945), but also functioned as a model for other popular film industries to emulate. Most famously, Universal's *Dracula* inspired the British Hammer studio. As Peter Hutchings notes, 'the norms in relation to which Hammer initiated its own distinctive horror cycle were primarily those of the American cinema, and particularly the type of horror associated with Universal Studios throughout the 1930s and 1940s' (1993: 19), but it is important to note that this Universal model was also influential on film studios in other contexts such as Abel Salazar's 'Cinematográfica ABSA' in Mexico and the Ramsay Brothers in India.

A comparative global model based around the structuring metaphor of the meme allows us to trace these influences, looking at the ways in which, for example, the Browning 1931 Universal film is the predominant model for subsequent remakes, until its influence is displaced by Terence Fisher's 1958

Hammer film. Moreover, while Fisher's film inspired a cycle of Dracula films within the UK, including *The Brides of Dracula* (1960), *Dracula: Prince of Darkness* (1966), *Dracula Has Risen from the Grave* (1968) and *Dracula A.D. 1972* (1972), it was also a significant influence in other popular film industries, the Hammer Dracula functioning as inspiration for *Zinda Laash* in Pakistan and *Batman Fights Dracula* (1967) in the Philippines, among others. In other words, these two cycles within the USA and UK were not only influential and significant within their domestic spheres but they were also exported widely and became models for other industries to emulate. Obviously, such an account only takes us to the early 1970s, and this is soon followed by an even greater abundance of Dracula films in that decade, such as: the cycle of Blaxploitation adaptations like *Blacula* (1972) and *Scream Blacula Scream* (1973); the numerous appearances in Hong Kong cinema including the Hammer/Shaw Bros. co-production *The Legend of the 7 Golden Vampires* (1974) and the Brucesploitation film *Bruce Lee: The Dragon Lives Again* (1977); the 1975 film *Deafula*, which remakes the Dracula story entirely in American sign language; and the return to Murnau's vampire story in Werner Herzog's 1979 remake of *Nosferatu*. In this chapter, it would, of course, be an impossible challenge to attempt to map out all of the innumerable ways in which Dracula has been adapted, reworked and remade throughout world cinema. My intention here, though, is not to be exhaustive but instead to illustrate how a comparative memetic model might be useful in helping us to investigate the spread of Draculas and to interrogate the factors underpinning his presence in such a diverse range of contexts. To return to the tree metaphor from earlier, most studies of Dracula tend to focus on the uses of the character within a specific national context – Peter Hutchings' work on *Dracula* (1993, 2003), for example, focuses primarily on the British context of the Hammer productions. A model based around memes, however, allows us to then trace the spread of these texts beyond that national context and interrogate the processes of cross-pollination that consequently complicate any notion of discrete national cinemas. Furthermore, it offers us a comparative model for not only tracking this movement but also investigating the ways in which differing cultural contexts may help shape differing forms of adaptation. Linda Hutcheon has argued as follows:

> To think of narrative adaptation in terms of a story's fit and its process of mutation or adjustment, through adaptation, to a particular cultural environment is something I find suggestive. Stories also evolve by adaptation and are not immutable over time. Sometimes, like biological adaptation, cultural adaptation involves migration to favourable conditions: stories travel to different cultures and different media. In short, stories adapt just as they are adapted. (2006: 31)

This is not to say that texts are necessarily adapted simply to conform with local cultural practices and traditions – these processes are more complex than such a limited model of localisation would imply – but nevertheless these adaptations are certainly shaped by the cultural environment in which they are produced and the myriad socio-historical forces at play. In the rest of this chapter, therefore, I am using my comparative memetic model to focus upon three contexts in which the Dracula story has travelled – Turkey in 1953, Mexico in 1957 and Pakistan in 1967 – and I am exploring this mid-twentieth-century transnational cycle of Dracula films to see what insights they can offer into the broader processes of globalisation and cross-cultural exchange that impact on the production of transnational film remakes.

DRAKULA İSTANBUL'DA (DRACULA IN ISTANBUL, 1953)

While the Turkish popular film industry known as Yeşilçam would gain a reputation in the 1970s for producing unlicensed remakes of imported Hollywood texts such as *Star Trek* (1966–9), *The Exorcist* (1973) and *Batman* (1966–8), this process of transnational adaptation was already flourishing in the 1950s with a series of imported characters being transplanted to Istanbul in films with titles that explicitly drew attention to that relationship: *Tarzan Istanbul'da* (*Tarzan in Istanbul*, 1952), *Görünmeyen Adam Istanbul'da* (*The Invisible Man in Istanbul*, 1955) and *Drakula Istanbul'da*. This latter transposition takes on especial significance given the relationship between Stoker's novel and the cultural imaginary of an orientalised East that I discussed earlier. Harker's journal opens with his account of leaving the West and entering the 'traditions of Turkish rule' (1997: 10) and this narrative of travel and cultural encounter takes on a quite different resonance when Harker (here renamed Azmi) is travelling not from London but from Istanbul. To some extent, therefore, it makes sense to read this remake through the lens of localisation – seeing how the filmmakers remade Dracula for Turkish audiences and the changes that they made to adapt it for the context of 1950s Istanbul.

Directed by Mehmet Muhtar, the film closely follows the Stoker narrative and visually references the Browning adaptation from 1931 by re-creating many of the iconic sequences from that source text, albeit on a lower budget. For example, after Azmi (Bülent Oran) arrives at the castle, Drakula (Atif Kaptan) ominously bids him welcome and, on hearing the howling of wolves outside, remarks on the beautiful sounds of these 'children of the night' – a sequence made iconic by Bela Lugosi two decades earlier. Yet, while Atif Kaptan's Drakula follows this exchange by bidding Azmi goodnight with the local phrase 'Allah rahatlık versin' (literally 'May Allah give you comfort'), it is notable just how few references to religion there are within the rest of this remake. Unlike later transnational adaptations produced in Turkey such as

Şeytan (Satan), a 1974 remake of *The Exorcist* in which symbols of Christianity are replaced directly with those of Islam, *Drakula Istanbul'da* removes all the Christian iconography from the Stoker story, such as the crucifix and holy water, and does not replace them with an Islamic equivalent. The historical context is significant here. The film was adapted from a 1928 novel by Ali Riza Seyfi (Seyfi 1928) called *Kazıklı Voyvoda* (*Impaler Prince*), which was written at 'a time when Turkey was undergoing a full-swing secularisation drive at the hands of the new Republican regime' (Özkaracalar 2012: 251). Seyfi's novel and Muhtar's subsequent adaptation reflect the forces of secularisation at play under Mustafa Kemal Atatürk's programme of reforms in the years following the establishment of the republic in 1923.

Our reading of *Drakula Istanbul'da* as a remake of the 1931 Universal *Dracula* is, therefore, very much complicated by this overlapping history of adaptations of Stoker's novel. While Browning's film was based on the 1924 stage adaptation by Hamilton Deane and John Balderston that had made significant changes to the source text, Mehmet Muhtar's film is based on the novel *Kazıklı Voyvoda* – principally a translation of Stoker into Turkish that makes very few changes to the source text. Indeed, *Drakula Istanbul'da* contains a number of details from the novel that do not appear in Universal's adaptation, including: Drakula's canine fangs (pre-dating Christopher Lee in the Hammer film by five years); Drakula's lizard-like crawl down the outer wall of the castle; and Drakula's offering up of a baby to the female vampire Sadan (Lucy). Moreover, both the Turkish novel and film take the brief reference by Van Helsing in Stoker's text to that 'Voivode Dracula who won his name against the Turk, over the great river on the very frontier of Turkey-land' (1997: 212) and develop this into a more explicit connection between Dracula and the historical Vlad Dracula, the prince (voivode) of Wallachia. As Dina Iordanova has noted, Stoker had never visited Romania, but after carrying out library research he discovered records of this fifteenth-century Vlad III, 'whom he used as a prototype for the literary character' (2007: 48). Therefore, the underlying dynamic in *Drakula Istanbul'da* in which Azmi travels from his home in Istanbul to the Castle in Romania takes on additional resonances within this context. No longer is Dracula associated primarily with an orientalised East as seen from the perspective of Victorian London, but rather Drakula now represents a Romanian prince who had battled against the Ottoman Empire numerous times throughout his life, and therefore represents a qualitatively different threat to our Turkish protagonist.

What we see here are the ways in which our framing of a transnational film remake such as *Drakula Istanbul'da* is complicated by an overlapping history of adaptations with numerous different source texts coming into play: each with their own cultural implications and meanings. While the film does not include certain elements from the novel, such as the character of Renfield who is replaced with a hunchback servant, it is nonetheless still much closer to Stoker's book than Browning's film, given its basis in an earlier Turkish translation of the novel, and it develops upon the novel's brief references to Vlad III to lend the entire tale a markedly different resonance. No longer embodying the anxieties surrounding the British empire during the Victorian period, Drakula is here more explicitly linked to the historical figure of Vlad III and his antagonistic relationship with the Ottomon Empire. In memetic terms, it is also important to note that this particular Dracula meme did not proliferate in its new cultural environment. The film failed to inspire further Dracula films in Turkey – indeed, the horror genre was nearly non-existent in Turkish cinema until the twenty-first century with the popularity of films such as *Araf* (Purgatory, 2006) and *D@bbe* (Creature, 2006) – although, as I will now discuss, the Dracula meme did continue its spread elsewhere.

EL VAMPIRO (*THE VAMPIRE*, 1957)

Four years later, the Mexican actor and producer Abel Salazar would produce *El Vampiro* (1957), a Dracula remake directed by Fernando Méndez. Up until this point in his career, Salazar had been focused on producing light comedies with himself in a leading role, such as *Matrimonio sintético* (*False Marriage*, 1948) and *Los tres amores de Lola* (*The Three Loves of Lola*, 1956), but in 1957 he made the decision to move into the horror genre by producing a Dracula adaptation. The inspiration for this shift came less from the Stoker novel or the Browning film than from the overarching production model represented by Universal Studios. Seeing that Universal had been able to support their broader production slate with the success of their monster films such as *Dracula, Frankenstein* (1931) and *The Mummy* (1932), Salazar decided it was time for him to move into the horror genre: 'That was what sustained Universal. Therefore, I decided to make a horror film and I chose *El Vampiro*. I basically made *Dracula*, located on a Mexican hacienda' (quoted in Wilt 1998: 142).

The film follows Marta Gonzalez (Ariadna Welter), who arrives at her family's hacienda in Sicomoros, Mexico to find that one of her aunts, Maria Teresa (Alicia Montoya), is dead, while her other aunt, Eloisa (Carmen Montejo), is under the control of the mysterious Mr Duval (Germán Robles). We soon learn that Duval is, in fact, the undead Count Lavud, and that he is planning to take control of the hacienda as part of a plan to resurrect his dead brother and to subsequently conquer the country together with him. While *El Vampiro* does not closely follow the plotline of the Stoker novel, nor the Universal film that Salazar cites as his inspiration, it is in the representation of Count Lavud that the film clearly displays its indebtedness. As we can see (Figure 4.1), Robles is dressed to resemble Lugosi with his black cape, white shirt, waistcoat,

Figure 4.1   Count Lavud (Germán Robles) and the iconic *Dracula* (1931) costume

slicked-back hair, and star pendant hanging from his neck. This costume and characterisation, however, have been transposed into a quite distinct narrative context. Within *El Vampiro*, the vampire is very much presented as an elegant, aristocratic man of European nobility who comes from abroad to threaten the Mexican peasantry. In one sequence early in the film, the Count supervises the delivery of a coffin filled with earth from his family cemetery in Bakony, Hungary. This soil is to be used to restore life and immortality to his brother Karol de Lavud, and the Count declares: 'We will go forth into this new country and once again impose the rule of the Lavuds.' The film is therefore playing with that long-established trope in which the vampire is positioned as a threating Other who is transgressing physical borders and taking root in another country – yet, within this context, he is framed as a European colonialist who wishes to impose his rule upon Mexico.

As Antonio Barrenechea has argued, the character of Count Lavud can productively be read as a 'harrowing manifestation of Mexico's past' (2009: 235), representing a threatening re-emergence of its colonial history. The opening sequence of the film depicts a vampire attack in the mid-1800s, a period in which Mexico was invaded by the French during the Maximilian

Affair, and it is therefore hardly a coincidence that the later reappearance of this vampire family goes by the French name Duval. This adaptation of the vampire story to the Mexican context echoes Moretti's analysis of Stoker's novel, in which he develops Marx's comparisons between vampirism and capitalism: 'Like capital, Dracula is impelled towards a continuous growth, an unlimited expansion of his domain: accumulation is inherent in his nature' (1982: 73). Within *El Vampiro*, we follow Count Lavud's attempts to expand his domain into Mexico and spread his vampiric control and influence to another country. This drive towards expansion and growth is reflected both within the narrative of the film and also, at an extra-textual level, in the global spread of Dracula films that resulted in a film like *El Vampiro* being produced. In other words, these are films which not only evoke the spread of capitalism at a narrative level with their depiction of a vampire expanding his domain into new national contexts, but also engage with it at an industrial level given their genesis in the intertextual dynamics of globally circulating popular cinemas.

This is part of the reason why Dracula remakes pose such a useful case study for a comparative approach to cinema. In his pivotal 2005 article, 'For a comparative film studies', Willemen puts forward the question: 'How do cinemas emerging from within different socio-historical formations negotiate the encounter between capitalist modernization and whatever mode of social-economic regulation and (re)production preceded that encounter?' (2005: 99). As I have been arguing, these films are not only reflective in narrative terms of that kind of cultural encounter but are themselves products of that engagement. This is not simply an account of the spread and influence of a particular narrative, but also of the spread and influence of a particular model of capitalist film production. It is therefore telling that Salazar was not merely desiring to create a localised version of Dracula but was intending this adoption of the Universal model to allow him to emulate the production structure of that Hollywood studio more broadly. After the success of *El Vampiro*, Salazar's production company 'Cinematográfica ABSA' focused its production slate on a cycle of monster films including the return of the vampire in *El ataúd del Vampiro* (*The Vampire's Coffin*, 1958) and *El mundo de los vampiros* (*The World of the Vampires*, 1961), a werewolf-like reworking of *Dr Jekyll and Mr Hyde* in *El hombre y el monstruo* (*The Man and the Monster*, 1959), and a brain-sucking beast in *The Brainiac / El barón del terror* (*Baron of Terror*, 1962). These monster films would quickly become the primary output of Salazar's production company and would also reach the export market via the American exploitation film producer K. Gordon Murray. Furthermore, Dracula himself would continue to make appearances in Mexican cinema in subsequent years – most notably in films in which he would be paired against the luchador El Santo in films such as *Santo en El tesoro de Drácula* (*Santo in The Treasure of Dracula*, 1969) and *Santo y Blue Demon vs Drácula y el Hombre Lobo* (*Santo and Blue Demon vs. Dracula and Wolf Man*, 1973). Unlike in Turkey where the Dracula character would disappear from domestic cinema production after *Drakula Istanbul'da*, the Mexican film industry was a hospitable cultural environment in which the Dracula meme flourished, spread and took on additional new meanings and resonances.

ZINDA LAASH (THE LIVING CORPSE, 1967)

While the 1931 Universal adaptation was the primary cinematic intertext for my two previous case studies, demonstrating its continued global influence two decades after its release, it was the 1958 Hammer film starring Christopher Lee that was to have the most memetic impact in subsequent decades. Even Pakistan, a national film industry with no prior horror film tradition to speak of, was not immune from this spreading influence, and in 1967 there was a Pakistani adaptation produced entitled *Zinda Laash* aka *Dracula in Pakistan*. As Tabish Khair notes in his study of South Asian vampires in literature, 'While India and Pakistan have various versions of the Undead . . . the vampire *qua* vampire is largely absent from English-language fiction written by Indians and Pakistanis' (2013: 105). It is therefore significant that, in a cultural context in which the vampire *qua* vampire is largely absent, producer/actor Habib was able to convince director Khwaja Sarfraz to follow up his 1965 adaptation of the classic Bengali romance novel *Devdas* with a film based around this unfamiliar character and genre.

The film borrows many of the central set pieces from Fisher's 1958 adaptation, albeit now with the setting shifted to Pakistan, and it is certainly the case that much of the film would be familiar to audiences conversant with Stoker's novel and Fisher's adaptation. As we can see (Figure 4.2), the appearance of the actor Rehan in the Dracula role is modelled specifically on Christopher Lee's animalistic incarnation of the character down to the manic expression and blood-dripping lips. Yet one of the crucial ways in which *Zinda Laash* differs from Fisher's adaptation is in the explanation provided for the antagonist's vampirism. The plot centres on Professor Tabini (Rehan), who is attempting to produce a new drug that will give him eternal life. After what appears to be a breakthrough, he tests the concoction on himself, only to discover that it has turned him into a bloodthirsty vampire. The sacrilegious nature of his experiments is alluded to in the opening credits, where the audience is warned:

> Life and death are only in the hands of Allah. There is no being in the world, whether of good or bad intention, who can challenge this right of Allah's. This film is the story of just such a professor, who with good intentions conducted experiments in order to gain power over death.

Figure 4.2 Professor Tabini (Rehan) evoking Christopher Lee's incarnation of Dracula

This is reminiscent of the caution that was appended to the opening credits of Universal's *Frankenstein* from 1931, in which Edward Van Sloan steps out from behind a curtain to explain: 'We are about to unfold the story of Frankenstein, a man of science who sought to create a man after his own image without reckoning upon God.' Indeed, this is a relatively common trope within the horror genre in which characters are punished for attempting scientific experiments that transgress religious codes. However, this narrative struggle between science and religion takes on additional layers of meaning within the Pakistan context given the numerous ways in which Tabani is coded as a Pakistani man who has lost his way through the influence of westernisation. As Sean Moreland and Summer Pervez have argued, 'his Western style of dress and his abandonment of religious and cultural mores in pursuit of knowledge and power [render] him a striking embodiment of anxieties surrounding the long-term effects of British colonial control, Western cultural influence, and unchecked technological change' (2009: 187). Rather than coding this Dracula figure as a threatening, transgressive Other entering Pakistan from a foreign nation, Tabini is instead presented as a local who has become too enamoured with Western culture, and the character therefore embodies many of the anxieties surrounding Pakistan's relationship with the West and with the legacy of

THE TRANSNATIONAL AFTERLIVES OF DRACULA

British colonialism. Within this context, it is the influence of the West that has become the invading vampiric force that is threatening to the local population.

Interestingly, however, there is a tension within the film between this ostensible desire to frame Western culture as a dangerous, corrupting influence and the numerous ways in which the film itself makes use of Western influences. Of course, there is the obvious point that the film is based on a Western source text, but, as I will now explore, the complex web of intertexts goes far deeper than that. In an early sequence in which the ostensible hero Aqil Harker (Asad Bukhari) meets the vampire bride (Nasreen), the film closely re-creates the moment in the 1958 Hammer film where Harker (John Van Eyssen) encounters one of Dracula's brides (Valerie Gaunt) before she attempts to bite his neck. Whereas the Fisher film portrays this as a dialogue scene with the bride begging Harker to help her escape, Sarfraz's film instead depicts this as a sequence of silent seduction with Nasreen dancing alluringly for Harker before moving in for the kill. This change is primarily due to the expectation for song and dance sequences in South Asian cinema, and these kinds of 'item numbers' in which an actress performs in a provocative dance sequence are prevalent throughout the cinemas of India and Pakistan. Before the 1970s when these dances began to be performed by the female star, it was an opportunity for cameos from actresses who specialised in playing screen 'vamps', and these women were often coded as being overly westernised. It is therefore quite fitting that Nasreen is here performing both as vamp and vampire – sexually alluring, transgressive, and otherworldly. Her dance is one of the elements that most clearly defines this film as breaking away from the imported Western template and incorporating South Asian generic patterns, and yet these very patterns are themselves reliant upon a depiction of sexual permissiveness and immorality that is being associated primarily with an imagined West. Moreover, these cultural engagements are further complicated by the fact that the music that Nasreen is dancing to is not a local composition but is instead a version of *In a Persian Market* by the British composer Albert Ketèlbey. As such an example demonstrates, the tensions within *Zinda Laash* between mimicry and oppositional critique of Western culture are reflective of a wider ambivalence underpinning this form of transnational film remake. Drawing attention to a sedimented history of exchange that complicates any notion of national or cultural fixity, these overlapping borrowings point to the necessity of a comparative model that can attend to the diverse ways in which cultural forms are reworked and the myriad factors shaping these processes.

CONCLUSION

Within this chapter, therefore, I have attempted to demonstrate the numerous ways in which transnational remakes of Dracula can act as a privileged site for exploring these processes of cultural exchange and borrowing, and can help us complicate existing models of intertextuality and global popular cinema. Focusing on the quasi-independent repetitions of a single story such as Dracula allows us to investigate their spread across diverse cultural contexts while keeping in view the larger macro-level phenomenon that underpins this memetic dispersal. Moreover, by interrogating the mid-twentieth-century cycle of Dracula films produced in Turkey, Mexico and Pakistan, I have demonstrated how a comparative memetic model can also function at the micro level to explore the specific impact of different social and historical contexts, and to problematise intertextual models based around discrete national cultures.

When Hutcheon wrote her influential monograph *A Theory of Adaptation*, she was attempting to challenge the critical denigration of film adaptations and remakes in which they are positioned as inferior works that detract from the value of their source text. Her choice of words in framing that defence is significant:

> An adaptation is not vampiric: it does not draw the life-blood from its source and leave it dying or dead, nor is it paler than the adapted work. It may, on the contrary, keep that prior work alive, giving it an afterlife it would never have had otherwise. (2006: 176)

By positioning the history of Dracula remakes as a series of memes circulating around the globe, I have been exploring this notion of an adaptation giving its source an afterlife that it would not have had otherwise. Building on this observation, I have proposed a model of transnational film remaking that focuses on these transnational afterlives to explore the various ways in which stories are adapted and reworked across national and cultural contexts. Investigating how a text has been localised to a particular local context while also looking at how it interacts with other globally circulating forms, this model can of course be applied to many case studies beyond Dracula. Yet, as I have outlined throughout this chapter, there is nevertheless something unique about the sheer memetic vitality of Stoker's tale and the myriad ways in which it has been adapted all across the globe. Perhaps it really is the case, as Jonathan Harker's travel companion whispered back on the trip to Count Dracula's castle: *Denn die Todten reiten schnell* (For the dead travel fast).

<h2 style="text-align:center">References</h2>

Abbott, Stacey (2007), *Celluloid Vampires*, Austin: University of Texas Press.
Andrew, Dudley (2006), 'An Atlas of World Cinema', in Stephanie Dennison and Song Hwee Lim (eds), *Remapping World Cinema: Identity, Culture and Politics in Film*, London: Wallflower Press, pp. 19–29.

Barrenechea, Antonio (2009), 'Hemispheric Horrors: Celluloid Vampires from the "Good Neighbor" Era', *Comparative American Studies*, 7: 3, pp. 225–37.

Beugnet, Martine (2007), 'Figures of Vampirism: French Cinema in the Era of Global Transylvania', *Modern & Contemporary France*, 15: 1, pp. 77–88.

Boehmer, Elleke (2004), 'Empire and Modern Writing', in Laura Marcus and Peter Nicholls (eds), *The Cambridge History of Twentieth-Century English Literature*, Cambridge: Cambridge University Press, pp. 50–60.

Brooker, Will (1999), 'Batman: One Life, Many Faces', in Deborah Cartmell and Imelda Whelehan (eds), *Adaptations: From Text to Screen, Screen to Text*, London: Routledge, pp. 185–98.

Browning, John Edgar and Caroline Joan Picart (2009) (eds), *Draculas, Vampires and Other Undead Forms*, Lanham, MD: Scarecrow Press.

Dawkins, Richard (1989), *The Selfish Gene*, Oxford: Oxford University Press. (Original work published 1976).

Fischer-Hornung, Dorothea and Monika Mueller (2016) (eds), *Vampires and Zombies: Transcultural Migrations and Transnational Interpretations*, Jackson: University Press of Mississippi.

Forrest, Jennifer and Leonard R. Koos (2002) (eds), *Dead Ringers: The Remake in Theory and Practice*, New York: State University of New York.

Horton, Andrew and Stuart McDougal (1998) (eds), *Play It Again, Sam: Retakes on Remakes*, Berkeley: University of California Press.

Hudson, Dale (2014), 'Vampires and Transnational Horror', in Harry M. Benshoff (ed.), *A Companion to the Horror Film*, Malden: Wiley Blackwell, pp. 463–82.

Hutcheon, Linda (2006), *A Theory of Adaptation*, London: Routledge.

Hutchings, Peter (1993), *Hammer and Beyond: The British Horror Film*, Manchester: Manchester University Press.

Hutchings, Peter (2003), *Dracula*, London: I. B. Tauris.

Joslin, Lyndon L. (2006), *Count Dracula Goes to the Movies: Stoker's Novel Adapted, 1922–2003*, 2nd edn, Jefferson, NC: McFarland.

Khair, Tabish (2009), *The Gothic, Postcolonialism and Otherness*, Basingstoke: Palgrave Macmillan.

Khair, Tabish and Höglund, Johan (2013) (eds), *Transnational and Postcolonial Vampires: Dark Blood*, Basingstoke: Palgrave.

Khair, Tabish (2013), 'The Man-Eating Tiger and the Vampire in South Asia', in Tabish Khair and Johan Höglund (eds), *Transnational and Postcolonial Vampires: Dark Blood*, Basingstoke: Palgrave, pp. 105–20.

Konigsberg, Ira (1998), 'How Many Draculas Does It Take to Change a Lightbulb?', in Andrew Horton and Stuart McDougal (eds), *Play It Again, Sam: Retakes on Remakes*, Berkeley: University of California Press, pp. 250–75.

Michaels, Lloyd (1998), 'Nosferatu, or the Phantom of the Cinema', in Andrew Horton and Stuart McDougal (eds), *Play It Again, Sam: Retakes on Remakes*, Berkeley: University of California Press, pp. 238–49.

Moreland, Sean and Summer Pervez (2009), 'Becoming Death: The Lollywood Gothic of Khwaja Sarfraz's *Zinda Laash* (*Dracula in Pakistan* [US title], 1967)', in John Edgar Browning and Caroline Joan Picart (eds), *Draculas, Vampires and Other Undead Forms*, Lanham, MD: Scarecrow Press, pp. 187–202.

Moretti, Franco (1982), 'The Dialectic of Fear', *New Left Review*, 136, pp. 67–85.

Moretti, Franco (2000), 'Conjectures on World Literature', *New Left Review*, 1, pp. 54–68.

Özkaracalar, Kaya (2012), 'Horror Films in Turkish Cinema', in Patricia Allmer, Emily Brick and David Huxley (eds), *European Nightmares: Horror Cinema in Europe Since 1945*, London: Wallflower Press, pp. 249–60.

Seyfi, Ali Rıza (1928), *Kazıklı Voyvoda*, İstanbul: Resimli Ay Matbaası.

Shapiro, Stephen (2008), Transvaal, Transylvania: Dracula's World-system and Gothic Periodicity, *Gothic Studies*, 10: 1, pp. 29–47.

Smith, Iain Robert (2016), *The Hollywood Meme: Transnational Adaptations in World Cinema*, Edinburgh: Edinburgh University Press.

Stoker, Bram (1997), *Dracula*, Norton Critical Edition, New York: W. W. Norton (Original work published 1897).

Verevis, Constantine (2006), *Film Remakes*, Edinburgh: Edinburgh University Press.

Willemen, Paul (2005), 'For a Comparative Film Studies', *Inter-Asia Cultural Studies*, 6: 1, pp. 98–112.

Wilt, David (1998), 'Masked Men and Monsters', in Pete Tombs (ed.), *Mondo Macabro: Weird and Wonderful Cinema Around the World*, New York: St Martin's, pp. 136–47.

PART II

GENDER AND PERFORMANCE

5. THE CHINESE CINEMATIC REMAKE AS TRANSNATIONAL APPEAL: ZHANG YIMOU'S *A WOMAN, A GUN AND A NOODLE SHOP*

Kenneth Chan

The past two decades have witnessed the resurgence of Chinese cinemas on the global stage. In an era of relative cultural and political 'openness' after the Cultural Revolution, and during and after Deng Xiaoping's leadership in the People's Republic of China, a number of the Fifth and Sixth Generation graduates from the Beijing Film Academy have become celebrity fixtures in the international film-festival circuit, with more iconic directors such as Chen Kaige, Zhang Yimou and Jia Zhangke entering the global cinematic mainstream. These filmmakers have joined their Hong Kong, Taiwanese and Asian American counterparts – the likes of Wong Kar-wai, John Woo, Tsui Hark, Johnnie To, Stanley Kwan, Peter Chan, Ang Lee, Hou Hsiao-hsien, Tsai Ming-liang, Chen Kuo-fu and Wayne Wang – in generating a substantive body of work that constitutes a discursive Chinese cinematic presence in the global film histories of the late twentieth and early twenty-first centuries. This Chinese cinematic presence seeps across national boundaries, as it rides transnational capitalist media flows, to permeate regional, diasporic and global networks. One could even go so far as to say, as Chris Berry does, that 'it is precisely because the transnational is a world order that it plays a role in shaping all Chinese film-making activities today' (2011: 15), producing both a material phenomenon and a critical perspective that Sheldon Hsiao-peng Lu has earlier classified as 'transnational Chinese cinemas' (1997). It is within this context that I locate this chapter's examination of transnational Chinese cinematic remaking and, specifically, its critical analysis of Zhang Yimou's 2009 remake of the Coen Brothers' feature film debut *Blood Simple* (1984) as *A Woman, a Gun and a Noodle Shop*.

Scholars of film remakes have rightly problematised the linear and hierarchical cultural relationship between an 'original' filmic source and its cinematic remake. Constantine Verevis, for example, questions how 'textual accounts of remaking risk essentialism, in many instances privileging the "original" over the remake or measuring the success of the remake according to its ability to realise what are taken to be the essential elements of a source text – the property – from which both the original and its remake are derived' (2006: 2). The complexity of this source–remake relation is further compounded in the case of cross-cultural remaking when one considers the cultural, economic and political power dynamics of filmic appropriation, reconfiguration and representation that such cross-cultural interaction demands. In his study of Hollywood's recent tinkering with Japanese horror cinema, Daniel Herbert argues that 'Hollywood's remakes of Japanese and other East Asian films should be seen as part of a larger reaction to the competition posed by them. This represents a strategic respatialization of Hollywood towards Asia, a redirection of the economic and cultural flow through which Hollywood operates and seeks to command' (2009: 154). As his remaking of the Hong Kong box-office hit *Infernal Affairs* (2002) into the Leonardo DiCaprio vehicle *The Departed* (2006) demonstrates, Martin Scorsese de-Asianises his film so that the Hong Kong version can be, as Verevis observes about these kinds of remakes, 'dispossessed of "local color" and "political content" to exploit new (English-language) markets' (2006: 3), thus eventually rendering the Hollywood iteration, in this particular case, much less effective in its narrative and emotional appeals than the Hong Kong version. One can draw some crucial theoretical lessons from these two recent examples: (1) the geopolitical power differentials between the national players involved in cross-cultural remaking colour the film's textual and representational configurations, as well as inflecting the modalities of production, marketing, distribution and consumption that constitute contemporary cinematic remakes as transnational capitalist commodities; (2) Hollywood as a hegemonic power in global cinematic industries asserts its cultural and economic might in a variety of (c)overt, (un)intended and/or reactive ways that consequently define the practices of transnational remaking; and (3) the processes of transnational, cross-cultural remaking involve various modes of cinematic appropriation, citation, hybridity, mimicry, translation, renarration, and reinterpretation, that are made even more complicated by the multidirectional flows of cultural exchange. Hollywood's recent incorporation of things Chinese – East Asia being the cultural flavour du jour of the last decade – is ironic in that Chinese cinema, especially Hong Kong film, has always been influenced by Hollywood trends, themes and genres in its history. 'A distinctive and long-standing feature of Hong Kong film', according to Patricia Aufderheide, 'is its voracious appetite for imitation, most boldly of Hollywood material but also of anything that has had international commercial success' (1998: 192).[1] It is, therefore, possible to describe this cultural exchange as a circular network of cross-pollination: Hollywood influencing Chinese cinemas influencing Hollywood (and now) influencing Chinese cinemas. This dizzying flow makes fuzzy and questionable the relational hierarchy of the original–remake paradigm in politically productive and insightful ways, in spite of, or maybe even as a result of, Hollywood's hegemonic role in the global cinematic industries.

This last point is particularly significant in light of the latest nascent trend of East Asian directors and production companies remaking American films into Asian versions, in counterpoint to and in reversal of what some critics see as Hollywood's appropriation and, even, cannibalisation of East Asian cinematic cultures. These include: director Sang-il Lee's 2013 treatment of Clint Eastwood's 1992 Oscar winner *Unforgiven* (*Yurusarezaru mono*), a Warner Bros. and historic Japanese company Nikkatsu co-production; a remake of the Patrick Swayze and Demi Moore hit *Ghost* (Jerry Zucker, 1990) by Japanese director Tarô Ohtani in 2010 (*Gôsuto*); and the transnational Chinese co-productions of *Connected* (Benny Chan, 2008 / *Cellular*, David R. Ellis, 2004), *What Women Want* (Daming Chen, 2011 / Nancy Meyers, 2000) and, of course, *A Woman, a Gun and a Noodle Shop*. Obviously, this rising trend is not a new phenomenon, as Aufderheide (1998) has shown. But, if the philosophy of Gilles Deleuze has taught us anything about the notions of difference and repetition, it is that repetition

> expresses at once a singularity opposed to the general, a universality opposed to the particular, a distinctive opposed to the ordinary, an instantaneity opposed to variation and an eternity opposed to permanence. In every respect, repetition is a transgression. It puts law into question, it denounces its nominal or general character in favour of a more profound and more artistic reality. (1994: 2–3)

To put it simply if not too reductively, (cinematic) repetition is never just about filming and projecting the same thing in the same way. While the point that Deleuze makes here has significant implications for an analysis of remakes, these ruminations on repetition should also encourage one to give theoretical pause to the cyclical nature of cinematic trends and not take them for granted. In other words, it is productive to give careful consideration to the shifting factors that condition the revival of a trend, to examine the distinctive textual features of these new films, and to scrutinise the politics of cultural representation that are coloured by the factors on the ground.

Because this recent phenomenon of Chinese (and Asian) remaking of Hollywood (and American) cinema is really in its infancy as a contemporary trend, and its impetus and its impact are still difficult to assess definitively at this point, I can only offer scattered and largely speculative observations about the possible conditions that have enabled these Chinese productions. First, Chinese audiences now constitute one of the largest mass markets in the world. In his book *Playing to the World's Biggest Audience*, Michael Curtin observes how

> media executives can, for the very first time, begin to contemplate the prospect of a global Chinese audience that includes more moviegoers and more television households than the United States and Europe combined. Many experts believe this vast and increasingly wealthy Global China market will serve as a foundation for emerging media conglomerates that could shake the very foundations of Hollywood's century-long hegemony. (2007: 3–4)

This Global China market not only consists of Mainland China but also encompasses Hong Kong, Taiwan and the global Chinese diaspora. Therefore, it makes business sense for media and studio executives to capitalise on this massive untapped market for Chinese film remakes of Hollywood titles. But I want to further argue that this essentialist corporate rationale of Chinese films for Chinese audiences is not one that just simplistically questions the audience's ability to appreciate culturally Hollywood narratives, themes and aesthetics; Hollywood's cultural hegemony is still indisputable in its transnational reach. Instead, the strategic appeal here achieves a doubling effect, where the remade film is believed to be able to not only capture audiences which the American one missed the first time round, but also, potentially, to recalibrate the latter into a culturally different kind of film altogether, with the hope of reaching both new audiences and those who are already familiar with the American version.

Second, China is emerging as the site for national and transnational productions and co-productions in terms of financing, facilities and industry infrastructure. In providing data to show how China has increased its film production output from 82 films in 1998 to 406 titles in 2008, Darrell William Davis theorises that 'marketization is not an end in itself but is rather intended to boost the quality and quantity of Chinese films, moving the PRC steadily toward a major soft-power role in the international arena' (2010: 122–3). He notes how China's strategic positioning of its film industry in the global marketplace has attracted companies 'from Hollywood, Europe, Japan, South Korea, and especially Hong Kong [to] hotly pursue joint ventures with the People's Republic of China['s] . . . production and exhibition outfits' (121). These Chinese production companies are making their mark as major players, with some of them involved in remaking American films. For instance, Benny Chan's *Connected* is co-produced by a number of companies including the

China Film Group and the Warner China Film HG Corporation. Sharing co-production credits with various international companies for the Chinese version of *What Women Want* is Bona Film Group. And, the Beijing New Picture Film Co. is responsible for co-producing *A Woman, a Gun and a Noodle Shop*. According to its corporate website, the China Film Group hails itself as 'the largest film distribution and co-production company in the People's Republic of China and Hong Kong and has been the sole government authorized importer of films' (China Film Group Corporation 2002–14). The China Film Group also made news in 2004 by partnering with Warner Bros. and Hengdian Group ('China's largest privately owned film and television enterprise') to form 'the first Sino-foreign joint venture filmed-entertainment company in the history of the People's Republic of China': Warner China Film HG Corporation ('China Film Group' 2004). The Bona Film Group describes itself as 'a leading film distributor in China, with an integrated business model encompassing film distribution, production, exhibition and talent representation' (Bona Film n.d.). And, the Beijing New Picture Film Co. is best known for its involvement in some of Zhang Yimou's recent films including *Hero* (2002), *House of Flying Daggers* (2004), *Curse of the Golden Flower* (2006), and *The Flowers of War* (2011) starring Christian Bale.[2] What is critical in this production boom in the PRC is that national governmental support, capitalist marketisation, and international funding and collaboration have contributed to an industry infrastructure that allows star Chinese filmmakers to create cinema with production values capable of competing with Hollywood releases. For example, critics writing for American news outlets have recently expressed their surprise at the impressive CGI in Hong Kong director Tsui Hark's *Young Detective Dee: Rise of the Sea Dragon* (2013),[3] a film co-produced by another important Chinese production outfit, Huayi Brothers Media. It is, however, significant to understand the emergence of Mainland Chinese production industry in terms of the transnational network it plugs into. Its connections to and collaborations with Hong Kong, Hollywood and the other sites of film production, postproduction technologies, and the creative media industries in global cities such as Seoul, Bangkok and Singapore must not be diminished. At the same time, these production possibilities grant Chinese filmmakers and producers a creative space to take on projects that they would not otherwise. I see this spate of remakes of American films as a minor effect of this transnational cinematic regime.

Third, and finally, the confluence of Global China as mass market and the PRC as production site has infused a cultural and creative confidence in Chinese filmmakers to be more ambitious in their projects. They are willing, for instance, to push the boundary on popular genres, take on less familiar ones, and be innovative in formulating new hybrid forms. (I am not uncritically celebrating here the commodified studio form, and am cognisant of its constraints on more experimental modes among independent filmmakers.) As Chinese directors confront the notion of remaking American films, they can do so with the assurance that there is a potential global market for their product, which in turn might foster a more creative reimagining of a Chinese version that can stand on its own artistic merits as transnational Chinese cinema. In my close analysis of *A Woman, a Gun and a Noodle Shop* as transnational Chinese cinematic remake, I demonstrate how the film confidently reinvents the Coen Brother's original as an original in its own right, infusing the film with Zhang Yimou's brand of cinematic pragmatism and co-opting a transgressive politics of gender and postcoloniality as the route towards transnational appeal.

THE CINEMATIC PRAGMATISM OF ZHANG YIMOU

As a critic and enthusiast of contemporary Chinese cinemas, I am deeply ambivalent about the work of Zhang Yimou. On the one hand, it is hard not to be enraptured by the powerful visual alchemy that he has been able to so magically distil. From *Raise the Red Lantern*'s atmospheric lighting and framing, used to evoke a sense of social confinement, to his fluid play with rainwater in *Hero*, and to the amazing kineticism of Zhang Ziyi's dance sequence in *House of Flying Daggers*, Zhang Yimou dazzles his audience with the artistry of his cinema. Complementing the brilliance of his art is also a personal survivalist back-story, which in the context of a stifling, bureaucracy-ridden, post-Cultural Revolution China only makes his rise to fame all the more compelling and inspirational a tale (see Gateward 2001 and Berry 2005: 108–40). On the other hand, the visual qualities, narratives and themes of Zhang's films are deeply problematic in that they lead audiences and critics to politically troubling conclusions; or, at best, they produce interpretative ambiguities that reflect a craven or calculated attempt to appeal to as many as possible, all at the same time. 'Zhang's first trio of films', as Michael Berry observes, 'drew criticism for presenting an orientalist vision that caters to Western audiences' fantasies and fetishes about China, and especially Chinese women' (2005: 110). This is despite the fact that one could also potentially read the same films as quasi-feminist attempts at highlighting the plight of women in Chinese society. In *Primitive Passions*, Rey Chow convincingly argues that Zhang constructs 'a "China" exaggerated and caricatured, in which the past is *melodramatized* in the form of excessive and absurd rituals and customs' (1995: 145). This cinematic ethnography lends itself to a process of 'self-subalternization [that] is unmistakably accompanied by the fetishization of women – a fetishization that can . . . be more accurately described as a *self-exoticization* through the tactics of visuality' (148). Tonglin Lu affirms and extends Chow's point by calling this process 'the Zhang Yimou model', where having 'turned into commodified images in a global market, women's oppression has become the symbol of China's Otherness' (2002: 168).

Critics in the West embraced Zhang as the *enfant terrible* of Chinese cinema, especially on account of the films he put out in the late 1980s and early 1990s, which the PRC government then rejected. But there was a specific tipping point in Zhang's career where, in contradistinction to his earlier reputation, he returned as the Chinese prodigal son to the good graces of the governmental authorities. That moment, one could argue, is signified by the release of his first martial arts film *Hero* in 2002. Independent filmmaker Evans Chan offers one of the more trenchant – and necessarily so – critiques by characterising 'the impulse behind the film . . . [as] fascist' and by highlighting its complicity in 'reinscribing an authoritarian old order, mythologized and naturalized through a perfect vehicle – the martial-arts film, the genre film *par excellence* to aestheticize combat and death' (2009: 269). Even the more sympathetic Paul Clark, who has acknowledged how Zhang's 'ability to reach broad popular audiences with serious artistic intent placed enormous pressure on [the director]' (2005: 164), draws the line with *Hero*, which he reads as an affirmation of 'the kind of authoritarian leadership tradition that the first emperor established for China', lamenting how, 'for a filmmaker who had grown up as the son of an "anti-revolutionary", the change in attitude and implied status that *Hero* suggested was startling' (2005: 185–6).

Of course, Zhang did not help his besmirched reputation when he assumed the role of artistic director for the opening and closing ceremonies of the 2008 Olympic Games in Beijing, reinforcing the notion that his keen sense of cinematic beauty and aesthetics could be easily co-opted into the political service of the state. When he was asked about the torrent of criticism lodged against him, his response was extremely telling (and deserves to be quoted at length):

> There is nothing I can do! I always feel that there are two schools of criticism out there when it comes to my films. They say that I'm trying to kiss either foreigners' asses or the Chinese government's ass . . . There are actually very few people who truly understand me as an artist . . . In the eyes of many, I am an opportunist. They think I sit around all day devising schemes to win the approval of foreigners or the Chinese government . . . If you repeat a lie enough times, it becomes true . . . After more than a decade of various criticisms of my work, the discourse has become a commentary on me as a person . . . You can say all I care about is kissing up to foreign audiences or the Chinese government. Fine, I don't care. But saying I have no love for the art of cinema and accusing me of using cinema as a tool to achieve my own personal objective is a fundamental negation of my commitment to the art form . . . You can hate my films, but no one can accuse me of not loving the art of film. (Berry 2005: 126–7)

The rhetoric of Zhang's response needs some brief unpacking. Zhang is careful to label the criticisms untruths, but he does not explain why his films lend themselves to the kind of political interpretations that they do. Instead, he hides behind the notion of filmic artistry, challenging anyone to question his 'commitment to the art form'. In a cursory survey of the English-language criticism, I have yet to encounter any major critic castigating him for 'not loving the art of film' (though such a criticism is possibly implied in the political *ad hominem* attacks he alludes to, and one can only take him at his word that he has indeed endured such accusations). In fact, even the staunchest critics often go out of their way to acknowledge the undeniable beauty and artistry of his work. What many of them struggle with, though, is the manner with which the shiny, spectacular object of cinematic form he places before them ultimately masks or deflects the politically problematic assumptions, implications and conclusions of his films. I want to argue further that the forms of Zhang's cinema have pragmatically shifted and morphed, though within the parameters of his personal aesthetic inclinations and strengths of course, to accommodate the demands of the transnational cinematic marketplace over the last two decades. Since China has also now become too big a market sector to ignore, *Hero* and even some of his earlier films began the process of pivoting towards a cultural nationalist discourse as filmic signifiers of his political rehabilitation.[4] Despite the seemingly sharp cultural political turns his oeuvre has taken, there is a certain consistency in his films. Many of them embody a cinematic pragmatism that can produce interpretative spaces of political ambiguity that multiplies the possibilities of audience appeal, and that can strategically latch on to political positions arrived at through a calculus of limited risk. It is within this specific understanding of Zhang's work that I would like to situate my close analysis of his transnational Chinese remaking of the Coen Brothers' film in the final segment of this chapter.

A Woman, a Gun and a Noodle Shop

In the publicity press kit for *A Woman, a Gun and a Noodle Shop*, Zhang Yimou describes his rationale for remaking the Coen Brothers' first feature in the following manner: 'I love all the works by the Coen Brothers. Some twenty years ago at a film festival, I saw their directorial debut *Blood Simple*, which left me with a great impression . . . One day, a curious idea struck me: what would it be like if *Blood Simple* was made as a Chinese story? That was how *A Woman, a Gun and a Noodle Shop* began to take shape' (Sony Pictures Classics n.d.: 5). The artistic sensibility of experimentation articulated here is reminiscent of the earlier cinema of Zhang Yimou, but with key differences: it is now infused with a professional and cultural confidence of a mature Chinese filmmaker who is willing to take on, comfortably, the daunting task of remaking an American film classic. The opening credits, for instance, tout the fact that the film is 'based on the motion picture "Blood Simple"',[5] a 'peritextual marker' indicating how the director is not shying away from its remade status (see Verevis 2006: 131). The project also marks a sensitivity to the levelling of cultural power and reputation: Zhang Yimou, as an award-winning global cinematic auteur, finds himself on a par with the film-festival and art-cinema giants such as the Coen Brothers. This sensitivity enables him to pitch his remake to the same transnational crowd, who adore the Coen Brothers, by enveloping it with an international art-film aura, hence lifting his film above the B-movie orbit of some cinematic remaking. But classification by association is clearly not sufficient for a filmmaker of Zhang's status. As he once noted in an interview very early in his career: 'No one is so stupid as to directly imitate a film and directly copy someone else's success. This tells everyone that you have no creative ability, that you're an idiot' (Jiao 2001: 10). So the route that the remake takes is to turn *Blood Simple* into 'a Chinese story', by infusing itself with 'a rich Chinese flavor' (Sony Pictures Classics n.d.: 5). How then is this Sinicisation achieved and how does it play into the mechanisms of transnational appeal? And, as a consequence, what are the cultural and political implications of this process and its results?

To answer these questions, I begin my analysis with the title of the film, both as a point of cultural signification and as a rhetorical framework. The ironic titular nuance of *Blood Simple* connotes the Coen Brothers' play on film noir conventions, and is lifted from Dashiell Hammett's novel *Red Harvest* (1929). In moving away from this specific American genre reference, the Chinese title of the remake, 三槍拍案驚奇, radically transforms the original cultural appeal by mobilising a specific Chinese literary allusion. 拍案驚奇 is the title of a Ming Dynasty literary work comprising unique short stories that surprise readers into 'banging the table' – 拍案 – as an expression of incredulity and wonderment. 三槍 literally means 'three guns', which in the context of the film narrative refers to the three bullets the wife finds lodged in the weapon she purchases from the Persian merchant. Hence, 三槍拍案驚奇 could be loosely translated as 'the incredibly surprising tale of three bullets'.[6] This complex cultural referencing in the title basically targets Chinese audiences as part of the film's 'rich Chinese flavor', which is true to the extent that Chinese audiences who are unfamiliar with *Blood Simple* will find the plot movements surprising and shocking in their unexpected twists and turns. In a similar fashion, the English title for the remake, *A Woman, a Gun and a Noodle Shop*, registers a specific cultural strategy in its appeal to non-Chinese, English-speaking audiences through its direct objectification of a woman, a gun and a noodle shop. Each of these objects provides me with a point of analytical focus from which to address the nature of the film's multiple cultural-political appeals, which I will now attend to, in reverse order, moving from the least to the most emphatic.

A Noodle Shop

The seemingly simple transformation of *Blood Simple*'s noirish locale of a sleazy small-town bar in the USA into a noodle shop (noodle restaurant) in a nondescript desert-like landscape within a remote part of the Chinese mainland is a culturally significant reconfiguration in Zhang's remake. Apart from the Chinese culinary association that this physical space suggests, I also see the noodle shop as metonymic of the exoticism, primitivism and Orientalism to which the film's setting and general *mise-en-scène* play. In the sequence where the local police arrive to investigate what sounded like cannon fire emanating from the noodle shop, the shop owner's wife (Yan Ni) offers to 'give . . . [the police captain] the tour' and further distract him and his officers by commanding the noodle shop employees to 'hurry up and make some noodles'. What follows is a tour-de-force spectacle of culinary expertise-as-martial-arts-on-display. Li (Xiao Shenyang), Zhao (Cheng Ye) and Chen (Mao Mao) launch into an acrobatic routine by taking turns to twirl the noodle dough into a giant flat pancake before cutting it up into thin strips and dunking them in boiling water. The camera then offers close-ups of the cooked noodles as they are ladled into outsized bowls and are subsequently covered over with a visually tantalising, spicy hot gravy: a delicious-looking entrée that the police officers enthusiastically slurp up. The exoticism of physical acrobatics is here concatenated with the exoticism of stunning gastronomic imagery to produce a touristic tableau of cultural China for global consumption.

The circus-like atmosphere of this entire sequence is further accentuated by the oddly coloured outfits and the strange Chinese-looking hairdos that the three of them don. The appearance of these three characters – and even shop owner Wang (played by Ni Dahong) and his wife – assumes a larger-than-life caricature, an exaggerated mode of cultural typology that is highly entertaining and comedic in its campy, carnivalesque playfulness. At the same time, the appearance of the characters is deeply disturbing in its descent into a historically indeterminate primitivism (to use Rey Chow's term). The stunning natural beauty of desert dunes and rust-red hilly terrain serves as a framing backdrop for the human morality tale acted out by these Chinese character puppets. Through his location shooting in Lanzhou ('Creating' 2009), Zhang spares no expense in conjuring a naturalist cinema of China's gorgeous vistas through his extensive and repeated use of extreme long shots, extended takes of these shots, and time-lapse sequences of solar and lunar cycles. In the midst of this vision of China-as-nature, he drops the noodle house and its denizens, further encasing them, rather claustrophobically, within a historically and geo-

Figure 5.1   Oddly coloured outfits and strange Chinese-looking hairdos of the characters in *A Woman, a Gun and a Noodle Shop* (2009)

graphically deterritorialised microcosm, which he captures with a wide-angle fisheye lens (every time the characters are seen moving within the compound of the noodle shop). This entire moving tableau of China as commodified nature and as commodified culture, removed from socio-political realities, entrances and enthrals the expectant touristic gaze.

A Gun

The sad ubiquity of the gun in American social and political culture makes its diegetic presence as the weapon of choice in *Blood Simple* unremarkable. But, for Zhang to retain its presence in his film (which is set deep in China's 'primitive' past) and within the film's title is a call to read this technology of violence as a symbol of the encroachment of Western modernity into Chinese culture. Additionally, it is a reminder of China's historical confrontation of the West's 'corrupting' influences and its technology's material impact on the politics of war. This postcolonial critique then takes a linguistic turn. The purveyor of this instrument of death is a flamboyant Persian merchant (Julien Gaudfroy), who sells the weapon to the wife only after they undergo a bartering exchange that comically takes place in English and Mandarin: both parties announce the amount in English and the currency 'guan' in Mandarin. There is even an extended play on the English phrase 'must die', words uttered by the merchant in extolling the capabilities of this 'technology for maximum violence', which Li and Zhao misread as 'moose die'. To anachronistically insert this culturally contemporary moment of linguistic humour, Zhang relies on the caricature of the bumbling Chinese buffoon who misreads and mispronounces the English language. The postcoloniality of this ambiguous moment in the film splits in its appeal to both Chinese and Western audiences. The gun can be seen as a disruptor of Chinese social order in the way it leads, directly or indirectly, to the deaths of Wang, Li, and Zhao, but it can also be interpreted as instrumental in freeing the wife from the patriarchal Wang. Also, the tacky linguistic humour verbally reifies the supposed cultural gulf separating China and the West, while reinforcing stereotypes of Chinese linguistic ineptitude in the English-speaking global marketplace. Comedy attenuates the discomfort of postcolonial criticism, thereby allowing critique-as-appeal to coexist with culture-as-commodity in Zhang's transnational remake.

A Woman

In Hollywood film noir of the 1940s, the iconic femme fatale is 'made to appear beautiful but also treacherous, criminally depraved and castrating in … [her] desires' (Boozer 1999/2000: 21). This female figuration did not remain static; for by the time one gets to the neo-noir films of the 1960s and 1970s, she has been transformed into 'usually the passive or incidental victim rather than active manipulator of her sexual-economic circumstance' (24). Frances McDormand's Abby in *Blood Simple* continues to embody the femme fatale's sexual mystery and threat, but the film *hints* at the fact that she has an affair with Ray (John Getz) only because she is unhappy with her marriage to a potentially abusive Marty (Dan Hedaya). In accordance with the noir narrative convention, Abby's trustworthiness is successfully questioned, which becomes a pivotal plot point, when Marty insidiously plants in Ray's head suspicions about Abby's motivations: 'what's really gonna be funny is when she gives you that innocent look and says, "I don't know what you're talking about, Ray. I ain't done anything funny."'

By shifting away from Hollywood's film noir and neo-noir traditions, Zhang's remake diminishes the sexual mystery of the wife and underscores much more explicitly, both in terms of character development and narrative revisions, her suffering under the perverse patriarchal dominance of her husband, Wang. In providing the back-story of how he 'bought' her for 'three *guan* and eight hundred *wen*' and how her 'womb is like a piece of junk' because 'it won't lay any eggs', Wang epitomises Chinese patriarchy's egregious treatment of women as social commodities and reproductive machines. To help further corroborate audience disgust with Wang, Zhang magnifies the shop owner's abuse of his wife by detailing, in the sexual role-play to which he subjects her, intimations of paedophilic fetishism. He burns her with his pipe when she challenges him. While *Blood Simple* only subtly insinuates Marty's mistreatment of Abby in the relationship prior to her affair, Zhang foregrounds and visually concretises in the narrative this aspect of the

Figure 5.2   The wife screams, 'You tell Wang he can't bully me anymore. I'm not afraid!' *A Woman, a Gun and a Noodle Shop* (2009)

relationship. This specific detail is necessary to justify the wife's fantasy of wanting to kill her husband and offers the emotional rationale for her overt expressions of anger at him. With great determination, she warns him that 'this will be the last time you abuse me like this'. She expresses a profound sense of purpose and self-understanding when she tells her lover Li that she intends to divorce her husband, unlike Abby's rather cautious revelation to Ray at the beginning of *Blood Simple* where she betrays her confusion about what to do with her failing marriage. The wife even confronts her feminised lover for being 'such a wimp', by expressing her emotional needs: 'As a woman, all I wanted was a shoulder to lean on, but there was none. Then I met you. I thought I found one. But I was wrong about you. You don't deserve my love.' The endings of the two films are also significantly different in tone. Abby rather calmly states 'I'm not afraid of you, Marty' after she shoots the hired assassin she mistakes for her husband, while the wife literally screams at the camera through the gunshot hole (in an iris, Dutch tilt shot): 'You tell Wang he can't bully me anymore. I'm not afraid!' Zhang, therefore, has chosen to remake the woman into the powerful modern feminist figure that she truly deserves to be.

In so foregrounding the 'woman' in *A Woman, a Gun and a Noodle Shop* and her oppressed status in Chinese society, Zhang has remade the Coen Brothers' film into a contemporary feminist version that resonates effectively with the gender politics of the new millennium. It necessarily articulates the need to address women's issues in China and Chinese society today. But, at the same time, do the progressive gender politics of the film risk its co-optation into the cinematic pragmatism of Zhang's work? Is the film simply returning to Lu's notion of 'the Zhang Yimou model' precisely because 'the oppressed Chinese woman ... as the object of a (Western) male gaze' appeals to the 'patriarchal nature of Western society' (2002: 168), just as this oppressed figuration can also reach out to the liberal sensibilities of feminist politics among contemporary global viewers? It is the fact that this remake lends itself too easily to these divergent, and even contradictory, interpretative possibilities that makes it an exemplary and appealing, albeit politically problematic, title in the recent offerings of transnational Chinese cinemas.

NOTES

1. While she devotes the remainder of her essay to an analysis of the Hong Kong film *Eastern Condors* and its possible Hollywood sources, Aufderheide also gestures to cinematic work from both Shanghai and Hong Kong to illustrate the extensive historical spread of this mode of cross-cultural 'imitation', including the films of Jackie Chan and Tsui Hark (1998: 192–3). Affirming the historicity of this phenomenon is also Stephen Teo's observation, for instance, that 'the ancient-costume film (*guzhuang pian*) [of Shanghai cinema in the 1920s] ... was influenced by Western costume pictures and adventure epics, particularly the swashbucklers of Douglas Fairbanks' (2009: 24). See also my essay on Shaw Brothers' 1977 attempt to offer a King Kong remake in the film *The Mighty Peking Man* (Chan 2009).
2. In recent news related to *A Woman, a Gun and a Noodle Shop*, the director was involved in a lawsuit in an attempt to retrieve US$2.5 million of the distribution fees supposedly due to him from the production firm ('Chinese Director' 2015).
3. Writing for *The Hollywood Reporter*, Clarence Tsui describes 'Tsui Hark's first deployment of stereoscopic cameras' as 'a visual spectacle from beginning to end' (2013). *Variety*'s Maggie Lee echoes this sentiment, by noting that, in 'raising the bar sky-high for Chinese blockbuster entertainment', the film 'lays out a gargantuan feast of 3D spectacle, high-wire martial arts, splendiferous period aesthetics, intelligent sleuthing and even an ancestor of "Pacific Rim's" kaiju' (2013). I have also encountered similar reactions to the film in my conversations with American audiences.
4. Evans Chan writes: 'Since *Hero* is essentially a film about self-laceration ... is there a parallel act of self-laceration, artistic, psychological, spiritual, going on for the filmmaker of *Ju Dou* and *Raise the Red Lanterns* [*sic*]? ... Zhang's dance with the state is a complex exercise of servitude, survival, and surging forth. After all, *To Live*, his most artful, politically audacious film, was made after *The Story of Qiu Ju*, his first conciliatory bow to the authorities' (2009: 275).
5. *A Woman, a Gun and a Noodle Shop*, DVD, directed by Zhang Yimou. USA: Sony Pictures Classics, 2009. I have relied mostly on the English subtitles in this US DVD release for all translations of credits and dialogue, making only occasional minor adjustments with my own translations of the original Chinese for purposes of clarity.
6. I want to thank my colleague Ting-Kai Su for assistance on this specific analytical point.

REFERENCES

Aufderheide, Patricia (1998), 'Made in Hong Kong: Translation and Transmutation', in Andrew Horton and Stuart Y. McDougal (eds), *Play It Again, Sam: Retakes on Remakes*, Berkeley: University of California Press, pp. 191–9.

Berry, Chris (2011), 'Transnational Chinese Cinema Studies', in Song Hwee Lim and Julian Ward (eds), *The Chinese Cinema Book*, London: BFI/Palgrave Macmillan, pp. 9–16.

Berry, Michael (2005), *Speaking in Images: Interviews with Contemporary Chinese Filmmakers*, New York: Columbia University Press.

Bona Film (n.d.), <http://www.bonafilm.cn/our-company.aspx> (last accessed 26 July 2015).

Boozer, Jack (1999/2000), 'The Lethal *Femme Fatale* in the Noir Tradition', *Journal of Film and Video*, 51: 3/4, 20–35.

Chan, Evans (2009), 'Zhang Yimou's *Hero*: The Temptations of Fascism', in Tan See-Kam, Peter X Feng, and Gina Marchetti (eds), *Chinese Connections: Critical Perspectives on Film, Identity, and Diaspora*, Philadelphia: Temple University Press, pp. 263–77.

Chan, Kenneth (2009), 'The Shaw–Tarantino Connection: Rolling Thunder Pictures and the Exploitation Aesthetics of Cool', *Mediascape: UCLA's Journal of Cinema and Media Studies*, <http://www.tft.ucla.edu/mediascape/Fall09_ShawBrothers. html> (last accessed 28 February 2016).

China Film Group Corporation (2002–14), <http://www.thechinafilmgroup.com/ #!about/cfp1> (last accessed 26 July 2015).

'China Film Group, Hengdian Group and Warner Bros. Pictures Partner to Create Warner China Film HG Corporation' (2004), 13 October, <http://www.warnerbros. com/studio/news/china-film-group-hengdian-group-and-warner-bros-pictures- partner-create-warner-china> (last accessed 26 July 2015).

'Chinese Director Zhang Yimou Sues Ex-Production Partner for $2.5M Share of Distribution Money' (2015), *US News & World Report*, 7 July, <http://www. usnews.com/news/entertainment/articles/2015/07/07/director-zhang-yimou-sues-ex- production-partner-for-25m> (last accessed 26 July 2015).

Chow, Rey (1995), *Primitive Passions: Visuality, Sexuality, Ethnography, and Contemporary Chinese Cinema*, New York: Columbia University Press.

Clark, Paul (2005), *Reinventing China: A Generation and Its Films*, Hong Kong: The Chinese University Press.

'Creating a Woman, a Gun and a Noodle Shop' (2009), *A Woman, a Gun and a Noodle Shop*, DVD special feature, Sony Pictures Classics, USA.

Curtin, Michael (2007), *Playing to the World's Biggest Audience: The Globalization of Chinese Film and TV*, Berkeley: University of California Press.

Davis, Darrell William (2010), 'Market and Marketization in the China Film Business', *Cinema Journal*, 49: 3, pp. 121–5.

Deleuze, Gilles (1994), *Difference and Repetition*, Paul Patton (trans.), New York: Columbia University Press.

Gateward, Frances, ed. (2001), *Zhang Yimou: Interviews*, Jackson: University Press of Mississippi.

Herbert, Daniel (2009), 'Trading Spaces: Transnational Dislocations in *Insomnia/ Insomnia* and *Ju-On/The Grudge*', in Scott A. Lukas and John Marmysz (eds), *Fear, Cultural Anxiety, and Transformation: Horror, Science Fiction, and Fantasy Films Remade*, Lanham, MD: Lexington Books, pp. 143–64.

Jiao Xiongping (2001), 'Discussing *Red Sorghum*', in Frances Gateward (ed.), *Zhang Yimou: Interviews*, Jackson: University Press of Mississippi, pp. 3–14.

Lee, Maggie (2013), 'Film Review: Young Detective Dee: Rise of the Sea Dragon', *Variety*, 18 September, <http://variety.com/2013/film/reviews/young-detective-dee- rise-of-the-sea-dragon-review-1200617362/> (last accessed 29 February 2016).

Lu, Sheldon Hsiao-peng, ed. (1997), *Transnational Chinese Cinemas: Identity, Nationhood, Gender*, Honolulu: University of Hawai'i Press.

Lu, Tonglin (2002), *Confronting Modernity in the Cinemas of Taiwan and Mainland China*, Cambridge: Cambridge University Press.

Sony Pictures Classics (n.d.), <http://www.sonyclassics.com/awomanagunandanoodle shop/presskit.pdf> (last accessed 29 July 2015).

Teo, Stephen (2009), *Chinese Martial Arts Cinema: The* Wuxia *Tradition*, Edinburgh: Edinburgh University Press.

Tsui, Clarence (2013), 'Young Detective Dee – Rise of the Sea Dragon (Di Ren Jie Zhi Shen Du Long Wang): Film Review', *The Hollywood Reporter*, 17 September, <http://www.hollywoodreporter.com/review/young-detective-dee-rise-sea-630670> (last accessed 29 February 2016).

Verevis, Constantine (2006), *Film Remakes*, Edinburgh: Edinburgh University Press.

6. TRANSFORMATION AND GLAMOUR IN THE CROSS-CULTURAL MAKEOVER: *RETURN TO EDEN*, *KHOON BHARI MAANG* AND THE AVENGING WOMAN IN POPULAR HINDI CINEMA

Michael Lawrence

The popular Hindi film *Khoon Bhari Maang* (*Blood-Smeared Forehead*, Rakesh Roshan, 1988) is an unofficial remake of *Return to Eden*, an Australian television mini-series broadcast in 1983.[1] An exemplary *masala*, *Khoon Bhari Maang* displays how Bombay filmmakers adapt foreign material for local audiences and 'consciously heighten and intensify the differences between their films and the "originals"' by expanding the narrative – adding back-story and a comic sub-plot – and inserting half a dozen song-dance sequences (Ganti 2002: 296, 290).[2] The implantation of Indian values also plays a part in this process: Sheila Nayar has suggested that the Hindi remake inevitably reflects how popular cinema is 'heavily circumscribed by the expectations and demands of its audience', observing that characters and relationships – and particularly family and gender roles – are 'rewritten to satisfy a culturally distinct ethos' (2003: 74, 75). In this chapter I focus on the representation of femininity in *Khoon Bhari Maang* to explore how this Hindi remake repurposes foreign material – in this instance, Australian rather than American – and transforms the original text into a traditional popular film format, but so as to challenge rather than endorse dominant cultural ideology.

As Iain Robert Smith has recently proposed, contemporary Bollywood remakes 'should not be seen as resulting from a simple process of "Indianisation" but as transnational cultural exchanges in which globally circulating media forms interact with local narrative traditions and industries' (2015: 118). Produced in the 1980s, *Khoon Bhari Maang* is an example of a transnational and trans-media adaptation that anticipates the more recent developments

Smith identifies as characteristic of popular Hindi cinema in the global era. This chapter will address how film remakes, as Robert Stam has suggested of novel-to-screen adaptations, 'can take an activist stance toward their source, inserting them into a much broader intertextual dialogism' (2000: 64) and even 'de-repress' their 'latent feminist spirit' (2005: 42). I shall discuss the global dialogism of the Australian source text and the local dialogism of the Indian remake, which complicate the central relationship between the mini-series and the film. Firstly, to refer back to Smith's terms, the 'transnational cultural exchanges' here precede the 'Indianisation' of the Australian mini-series since *Return to Eden* was itself a self-conscious emulation of the melodramatic style of US prime-time soap operas, and in particular *Dynasty* (ABC, 1981–9), and was subsequently extremely popular with both local and international audiences, and especially women. Ien Ang states that the global popularity of US soap operas in the 1980s was widely perceived as 'evidence of the threat posed by American-style commercial culture against "authentic" national cultures and identities' (1985: 2). But *Return to Eden* has been understood as a successful 'indigenisation' of a foreign format in response to the cultural imperialism of US television. Alan McKee describes it as 'a metaphorical narrative for the reconciliation of "Australian" and "American" elements in Australian television' (2001: 226). Secondly, the interaction with 'local narrative traditions' here exceeds the remake's 'Indianisation' of the 'Americanised' Australian mini-series (or 'Australianised' American soap opera). This is because its critical relation with earlier examples of what Lalitha Gopalan (2002) has called the 'avenging woman' film, and in particular *Tarazu* (*Scales of Justice*, B. R. Chopra, 1980), provides a spectacular critique of the conservative ideologies of popular Hindi cinema. Since *Return to Eden* was not broadcast in India, the remake's relationship with local narratives was arguably more important for audiences than its relationship with its source text. This chapter examines the politics of transformation by considering first the Australian show's indigenisation of *global* media texts, and then the more significant changes that constitute its 'Indianisation' as *Khoon Bhari Maang*, and finally the Hindi remake's subversion of *local* media texts through its radical reconfiguration of the source text. *Khoon Bhari Maang* was particularly meaningful for feminist audiences in India: Shohini Ghosh, for example, suggests that the film remains significant owing to the 'active resistance' of its heroine (1996: 153). She argues that it is a rare example of a popular film which seeks to 'liberate women from traditional frameworks of representation' and which exploits the popular format to '"activate" the fantasies of women's rage and autonomy' (175). As I shall suggest, this is due to the remake's 'activist stance' towards its source.

Glamour is the most important factor in both the processes described above – the Americanisation of the Australian mini-series and the subversion of the avenging woman film – and is arguably central to the success of both the original mini-series and the Hindi remake. Glamour also plays a pivotal role in the story, which concerns the dramatic physical transformation of the frumpy female protagonist necessitated initially by her husband's attempt on her life – she requires plastic surgery after being pushed overboard and ravaged by a crocodile while on her honeymoon – and subsequently by her desire for retribution – she changes her name, has a makeover and becomes a successful fashion model in order to get revenge on her husband and his mistress. Andrew Horton has described the 'makeover' as 'a particular form of remake that purposely sets out to make significant changes' (1998: 174). And for Rashna Wadia Richards the 'cross-cultural makeover' invites us to 'explore how cultures embrace and resist, borrow from and interact with each other' (2011: 344). While the heroine's recourse to the makeover in the Australian mini-series can be understood as an allegory of the show's own tactical appropriation of the conventions of the US soap opera, whereby, as McKee suggests, the heroine survives her ordeal by 'understanding . . . how the glamour of American culture might be experienced as an opportunity rather than a threat', in the Hindi film her makeover not only refers to the strategic transformations that characterise the remake itself but, more significantly, intervenes in the ideological representations of traditional (Indian) and foreign (Western) modes of femininity in the avenging woman film and popular Hindi cinema more generally (2003: 235). The 'Indianisation' of the Australian mini-series inevitably reproduces that show's own appropriation of American television, with the result that the Australian features privileged in the earlier indigenisation or 'Australianisation' process are inevitably lost. The explicit female address and melodramatic style, derived from the US prime-time soap opera, remain. And while the melodrama transmutes easily into the extravagances of the popular *masala* format, the female address, far less common in Hindi cinema, is actually intensified and politicised in the remake.

The centrality of glamour and fashion to the narrative's conventionally elaborate convolutions – and the role masquerade plays in the heroine's machinations – also invite a consideration not only of the reception of certain popular Hindi films as camp, but also of the transnational circulation of codes of popular melodrama and signs of glamorous femininity. In her discussion of *Dynasty* Jane Feuer implies that the privileging of female characters and the ostentatious display of women's fashion was of particular significance to those for whom the show had 'an intentional camp sensibility' (1995: 118): 'the two groups that became obsessed with *Dynasty* in the mid-1980s', she writes, 'were gay men and heterosexual women . . . the two groups most connected to . . . notions of femininity as a commodity to be purchased' (131). As Jack Babuscio suggests in 'Camp and the Gay Sensibiity', 'camp emphasizes style as a means of self-projection . . . Style is a form of consciousness; it is never "natural", always acquired': 'Clothes . . . can be a means of asserting one's identity, as well as a form of justification in a society which denies one's essential validity' (1993: 23). The makeover, which enables the heroine's self-empowerment, thus resonates with the gay man's 'cultivation of exquisite taste' as 'a means of making something positive from a discredited social identity' (23). Camp appreciations of the heroine's taste in fashion, and references to the film's soapy sensibility and trashier excesses, are frequent in online appraisals by fans of *Khoon Bhari Maang*. The UK blogger 'Bollywooddewanna', for example, describes the film as 'camp' 'soap opera *masala*', 'high on glamour [and] fabulous over the top fashion', and then presents a convincing case for the lasting influence of the heroine's taste in turbans, sunglasses and clutch bags on contemporary style icons such as Kate Moss, Rihanna and Lady Gaga (2009).

The dramatic makeover of the heroine in the remake is inflected at an extra-textual level by the casting of Rekha in the role of Aarti/Jyoti. Local audiences were familiar with popular accounts of the actress's transformation from gawky 'ugly duckling' to screen goddess, fashion icon and fitness guru; she was 'perhaps the only actress who made over her physical appearance from ordinary to alluring' (Somaaya et al. 2012: 145). As Lucia Krämer has argued, when 'tailoring remakes as star vehicles', 'roles are adapted to fit the image and talents of particular stars, which allows them to play up to audience expectations': 'wardrobe and make-up choices' can thus contribute to the remake's 'showcasing of the star' (2015: 84–5). The makeover is a narrative convention and camp trope of the women's film in which the heroine transforms her appearance – her weight, her hair, her make-up, and her clothes – so as to assert hitherto inexpressible but now irrepressible dimensions of her personality; the star playing the heroine is usually 'unrecognisable' before the makeover, after which character and actor converge: for example, Bette Davis in *Now, Voyager* (1942) and Barbra Streisand in *The Mirror Has Two Faces* (1996). According to Suzanne Ferris, 'with its persistent emphasis on appearance and display, the makeover film inevitably and irrefutably puts the woman at the centre. As such, it also capitalizes on the role fashion and commodification played in the classic woman's film' (2008: 42). Whereas the makeover film typically concludes with the woman being recognised by the man she desires for her inner qualities rather than her outward appearance, the makeover trope is here inverted since the narrative revolves around revenge rather than romantic union. Owing partly to the Hindi remake's showcasing of its star, the representation of the heroine's makeover and labours in the fashion industry is strikingly different from the Australian original, as is the use she makes of her glamour in her quest for justice. While in *Return to Eden* the heroine uses her glamorous new image to seduce her husband, with the intention of exposing his hypocrisy, in *Khoon Bhari Maang* the heroine's makeover is from the outset a weapon in her plans for violent retribution.[3] It is arguably *Khoon*

Bhari Maang's reconfiguration of the role of glamour in *Return to Eden* that constitutes its significance as a feminist text, since, as Ferris suggests, female audiences 'have access to the same tools of transformation' as the heroines of makeover films (2008: 44). The representation of the makeover in the Hindi remake corresponds to the film's radical intervention in the avenging woman cycle: beyond simply yet paradoxically enabling the expression of an authentic identity, the makeover becomes the means for a powerful assertion of feminist agency.

RETURN TO EDEN AND THE FEMINISATION OF THE AUSTRALIAN MINI-SERIES

Return to Eden, broadcast as three 90-minute episodes on consecutive nights on Network 10 during September 1983, was the top-rating mini-series of the year, and the third most successful of the decade.[4] A brief synopsis is necessary. In Sydney, the meek and dowdy heiress Stephanie Harper (Rebecca Gilling), a divorced mother of two and 'Australia's wealthiest woman', marries the handsome and considerably younger tennis champion Greg Marsden (James Reyne). On their honeymoon at Eden, the Harper family estate, Greg pushes Stephanie out of their boat and into the jaws of a nearby crocodile. Miraculously, Stephanie survives. An old hermit drags her to his shack and slowly nurses her back to health with Aboriginal remedies. Unable to remember her name, Stephanie calls herself Tara (after the house in *Gone with the Wind*, her mother's favourite film). Tara spends the next six months recuperating at an island clinic, where she asks plastic surgeon Dan Marshall (James Smilie) to redesign her face. Dan falls in love with Tara, but she returns to Sydney, having finally remembered what happened. She further transforms her image and within six months is a successful and glamorous fashion model. She then begins to date Greg, who fails to recognise her, and is reacquainted with her former best friend Jilly (Wendy Hughes), Greg's mistress and accomplice. Dan comes to Sydney and proposes to Tara, but she declines. Tara returns with Greg to Eden. A desperate Jilly arrives soon afterwards. Tara and Greg make love, after which she reveals her real identity to both Greg and Jilly. Greg tries to strangle Stephanie in the swimming pool, but Jilly shoots him in the arm with his rifle. He attempts to escape in a plane, but he loses control and is killed when it crashes and explodes. Dan, who has since discovered that Tara is actually Stephanie, arrives at the estate with her two children. Jilly is arrested.

Stuart Cunningham and Toby Miller have referred to a 'golden age' of television drama in Australia during the 1980s 'when finances, creative endeavour and audience following coalesced in making prestige national fictions a source of pride and profit at home and of recognition and acceptance abroad' (1994: 140). The big-budget mini-series was the most popular format for exploring

Figure 6.1 Tara (Rebecca Gilling) strikes a pose during a photo shoot in *Return to Eden* (1983)

'serious historical themes of nation-formation' – there were 'more than 100 of them in the decade to 1988' – and almost all 'were treatments of significant moments in Australia's past' (140). As the above description makes clear, *Return to Eden* is much more interested in a woman's personal transformation than in 'historical themes of nation-formation'. But if, as Albert Moran claims, the show 'broke decisively with the pattern of the Australian mini-series up to that point', this had as much to do with its relation to mainstream modes of popular entertainment as with its contemporary setting and focus on female identity (1993: 140). In a 'stylistic and generic map of the Australian mini-series', Cunningham argues that the form was marked by a 'textual and production rhetoric of quality', 'analogous to that of the art cinema in relation to mainstream commercial cinema' (1993: 118–19). *Return to Eden*'s apparent lack of concern with Australian history is compounded by its preference for melodrama over realism; for McKee, 'an ethos of anti-realist excess . . . informs the production' (2001: 222). This, however, is related to the viewers it sought most self-consciously to satisfy. McKee avers that *Return to Eden* was 'exceptional' precisely owing to its 'feminised address' (2001: 220, 224).

Rather than present the nation's past in a legitimate aesthetic register, then, *Return to Eden* presents a modern woman's passions in an ostentatiously melodramatic manner.

Cunningham and Elizabeth Jacka note that *Return to Eden*'s 'far-fetched plot' resembled more than anything else US prime-time soap operas (1996: 173). *Return to Eden* is indeed a strikingly self-conscious deployment and display of the form and address associated with shows such as *Dallas* (CBS, 1978–91) and especially *Dynasty*, in particular their combination of glamorous characters, opulent settings and elaborate plots. 'Although its production values are high', McKee admits, *Return to Eden* 'is more likely to be described as "trashy" than "quality"' (2001: 220). But the mini-series also localises the foreign soap opera by emphasising its Australian setting and character even as its heroine embraces her new career as a fashion model (she stubbornly retains her penchant for beer). Several fashion shoots take place in and around Sydney harbour, and during one fashion show Tara struts down the catwalk arm in arm with Bondi Beach surfers. The foregrounding of such banal and stereotypical signs of 'Australia' suggests a tactical and even a knowing recourse, rather than a total relinquishment, to the narrative and affective codes of American popular culture. Despite Tara's glamorous new image, for example, the Aboriginal servants at the family estate instantly recognise her as Stephanie. Her new look is first revealed when she walks into a modelling agency and asks for 'someone who can get [her] on the front cover of *Vogue* in six months'. But it is of course the cover of the Australian edition of the fashion magazine on which Tara's face appears, a local variation of the international style bible. As such, Tara's success as a model reflects a national iteration of globally circulating signs of glamour, and thus refers to the show's own hybrid form. Indeed for McKee, the heroine's recovery, reinvention and triumphant 'return' embody how *Return to Eden* 'negotiates . . . two imperatives', namely American popular melodrama and Australian national identity (2001: 220). In the following section I will examine the 'Indianisation' of *Return to Eden* by focusing in particular on the remake's representation of the heroine's dramatic makeover and fashion career as well as her quest for vengeance, which evolves into a more expansive and aggressive exercise in retaliation and retribution, indigenised via feminist invocations of Indian history and Hindu mythology.

KHOON BHARI MAANG AND THE 'INDIANISATION' OF RETURN TO EDEN

The Hindi makeover of *Return to Eden* involves a number of 'significant changes' related to the heroine's original situation, her dramatic transformation, and her ultimate course of action. While in *Return to Eden* the heroine, Stephanie, is a divorcee whose father died seventeen years earlier, the heroine of *Khoon Bhari Maang*, Aarti, is a widow whose father (Saeed Jaffrey) is murdered by his business partner Hiralal (Kader Khan) at the beginning of the film. Stephanie's ex-husbands don't appear in *Return to Eden*, and her two children feature in only a few scenes, whereas in *Khoon Bhari Maang* flashbacks and a song sequence represent Aarti's memories of her husband (played by the film's director) and the children are prominent throughout. *Return to Eden* begins with Stephanie marrying Greg – his treachery is revealed soon afterwards – whereas Aarti marries Sanjay (Kabir Verdi) about halfway through the remake. But we know from the start that he intends to kill her for her fortune; he is in fact in cahoots with Hiralal, his uncle, as well as Aarti's best friend Nandini (Sonu Walia), a famous model. Narrative symmetry in *Khoon Bhari Maang* balances Sanjay's scheme to trick Aarti – she is persuaded he would make an ideal husband and father to her children – with Jyoti's plan to destroy Sanjay: he remains unaware she is his wife and the mother of 'his' children. While *Return to Eden* devotes a lot of time (the entire middle episode) to Stephanie's recovery at the clinic, and has her plastic surgeon fall in love with her and then follow her to Sydney, in *Khoon Bhari Maang* the heroine returns home immediately after her operation (midway through the film), and it is JD (Shatrugham Sinha), her photographer at the modelling agency, who develops protective feelings towards her. While Sanjay simply wants to possess Jyoti after seeing her image in the fashion magazines, JD apparently wants to 'help her as a friend' after getting to know her at the agency. However, while Stephanie appears genuinely torn between her desire for Dan and her need to confront Greg, especially after Dan's proposal, Aarti remains much more focused on avenging Sanjay, and JD is not presented as a potential future husband, though both Dan and JD deliver the children to the heroine at the end.[5] In *Return to Eden* Stephanie spends six months at the clinic and a further six months working as a model before she is reconciled with her children, but the Hindi remake dispenses entirely with the recovery sequences and Jyoti's rise to fame takes very little time indeed.[6] In *Khoon Bhari Maang*, Ramu Kaka (A. K. Hangal), Aarti's old manservant, overhears Sanjay and Hiralal discussing their schemes; Hiralal promptly orders Sanjay to kill Ramu Kaka. When Sanjay invites Jyoti over for lunch, her frightened children tell her everything, unaware that she is actually their mother. Without revealing the truth, Jyoti tells her children to regard her as their mother, returned to punish both Sanjay and Hiralal for their crimes.

In *Return to Eden*, when Stephanie returns to Eden as Tara, she initiates sex with Greg during a thunderstorm the night before she reveals her identity; she is determined to let him satisfy his desire for her since he had earlier that day told her that his former wife was 'old, fat and boring' and that he had to be 'half-drunk' before he could make love to her. In *Khoon Bhari Maang*, however, Aarti and Sanjay don't even consummate their marriage (she spends their wedding night with her children) and, when she returns to the estate as Jyoti, after having killed Hiralal, she confronts Sanjay the very same day. Dressed in leather and armed with a rifle and a whip, she tells him God kept her alive so she could sign his death warrant; she snags Sanjay with her lasso, drags him to the river, beats him with a stick, and watches him plunge into the water to be devoured by a crocodile. Aarti intended this from the very beginning: while recovering in the old hermit's shack, she stands before an image of Kali, the goddess of destruction, and declares her desire to 'throw [Sanjay] to the crocodiles and watch him die'. While the old hermit tells Aarti that *God* will punish Sanjay, Aarti declares that *she* will personally take revenge, and 'show the world that woman isn't weak'. When she eventually confronts Sanjay at the estate, she invokes Kali once again, as well as Durga (the goddess of creation and annihilation, and of the victory of good over evil), the Rani of Jhansi (a.k.a. Lakshmibal [1828–58], an Indian Queen celebrated for her role in the Rebellion of 1857) and Razia Sultana (Raziyya al-Din [1205–40], a thirteenth-century ruler of the Delhi Sultanate).

The differences noted above demonstrate how the remake reconfigures the original heroine so as to present a conventional and traditional Indian woman: Aarti/Jyoti is explicitly defined as a both a daughter and a mother, and since she remains untroubled by romantic desire she can remain 'faithful' to her dead husband. At the same time, however, she is relentless in her pursuit of vengeance, and assumes personal responsibility for the restoration of justice, rather than involve the law, despite discovering that Hiralal and Sanjay have murdered her father and Ramu Kala. Rather than report these crimes to the police, or ask her friend JD for help, Aarti/Jyoti kills the two villains herself. *Khoon Bhari Maang* thus offers a heroine who is both devoted to her father and her children yet defiant and active in her desire for revenge; as Shohini Ghosh has suggested, the film 'shattered the myth about women's pacifism and showed her as an agent of violence' (2015).

At first it would appear that the somewhat unlikely friendship between the professional model and nightclub singer Nandini and the dowdy and demure Aarti is simply a conventional and conservative ideological device for contrasting 'proper' and 'improper' modes of femininity. However, the traditional opposition between virtuous heroines and delectable but degraded vamps is precisely what the film subverts via Aarti's dramatic makeover, her embrace of glamour, and her tactical infiltration of the fashion industry. By becoming a model, Jyoti threatens Nandini both professionally and personally, and is regarded as competing with Nandini for first JD's and then Sanjay's attention. JD stages a public competition to determine which of the models is the most popular: Jyoti and Nandini duke it out in a deliriously demented song-dance sequence, involving several costume changes (including Jyoti's turn as a flamenco dancer), at the end of which Jyoti's victory seems assured when she throws a gold necklace off the stage and around Sanjay's neck, anticipating the lasso from the final act.

During the climactic confrontation at the estate, Nandini dies after leaping in front of a bullet Sanjay intended for Aarti. While the vamp was typically killed off in the popular cinema of the 1970s, *Khoon Bhari Maang* also subverts this tradition since Aarti's righteous vengeance is actually enabled by her glamorous new image: it is by assuming the appearance of the vamp that the heroine can settle her scores. The film reflects how, as Jyotika Virdi has suggested, by the 1980s 'the sexualized Hindi film heroine was no longer punished as was the phallic vamp for satisfying specular desires' (1999: 35).[7] Indeed, Aarti/ Jyoti uses her glamorous image to punish others. Anustup Basu describes the representation of women in popular Hindi cinema as an anxious negotiation of the 'indigenous' and the 'worldly' (2010: 9), which necessarily involves 'a complex process of "distilling" visibilities . . . into a postulate of "traditional" patriarchy or of its intimate enemy, the modern' (29). The heroine's makeover mission in *Khoon Bhari Maang*, however, results in a spectacular refusal of the earlier tendency whereby 'the female body is . . . reified into both the spirit of the nation and its torrid others', divided between 'theorems of modernity and tenets of tradition', 'the ceremonial interiors of the home and the shock and the traffic of money and bodies in urban space' (29, 31).

The representation of the heroine's makeover and her work as a fashion model in the remake reflects how, as Kasbekar has suggested, popular Hindi cinema of the 1980s 'solicited [the female gaze] by the kaleidoscopic changes of extravagant sets, sumptuous costumes, fashionable jewellery, imaginative hairstyles and daring make-up, so that [quoting Mary Ann Doane] "the film frame is a kind of display window and spectatorship consequently a form of window-shopping"' (2001: 124). In *Return to Eden*, after Stephanie returns to Sydney, she is shown wandering through a shopping mall and then visiting a hair salon; her glamorous new image is revealed for the first time at the modelling agency in the next scene. *Khoon Bhari Maang*, in contrast, offers a spectacular montage sequence in which a succession of extreme close-ups emphasises the labour required to construct a glamorous appearance, as consecutive shots show Aarti applying first her lip gloss, then her eye shadow, then her blusher, and then her nail varnish, and finally her contact lenses. In the fashion shoot sequences in *Return to Eden* Tara strikes curious poses beside Sydney's public sculptures, with a serious expression on her face, but then suddenly laughs and teases her photographer Jason, mocking the style of modelling associated with fashion photography, and suggesting an ironic detachment from her new glamorous image. In the fashion shoot sequence in *Khoon Bhari Maang*, on the other hand, Jyoti stares directly into the camera – the photographer is nowhere to be seen – and never smiles. The heroine's work as a model in the story is collapsed with the showcasing of the star by the film itself, as

Figure 6.2 Jyoti (Rekha) stares into the camera during the photo shoot in *Khoon Bhari Maang* (1988)

Jyoti/Rekha is presented in a succession of increasingly bizarre 'looks'. This sequence resonates with Babuscio's suggestion that camp is produced when 'one aims to become what one wills, to exercise some control over one's environment' and particularly 'when the stress on style is "outrageous" or "too much"' (1993: 23–4). While Jyoti is shown working with Jason on the streets of Sydney, Tara is shown for the most part alone in the abstract and more symbolic space of the empty studio. Jyoti's labours as a model are marked by a seriousness that suffuses her entire scheme, and her mission is clear, as shown by the gigantic golden cobweb which features in the fashion shoot. As I discuss in the following section, the remake's representation of glamour and the labours of the fashion model are integral to its significance as a subversive intervention in the avenging woman film cycle.

KHOON BHARI MAANG AND THE AVENGING WOMAN FILM

In her discussion of Hollywood's rape-revenge films, Jacinda Read argues that 'insofar as feminism can be defined as involving a struggle over the meanings of femininity, it is in its on-going articulation of these struggles that the rape-revenge film can be seen to be attempting to make sense of feminism' (2000: 10). Indeed, Basu suggests that popular Hindi rape-revenge cinema reflects how in the 1970s 'the circulation of female bodies in different public avenues' became 'worrying for a patriarchal custodianship of culture' and reveals the 'difficulties in customizing womanhood' in relation to the 'gathering storm' of feminism (2010: 32). *Khoon Bhari Maang* is often included in critical accounts of avenging woman cinema, female vigilante films and the rape-revenge cycle, and is regularly mentioned alongside other women's films such as *Pratighaat* (*Retribution*, N. Chandra, 1987), *Sherni* (*Lioness*, Harmesh Malhotra, 1988), and *Zakhmi Aurat* (*Wounded Woman*, Avtar Bhogal, 1988, a remake of the American rape-revenge film *The Ladies Club* [Janet Greek, 1986]). In her consideration of 'Hindi cinema's dramatic re-inscription of women as avenging daredevils' Virdi asks: do 'the victim-heroines masquerade as avenging women, or do they indeed represent a politics of transformation and agency, dare I say a feminist one?' (1999: 17). *Khoon Bhari Maang* exploits its make-over melodrama to present a popular politics of female autonomy. Ghosh maintains that the 'very signifiers of "artificiality"' in the popular Hindi film, its 'masquerades' and 'excesses', 'provide greater space for the expression of subjectivity and unconscious operations than a rigid fidelity to "realism"' (1996: 174).

Rajeswari Sunder Rajan has read *Khoon Bhari Maang* in relation to 'the socially sanctioned violence against women that reinforces and is reinforced by the ideology of husband-worship' (1993: 83), and argues that its significance inheres in the fact 'that it envisages "action" as an option available to the oppressed, that it views this action as violent and revengeful but just, that its agent is a married woman, and that her victim is her husband' (96). Sanjay's attempt to kill Aarti by pushing her into the jaws of a crocodile is, of course, patently preposterous (as unlikely as her seeking vengeance by becoming a fashion model), but the scene itself presents a powerfully symbolic image of violence owing to the conspicuous absence of the crocodile – in contrast to the equivalent sequence in *Return to Eden* – in the shots that show Aarti screaming and struggling in the river and then slowly sinking beneath the bloody water. While this might appear at first to be simply a poverty of resources, the fact that the male actor (or his stunt double) is clearly shown wrestling with a model crocodile when Sanjay is killed at the end of the film suggests rather a deliberately ambiguous staging of the attempt on Aarti's life.

While the crocodile attack on the heroine is reconfigured in the Hindi remake so as to present a less realistic yet more expressive spectacle of women's victimisation, the makeover and fashion career are emphasised so as to offer a 'politics of transformation and agency' that is decidedly feminist. More specifically, the film inverts the relation between glamour and violence presented in *Insaf Ka Tarazu* (1980), 'the inaugural moment in the avenging woman genre' (Gopalan 2002: 44). In that film, we first encounter the heroine Bharati, played by beauty queen turned actress Zeenat Aman, working modelling swimwear on a beach. She is then brutally raped by an obsessive fan, and after being humiliated in court – her rapist is acquitted – she assumes a new identity as a modestly attired woman and begins a new career as a secretary. After her younger sister is raped by the same man

Bharati pursues and then shoots dead their attacker. When the tradition-ally dressed and demure Bharati is back in court and on trial for the double rapist's murder, the judge fails to recognise her. At the original rape trial the judge had agreed that her glamorous appearance and choice of career was incontrovertible evidence that she must have deliberately aroused and even seduced her attacker.

In *Lipstick* (Lamont Johnson, 1976), the American mainstream rape-revenge film on which *Tarazu* is based, the heroine, Chris, played by model turned actress Margaux Hemingway, continues to work as a model after her rapist is acquitted. Significantly, it is during a fashion shoot that Chris learns that her rapist has attacked her younger sister Kathy (Mariel Hemingway) and proceeds, still wearing a glittering crimson evening gown, to shoot him dead with a rifle as he attempts to drive out of the parking lot. The Hindi remake of *Lipstick*, in other words, departs from its source material by having the heroine switch careers and suppress her sexuality. Fareed Kazmi refers to how 'behind [the film's] iconoclastic exterior lies a severely compromised inner core' insofar as Bharati 'imbibes' the values of patriarchy and decides to 'lead the life of a recluse' (2010: 234–40). In stark contrast, in *Khoon Bhari Maang*, the heroine starts working as a model as a response to her being victimised by her husband. Bharati's and Aarti's makeovers transform their lives – and also conceal/reveal the actress' star images – in diametrically opposed fashion. Where Zeenat dis-appears into Bharati's dowdy drag, Aarti's masquerade offers an outrageous incarnation of Rekha's own glamorous personality. Where Bharati's glamour is the apparent cause of her victimisation, Jyoti's glamour is the vehicle for her vengeance; when she confronts Sanjay at the estate, she appears to be wearing the leathers that in the earlier fashion shoot montage she had modelled while sitting astride a motorbike. Aarti's glamour makeover, and her tactical deploy-ment of foreign and modern modes of femininity, thus refers to the film's stra-tegic repurposing of *Return to Eden*'s original appropriation of global forms of women's media, but also embody this remake's fantastic and fabulous but undoubtedly feminist politics of transformation.

Notes

1. In the summer of 2015 there were rumours, widely debated online, of a planned remake of *Khoon Bhari Maang*, to star Deepika Padukone. Another (but much less popular) example of a Hindi adaptation of a foreign television mini-series is *Dil Aashna Hai* (*The Heart Knows the Truth*, Hema Malini, 1992), an unofficial remake of the American mini-series *Lace* (ABC, 1984), itself adapted from the 1982 novel by British author Shirley Conran.
2. Anticipating the eclectic combinations of multiple source texts found in contempo-rary Bollywood remakes, one of the film's songs ('Main Teri Hoon Janam . . .') is based on the famous theme music by Vangelis from the British heritage film *Chariots of Fire* (1981).

3. In a subsequent avenging woman film, *Phool Bane Angary* (K. C. Bokadia, 1991), Rekha's character Namrata becomes a police officer so as to bring her rapists (who also murdered her husband) to justice.
4. *Return to Eden* returned to the screens as a weekly television show – comprising twenty-two 60-minute episodes – in 1986.
5. In the spin-off series Stephanie and Dan are married; it transpires that Jilly is Stephanie's half-sister; Jilly schemes with Greg's long-lost brother to take over the Harper business.
6. In an interview on the *Return to Eden* DVD, Rebecca Gilling, who played Stephanie, admits that the most unbelievable aspect of the story for her was the length of time the heroine was willing to spend apart from her children.
7. This development was short-lived. Gohar Siddiqui suggests that the increasing conservatism of the industry in the 1990s ensured that 'the avenging woman protagonist was replaced with the ideal wife in mainstream films' (2013).

References

Ang, Ien (1985), *Watching Dallas: Soap Opera and the Melodramatic Imagination*, London: Methuen.
Babuscio, Jack (1993 [1977]), 'Camp and the Gay Sensibility', in D. Bergman (ed.), *Camp Grounds: Style and Homosexuality*, Amherst: University of Massachusetts Press, pp. 19–38.
Basu, Anustup (2010), *Bollywood in the Age of New Media: The Televisual Aesthetic*, Edinburgh: Edinburgh University Press.
Bollywooddeewana (2009), '*Khoon Bhari Maang* (1988)', 4 July, <http://bollywood-deewana.blogspot.co.uk/2009/07/khoon-bhari-maang-1988.html> (last accessed 30 June 2015).
Cunningham, Stuart (1993), 'Style, Form and History in Australian Mini-series', in J. Frow and M. Morris (eds), *Australian Cultural Studies: A Reader*, Urbana and Chicago: University of Illinois Press, pp. 117–32.
Cunningham, Stuart and Toby Miller (1994), *Contemporary Australian Television*, Sydney: University of New South Wales Press.
Cunningham, Stuart and Elizabeth Jacka (1996), *Australian Television and International Mediascapes*, Cambridge: Cambridge University Press.
Ferris, Suzanne (2008), 'Fashioning Femininity in the Makeover Flick', in S. Ferris and M. Young (eds), *Chick Flicks: Contemporary Women at the Movies*, New York and Abingdon: Routledge, pp. 41–57.
Feuer, Jane (1995), *Seeing Through the Eighties: Television and Reaganism*, Durham, NC and London: Duke University Press.
Ganti, Tejaswini (2002), '"And Yet My Heart Is Still Indian": the Bombay film industry and the (H)Indianization of Hollywood', in F. D. Ginsburg, L. Abu Lughod and B. Larkin (eds), *Media Worlds: Anthropology on New Terrain*, Berkeley: University of California Press, pp. 281–300.
Ghosh, Shohini (1996), 'Deviant Pleasures and Disorderly Women: The Representation of the Female Outlaw in *Bandit Queen* and *Anjaam*', in R. Kaur (ed.), *Feminist Terrains in Legal Domains: Interdisciplinary Essays on Women and Law in India*, New Delhi: Kali for Women, pp. 150–83.
Ghosh, Shohini (2015), 'A Daughter's Toast', *The Book Review*, 39: 2 (February), <http://www.thebookreviewindia.org/articles/archives-4351/2015/february/2/a-daughters-toast.html> (last accessed 20 March 2016).
Gopalan, Lalitha (2002), *Cinema of Interruptions: Action Genres in Contemporary Indian Cinema*, London: BFI.

Horton, Andrew (1998), 'Cinematic Makeovers and Cultural Border Crossings: Kusturica's *Time of the Gypsies* and Coppola's *Godfather* and *Godfather II*', in A. Horton and S. Y. McDougal (eds), *Play It Again, Sam: Retakes on Remakes*, Berkeley: University of California Press, pp. 172–90.

Kasbekar, Asha (2001), 'Hidden Pleasures: Negotiating the Myth of the Female Ideal in Popular Hindi Cinema', in R. Dwyer and C. Pinney (eds), *Pleasure and the Nation: The History, Politics and Consumption of Popular Culture in India*, New York: Oxford University Press, pp. 286–308.

Kazmi, Fareed (2010), *Sex in Cinema: A History of Female Sexuality*, New Delhi: Rupa Publications.

Krämer, Lucia (2015), 'Hollywood Remade: New Approaches to Indian Remakes of Western Films', in R. Heinze and L. Krämer (eds), *Remakes and Remaking: Concepts – Media – Practices*, Bielefeld: Transcript Verlag, pp. 81–96.

McKee, Alan (2001), '*Return to Eden*: Australianising America', *Australian Television: A Genealogy of Great Moments*, Melbourne: Oxford University Press, pp. 218–36.

Moran, Albert (1993), *Moran's Guide to Australian TV Series*, North Ryde, NSW: Australian Film, Television and Radio School.

Nayar, Sheila (2003), 'Dreams, Dharma, and Mrs Doubtfire: Exploring Hindi Popular Cinema Via Its "Chutneyed" Western Scripts', *Journal of Popular Film and Television*, 31: 2, pp. 73–82.

Rajan, Rajeswari Sunder (1993), *Real and Imagined Women: Gender, Culture and Postcolonialism*, London and New York: Routledge.

Read, Jacinda (2000), *The New Avengers: Feminism, Femininity and the Rape-Revenge Cycle*, Manchester: Manchester University Press.

Richards, Rashna Wadia (2011), '(Not) Kramer vs. Kumar: The Contemporary Bollywood Remake as Glocal Masala Film', *Quarterly Review of Film and Video*, 28: 4, pp. 342–52.

Siddiqui, Gohar (2013), '"Behind Her Laughter . . . Is Fear!": Domestic Abuse and Transnational Feminism in Bollywood Remakes', *Jump Cut: A Review of Contemporary Media*, 55, <http://ejumpcut.org/archive/jc55.2013/SiddiquiDomesticAbuse India/indexhtml> (last accessed 15 June 2015).

Smith, Iain Robert (2015), '*Memento* in Mumbai: "A Few More Songs and a Lot More Ass Kicking"', in R. Pearson and A. N. Smith (eds), *Storytelling in the Media Convergence Age: Exploring Screen Narratives*, Basingstoke: Palgrave Macmillan, pp. 108–21.

Somaaya, Bhawana, Jigna Kothari and Supriya Madangarli (2012), *Mother Maiden Mistress: Women in Hindi Cinema, 1950–2010*, New Delhi: HarperCollins/The India Today Group.

Stam, Robert (2000), 'Beyond Fidelity: The Dialogics of Adaptation', in J. Naremore (ed.), *Film Adaptation*, London: Athlone, pp. 54–76.

Stam, Robert (2005), 'Introduction: The Theory and Practice of Adaptation', in R. Stam and A. Raengo (eds), *Literature and Film: A Guide to the Theory and Practice of Film Adaptation*, Malden MA and Oxford: Blackwell, pp. 1–52.

Virdi, Jyotika (1999), 'Reverence, Rape – and Then Revenge: Popular Hindi Cinema's "Woman's Film"', *Screen*, 40: 1, pp. 17–37.

7. TRANSLATING COOL: CINEMATIC EXCHANGE BETWEEN HONG KONG, HOLLYWOOD AND BOLLYWOOD

Rashna Wadia Richards

When the heist goes terribly wrong, the gangsters suspect a mole within their midst. Who else could have alerted the police about their robbery but a cop masquerading as a criminal? The newest member of the posse comes under suspicion. But the expectation that the jig is up makes all the gangsters turn on each other. This denouement concludes Sanjay Gupta's *Kaante* (2002), an unabashed re-creation of Quentin Tarantino's *Reservoir Dogs* (1992), which closes with the familiar Mexican stand-off as well. Although there are some differences between them, Gupta's is clearly a replication of Tarantino's film. We might even think of *Kaante* as a good example of what Thomas Leitch calls a 'true' remake, as it reproduces its source so closely that it both invokes and disowns it completely. One might argue that *Kaante* imitates *Reservoir Dogs* too well, seeking 'to annihilate the model' by 'eliminat[ing] any need or desire to see the film [it] seek[s] to replace' (Leitch 2002: 50). In the process, *Kaante* establishes Bollywood on the global screen by replicating and then outdoing *Reservoir Dogs* in Los Angeles itself.

But to truly understand the relationship between *Kaante* and *Reservoir Dogs*, we must first acknowledge that Gupta's twice-told tale is actually a thrice-told tale, because, as is now well known, Tarantino's film is itself a mostly true remake of Ringo Lam's *City on Fire* (1987), which ends with a similar Mexican stand-off. Both Tarantino and Gupta have engaged overtly in the kind of avowal and disavowal that Leitch considers central to true remakes. When asked about its source text, Gupta does not deny Tarantino's influence, but then swiftly undercuts that claim by arguing that *Kaante* is 'in the genre

of films like *Reservoir Dogs, The Asphalt Jungle, The Killing, City on Fire*
. . . [and] not a remake of any one film' (quoted in Desser 2005: 221). Gupta,
however, does not fail to remind us that *Reservoir Dogs* is itself a remake of
City on Fire. Ironically, early reviewers of Tarantino's film didn't immediately
notice that connection. When asked later by his biographer about Lam's influence, Tarantino admits his admiration for *City on Fire*, even acknowledges
that 'it's a great movie', but then undermines that singular inspiration by pro-
fessing a penchant for 'steal[ing] from every single movie ever made' (quoted
in Dawson 1995: 91). While somewhat exaggerated, per Tarantino's hyper-
bolic style, this notion of borrowing from a series of films applies to all three
versions. For although there are remarkable visual and thematic replications
in each version of a failed theft, Gupta's version is not a simple imitation of
Tarantino's, just as Tarantino's film does not solely copy Lam's. And Lam's
film itself is not free of imitations of other films from the international canon.
By drawing on this thrice-told tale of a botched robbery, this essay explores the
complex processes of copying, borrowing, stealing, and adapting that transnational remakes engage in. Each version pivots on the performance of 'cool'. By
invoking the notion of cool, I am referring not just to characters who look cool
or remain cool under pressure, nor only to film styles that foreground hipness.
Coolness in this triad is closely linked to the idea of borrowing from earlier
cool sources, of highlighting one's imitations, and of participating in a global
circuit of cool. How does 'cool' travel across industries and cultures? What
can its imitation tell us about the cinematic exchange between Hong Kong,
Hollywood and Bollywood?

To think about this kind of multidirectional imitation, I would like to draw
on the paradigm of translation. Translation is an apt metaphor for transnational remakes, although it has not been adequately theorised. Writing about
translation, Walter Benjamin makes this analogy with a broken vessel. Just as
reassembling the shattered vessel exactly is impossible, 'a translation, instead of
reassembling the meaning of the original, . . . mak[es] both the original and the
translation recognizable as fragments of a greater language, just as fragments
are part of a vessel' (1969: 78). Translation does not imply making the original
text whole or lending it primacy. The translated text remains a fragment, and it
draws attention to the fact that the original was ever only a fragment too. Paul
de Man breaks down the metaphor further, arguing that 'translation is the
fragment of a fragment, is breaking the fragment – so the vessel keeps breaking, constantly – and never reconstitutes itself' (1986: 91). Thus, translation
demonstrates that 'there was no vessel in the first place' (1986: 91). De Man's
reading of Benjamin suggests that in translation we are left with nothing but a
collection of fragments that were never part of a complete whole to begin with.
Developing this breakdown, Burghard Baltrusch argues that 'translation can
be both a process that enables the "continuing life" (*Fortleben*) of any cultural

phenomenon held to be the original, and an act of resistance to and subversion of totalitarian practice' (2010: 124).

It is this reading of translation – as one among many copies that embrace and defy – that we can use for analysing transnational remakes. Robert Stam has made a similar case for rethinking film adaptations, which for too long were studied for their degree of conformity to source texts. Stam notes that 'translations invariably miss a nuance, smooth over an aggression, or exclude an ambiguity'; these are not features of 'bad' translations – 'in art as in language, "traduire, c'est trahir"', to translate is to betray (2000: 62). Only by betraying the source text can an adaptation produce new meanings and readings. If we think about remakes in this way, we can see that *Kaante*'s source texts are already translations. What we end up with in this triad, then, is a series of imitations without a single clear original. This methodology allows us to circumvent the linear search for cinematic roots or ancestries. As Lucy Mazdon notes, 'the unbroken vertical axis which leads from the "original" text to the remake as "copy" is replaced by the circles of intertextuality and hybridity' (2000: 27). Thus, drawing on multiple iterations of a bungled heist that ends in a Mexican stand-off, we can trace, instead of a linear movement of cinematic cool from one continent or culture to another, multi-dimensional media flows of simultaneous appropriation and opposition between Hong Kong, Hollywood and Bollywood, with nods to other cinemas along the way.

In order to undermine the notion of originality, let us begin with Lam's tale of an undercover cop who infiltrates a gang of jewel thieves. Racked with guilt over his partner's death, Ko Chow (Chow Yun-Fat) goes undercover but ends up developing a deep bond of friendship with Sam Fu (Danny Lee), the gangster he is supposed to arrest. Ambivalent about the value of duty over loyalty, he participates in the gangsters' plan to rob a jewellery store. When the heist goes awry, they suspect a traitor in their midst and end up in the iconic Mexican stand-off. *City on Fire* belongs to the 'heroic bloodshed' cycle of Hong Kong action films. Unlike kung fu or swordplay films, these movies foreground stylised action sequences and moral ambiguity in their tragic heroes. This cycle was influenced as much by anxiety over the impending handover of Hong Kong to Mainland China as it was by rising crime, corruption, and fast-paced late capitalism. It was inaugurated by John Woo's *A Better Tomorrow* (1986), although Lisa Stokes and Michael Hoover point out that in place of 'Woo's romanticized protagonists and dream-like settings', Lam offers 'conflictive characters and hard-hitting urban realism' (1999: 64). But if its main conflict is initiated by local conditions, *City on Fire* is, from the start, involved in transcultural exchange on a global scale.

The film opens by drawing on the aesthetic of classic noir. A saxophone plays as the credits roll, and a slow pan takes us into a night-time city lit with neon lights, a moment evocative of post-war American noir. Barbara Mennel

(2008) suggests that its opening scene is reminiscent of Robert Siodmak's *Criss Cross* (1949). Unlike that film's clandestine meeting, however, Lam takes us right to the heart of the action: an undercover cop being pursued by a group of criminals is brutally stabbed to death in the heart of Kowloon market. Hong Kong comes to life as a lawless, hard-boiled space, where cops are feckless and witnesses are too terrified to speak out. Thus, Lam imitates classic noir's romance of loneliness but adds to it a harsh critique of modern Hong Kong. Later, when Chow is haunted by his partner's death, his nightmares adopt the surreal atmosphere of noir. However, this isn't just a simple copy of post-war American cool. Although the blue tones, slow motion cinematography and chiaroscuro lighting are evocative of noir, the nightmares blend this classic aesthetic with 'older Chinese-inflected narrative traditions' (Mennel 2008: 100). Chow's guilt-laden dreams aren't merely steeped in Freudian guilt; they are also saturated with 'the Chinese culture of ancestor worship and parallel ghost worlds' (100). Lam's film borrows the noir look and localises it, translating classic noir for the contemporary Hong Kong moment.

As it goes along, *City on Fire* borrows from a wider range of sources, becoming an international fusion, particularly during its action sequences. During the first daytime robbery, the interior shots are tense, with short shots registering disruptions by the building manager, a delivery boy, customers and beat cops. Once the action moves outside, mayhem ensues. Two police cars collide and explode; while fire trucks spray chemicals all over the streets to prevent the fire from spreading, it appears as if the city is erupting in flames. The shots remain short and choppy, and the narrative takes a break in favour of fast-paced, jerky action. Later, during the heist in which Chow participates, this kind of interruptive action becomes more intense. As residents of a bustling Hong Kong engage in Christmas shopping, the gang attempts to rob a jewellery store. But the plan goes awry after the alarm sounds, and there is a full-blown shoot-out with the cops on the streets. The violence of this muddled heist is graphic, erratic, and unrestrained, as 'dozens of cuts and camera positions register the rapid-fire action as well as the ensuing confusion and out-of-control feeling' (Stokes and Hoover 1999: 68). But this is hardly a quick reworking of Hollywood blockbusters, as Hong Kong films are often accused of doing. These action shots combine the elliptical, jump-cut action of Jean-Luc Godard's *Breathless* (1960) with the excessive gore of Arthur Penn's *Bonnie and Clyde* (1967). Moreover, the inexplicability of violence is evocative of Akira Kurosawa's samurai epics.

Perhaps the most interesting instance of borrowing occurs in the film's epic finale. When the heist goes awry, the gangsters retreat to an abandoned warehouse. Chow has been shot in the stomach during the robbery, but the Triad boss, Nam (Fong Yau), suspects him to be a traitor, while Fu tries to convince him of Chow's innocence and loyalty to the group. But the second-in-command, Song, backs up Nam as Fu tries to protect Chow, and the three of them end up in the iconic Mexican stand-off. Lam frames the scene tightly. While accusations fly, quick medium shots cut back and forth to capture the tightening of space and the narrowing of options, and then the camera pulls back to show that, given their three-way stand-off, nobody is at a tactical advantage. This scene is often cited as the original to Tarantino's (and Gupta's) copy, but Lam's film is hardly the first to use the Mexican stand-off. Most famously, this motif is used during the cemetery showdown among three bandits in Sergio Leone's *The Good, the Bad, and the Ugly* (1966). Blondie (Clint Eastwood) knows the name of the grave where a cache of Confederate gold is buried; he pretends to write it on a rock that he places at the centre of the circular cemetery, thus forcing Angel Eyes (Lee Van Cleef) and Tuco (Eli Wallach) into a Mexican stand-off. Long shots register the painstakingly slow process of positioning among the three adversaries, then close-ups show them sizing each other up. Almost five minutes later, Angel Eyes draws his gun, but Blondie makes short work of him, while Tuco realises his gun contains no bullets. Leaving Tuco to die over his share of the gold, Blondie rides off at the end. Lam offers a condensed version of this Mexican stand-off. After the camera pulls out to reveal how all the gangsters are boxed in, merely waiting for the endgame as cops surround the warehouse, nobody shoots. Instead, the shoot-out happens a few moments later, with the cops, where Song and Nam perish in a hail of gunfire, and Chow succumbs to his injuries after confessing his disloyalty to Fu, who is arrested and hauled away. Here the Mexican stand-off does not offer the neat resolution that it does in *The Good, the Bad, and the Ugly*. Rather, Lam's swift imitation borrows the motif's cool energy, only to let the air out of its intensity.

That Lam imitates so many films should come as no surprise. After all, Hong Kong cinema is notorious for its insatiable borrowing. As Patricia Aufderheide points out, '[a] distinctive and long-standing feature of Hong Kong film – perhaps one indicator of Hong Kong's unusual positioning as an international business crossroads – is its voracious appetite for imitation, most boldly of Hollywood material but also of anything that has had international commercial success' (1998: 192). But there's something peculiar about these borrowings. In a sense, *City on Fire* functions like a late entry in the Hong Kong New Wave. Throughout the 1970s and early 1980s, a younger group of filmmakers, most of them trained in film schools overseas, began leading the Hong Kong film industry. These filmmakers, like the iconoclastic French New Wave directors before them, were technically audacious and un-shy about citing varied influences. More than mere cinematic quotation is at work here, however. Unlike traditional homages, like De Palma's to Hitchcock or Fassbinder's to Sirk, New Wave films cite promiscuously. Take, for example, Tsui Hark's *We're Going to Eat You* (1980), which blends zombie horror and dark comedy into a kung fu film. *City on Fire* is a product of these transnational reconfigurations, embracing and resisting, recycling and transforming its sources.

If Lam undercuts the traditional notion of the original, showing how translation is always already at work, then Tarantino overtly re-creates the idea of a transnational remake. Tarantino's arrival on the American independent cinema scene overlaps perfectly with a significant development in world cinema. David Desser (2005) offers a valuable study of how the availability of films on videotape in the 1980s led to the rise of a new kind of cinephilia. Unlike classical cinephilia, practised most ardently after World War II at *Cahiers du Cinéma* by critics who would later form the French New Wave, this renewed love of cinema is more global in its reach. It is focused not only on praising old masters but also on finding new auteurs, sometimes celebrated precisely because they are not popular among mainstream (American) audiences. Hong Kong cinema was at the heart of this renaissance. Desser argues that while films from a range of non-Western regions began to gain popularity, Hong Kong 'captured the imagination of a type of white, adolescent male subject in Euro-America who soon found himself identifying with non-white . . . characters. The kinetic montages, sometimes termed "bullet ballets", appealed to the increasing fragmentation of the mise-en-scene . . . and the overt play of cinema stylistics' (2005: 212). Tarantino's early films grow out of this context. After quitting school at the age of fifteen, Tarantino moved to the West coast and in his early twenties began working at a video rental store in Manhattan Beach. That job enabled him to indulge his cinephilia unrestrainedly, since he had access to popular as well as obscure films from all around the world. On one shelf of the store, Tarantino hosted a 'revolving film festival', which would change weekly, from Sam Fuller week to motorcycle movies week to heist film week (Dawson 1995: 43). Soon he made friendships with fellow film buffs; now he wasn't just screening films but also about to make them.

Drawing on his voracious viewings, Tarantino's films are said to emphasise direct quotation. Since his work is more postmodern, his images are flatter and more stylised, and his theft is more explicit. Addressing accusations of theft, Tarantino is reported to have said that 'great artists steal, they don't do homages' (Dawson 1995: 91), a line that echoes T. S. Eliot's aphorism 'immature poets imitate; mature poets steal'. But more than embezzlement is at work here. If, by the early 1990s, Hong Kong cinema became the new cool among Western cinephiles, how does Tarantino translate it for the American indie scene to create his own brand of cool? Though the term 'cool' has various origins, here is how it came to be used in American popular culture. Its use is typically attributed to tenor saxophonist Lester Young, who began using 'cool' as a term of approval. The term then began being used by journalists in the expression 'cool jazz' to distinguish post-war jazz's relaxed tempo and understated feeling from an earlier era's harder bebop sound. Miles Davis recorded

Birth of the Cool between 1949 and 1950 to codify this shift, a seminal album released in 1957. As Dick Pountain and David Robins suggest, 'in the '50s Hip had been a synonym for Cool, signifying knowingness, or a shared knowledge of secrets denied to squares' (2000: 71). This shared knowledge of secrets is similar to the new cinephilia that *Reservoir Dogs* adopts; by blending hip extracts that would be easily recognisable to fellow cinephiles, Tarantino creates his brand of cool.

Unlike the translation of noir cool in *City on Fire*, then, the opening credits of *Reservoir Dogs* feature eight gangsters slowly striding towards the camera, six of them wearing black suits, skinny ties and sunglasses, a look stolen from John Woo's *A Better Tomorrow II* (1987). Tarantino never failed to mention his debt to John Woo. Karen Fang points out that 'Tarantino, like the Hong Kong and Korean adolescents who had first emulated Mark Gor, was himself inspired to dress in sunglasses and trenchcoats for weeks after seeing *A Better Tomorrow*' (2004: 79). But if we look at the opening credits more carefully, we can see that Tarantino's work is not a direct copy. While the black suit/skinny tie ensemble is lifted from Woo's *A Better Tomorrow II* (1987), that look was itself a sartorial nod to Jean-Pierre Melville's *Le Samouraï* (1967). Similarly, the slow motion stride of the gangsters is 'the very picture of *Magnificent Seven* cool' (Bernard 2008: 32). In addition, the gangsters' colour-coded names are derived from Joseph Sargent's *The Taking of Pelham 123* (1974), and even the film's outrageous ear-cutting scene comes from Sergio Corbucci's *Django* (1966).

But the most overt source for Tarantino's text is Lam's *City on Fire*, which was not as popular as Woo's films in the West, although its translation in *Reservoir Dogs* would be impossible to miss for the initiated. In addition to the basic plotline of a heist thwarted by an undercover cop, Tarantino lifts specific moments from Lam's film, such as Mr White (Harvey Keitel), like Fu, unflappably shooting at cops with pistols in both hands in the aftermath of the botched heist and Mr Orange (Tim Roth), like Chow, getting shot in the stomach. When the heist fails, the surviving gangsters also retreat to an abandoned industrial warehouse and end up in a Mexican stand-off. While it is true that Tarantino has copied this final scene, which at first viewing may seem like a shot-for-shot rip-off, his Mexican stand-off is quite different. Tarantino translates the brief climactic moment of impasse in *City on Fire* by extending its personal implications. As we've seen, Lam's film is focused on localising its borrowings to critique contemporary Hong Kong. Tarantino does not offer such a broad cultural assessment. His remake, and especially its finale, emphasises the personal relationships between near strangers. Moreover, if we look closely, we can see subtle formal differences that demonstrate how this isn't plagiarism so much as a complex replication partaking in the push and pull of translation. Showing how it draws on Jean-Paul Sartre's *No Exit*,

Thomas Belzer has argued that Tarantino's film is 'staged in an unreal, timeless environment' (2000: no pag.). In that environment, an abandoned warehouse resembles hell. Tarantino's warehouse is larger and far less cluttered than Lam's. His tight medium shots expose an empty space, which is not just a site for confrontation with the police – a confrontation that is central to Lam's film. In fact, in *Reservoir Dogs* the police don't even show up on screen. The emphasis remains on the individual gangsters. In Tarantino's telling, Joe Cabot (Lawrence Tierney) accuses Mr Orange of being an undercover agent; his son, Nice Guy Eddie (Chris Penn), backs him up; and Mr White tries to convince them both that Mr Orange is a 'good kid'. But this is not a moment for a logical conversation. Four fatal shots are fired. Joe and Eddie fall first, while Mr Pink (Steve Buscemi), who remains neutral in the showdown, exits the warehouse stealthily. When Mr White crawls over to comfort him, Mr Orange apologises for being a cop. Heartbroken over his infidelity, Mr White shoots Mr Orange dead for his betrayal, before being gunned down by the cops, whose late arrival is indicated only aurally. The Mexican stand-off is employed here to show the futility of the power struggle that it initiates. If Lam borrows Leone's ending but condenses it by refusing its neat resolution, then Tarantino expands on Lam's ending's personal consequences. It is as if Tarantino underscores the Mexican stand-off by slowing down its pace, by letting it stay on screen longer, so we may appreciate his translation of Lam's set piece. In that sense, Tarantino's remake ends up 'both replicating the original cultural idea or moment and creating a new object which is both text and meta-text' (Desser 2005: 217). For Tarantino's film works as a remake of Lam's film as well as a commentary on Hong Kong becoming the new cool in international cinema. Indeed, Tarantino performs cool by re-performing moments he considers cool, inserting them in a virtually endless circuit of replays, thereby distinguishing his work from mainstream American cinema.

Replays and remakes are very common in Bollywood cinema. Such copies make economic sense, given that the industry churns out hundreds of films each year with rushed production schedules, relatively tiny budgets and, until very recently, no real threat of being cited for copyright violations. In fact, the history of popular Hindi cinema is replete with instances of uncredited borrowings, particularly of American films: for instance, Frank Capra's *It Happened One Night* (1934) inspired Anant Thakur's *Chori Chori* (1956), Stanley Donen's *Seven Brides for Seven Brothers* (1954) was re-created in Raj N. Sippy's *Satte Pe Satta* (1982), and Francis Ford Coppola's *The Godfather* (1972) was appropriated by Feroz Khan's *Dharmatma* (1975). But there is something distinctly different about Bollywood remakes in the era of globalisation, where they offer 'a historically specific response to a postmodern circulation and recirculation of images and texts' (Verevis 2006: 23). How does *Kaante* engage in such circulations and recirculations?

Like its predecessors, *Kaante* borrows promiscuously from a range of films, including Jules Dassin's *Rififi* (1955), Bryan Singer's *The Usual Suspects* (1995) and Michael Mann's *Heat* (1995). Still, at the heart of this bungled heist film, *Kaante* works as a transnational makeover of *Reservoir Dogs*. Just as Tarantino makes his citation of Hong Kong cinema explicit, Gupta attempts to copy Tarantino's film as blatantly as possible. Consider the film's opening credit sequence. Like the reservoir dogs going to work, we have six, hip, sun-glasses-clad men walking in slow motion towards the camera, with faint traces of Los Angeles in the background. Given that Gupta does not conceal his imitation at all, one might argue that this scene lies closer to homage. But contrary to the minimalist costuming of Tarantino's characters, these men wear designer suits, leather jackets and heavy gold jewellery. Moreover, this sequence lasts for two minutes, which is more than twice as long as its predecessor, and it includes several rapid zooms to the men's faces or jackets or shoes. This moment attempts to overlay the cache of American cool on a Bollywood film by setting it in Los Angeles itself. Interestingly, the film was shot in and around Los Angeles, using a primarily American crew and Hollywood technology, thus suggesting that a Bollywood film can not only borrow Hollywood cool but also embody it and move beyond it. As Nitin Govil puts it, *Kaante* 'engages an international division of cultural labor that supports the invigoration of new markets and commodity forms' (2015: 72). For by engaging with and then exaggerating Tarantino's own dramatic action, *Kaante* also offers more than replication. It is as if it performs its source text too well. In its hyperbole, the opening sequence appears almost campy. And this sense of camp recurs throughout the film. During the brutal showdown with the cops after the heist fails, Gupta shoots the scene with rapid gunfire, whizzing bullets and high-rigged explosions. Images overlap, camera angles are distorted, and shots and sound effects are recycled, creating an over-the-top action spectacle. Similarly, during the abducted police officer's interrogation, Gupta uses canted angles and ground-level shots to create a feeling of spectacular chaos. Though it first appears to be copying its American precursor too well, in fact its imitation lies somewhere between homage and parody. Thus, if Tarantino's cinephilic poaching on Lam's version of cool functions as a replication that is 'both text and meta-text', then we might say that Gupta's translation amounts to a deconstruction. If cool signified a shared knowingness in the 1950s, Pountain and Robins (2000) argue, it became more oppositional during the countercul-ture era. *Kaante* evinces this evolved representation of cool.

With that in mind, let us turn to Gupta's version of the Mexican stand-off, where Ajju (Sanjay Dutt) singles out Mak (Lucky Ali) as the rat. After all, Mak has just shot his own partner, Bali (Mahesh Manjrekar), for torturing a cop (Jeff Davis). To Ajju, Mak is the odd one out; his background remains a mystery to the team, as they've known him for fewer than six months. But

Major (Amitabh Bachchan) cannot imagine that the guy who took a bullet for him during the botched holdup could be a traitor. To him, Mak is the quintessential team player. Of the remaining members, Andy (Kumar Gaurav) remains neutral, arguing for fleeing with equal shares of the loot, but Marc (Sunil Shetty) backs Ajju's hunch. And therein lie the makings of a classic Mexican stand-off, Bollywood-style. As Ajju raises his gun to shoot Mak, Major challenges him to stand down, but Marc backs up Ajju, while Mak has a clear shot at Marc. A wide-angle shot of the warehouse shows that nobody holds an advantage, and everybody is killed. Given how closely this parallels Tarantino's climax, we might at first call it a direct copy. But this scene extends the sequence by capturing the mayhem of multiple bullets flying in slow motion, and it involves four characters, not three, with two guns apiece. This amplification embodies the sensationalised cool that is Tarantino's trademark but then implodes it from within. Neelam Sidhar Wright argues that *Kaante* 'becomes a mocking caricature' (2009: 201). However, Gupta's film offers more than mockery. It does the work of translation by reaching beyond Tarantino's love and theft of Hong Kong cinema to offer resistance more directly.

During *Kaante*'s hyperbolised Mexican stand-off, Ajju and Marc fall first, while Andy sneaks out with the swag. Major, though lethally wounded, walks over to Mak to apologise for not being able to save his life. Mak apologises too, claiming he was 'only doing [his] duty', a betrayal so grave that Major shoots him dead before succumbing to his own wounds. As the camera pans over their wasted bodies, Mak's voice-over promises to meet them all again in hell. But, unlike *Reservoir Dogs*, the film doesn't end there. Rather, it ends with a return to an earlier shot, of the six gangsters hanging out on a hotel rooftop. This is the rooftop where the heist plans originated. Their smiling faces, which echo the final shot of *City on Fire* when Chow smiles post-mortem, make them appear innocent – certainly not like Tarantino's gangsters who remain frozen in hell. Such culminating sympathy reminds us that this heist begins as an act of cultural resistance. The gangsters originally plan the bank robbery as retaliation for being the usual suspects. As Major laments when they're being initially held together in a jail cell, Indians are 'made to wear the turban of crime' by the LAPD because they don't have a syndicate to bail them out; robbing a bank that serves such a corrupt police force, and using that money to 'buy innocence', seems like the perfect payback. Thus, Gupta's criminals are not just petty crooks trying to make it big. If we read their heist as resistance, they become victims of an unjust system who get 'screwed' trying to challenge it. *Kaante* itself might be read as a kind of imitation rooted in resistance. Instead of 'evidence that Bollywood really ha[s] nothing new to offer by rehashing Hollywood' (Govil 2015: 68), which was the predominant critique of the film upon initial release, we might see Gupta's transnational remake as an imitation that produces more than a copy.

Thinking about translation as a breaking and remaking might enable us to respond to Heather Tyrell's provocative question: 'But is Bollywood named in imitation of Hollywood, or as a challenge to it?' (1999: 265). It is both – or rather that challenge, especially in the era of globalisation, is built into imitation. In the last two decades, Indian cinema has evolved to become a global brand. Sangita Gopal points out that the roots of what we might call New Bollywood can be traced back to the 1970s, when the industry began 'promiscuously embrac[ing] a range of foreign styles as it move[d] from a "nativist" to a globalized art form' (2011: 12). This embrace accelerated exponentially after India's economic liberalisation, which lifted restrictions on imports and foreign capital, relaxed licensing laws, and transformed the cultural environment. In this milieu, the Bombay-based film industry began asserting itself globally. Indeed, as Tejaswini Ganti argues, Bollywood 'has been an important accoutrement of India's resignification in the global arena, one that is deployed both by the Indian state and the corporate sector in efforts to brand the country as an economic powerhouse' (2012: 2). Moreover, Bollywood is now signified as cool, an adjective used to describe 'a general state of improvement marked by higher production values as well as a visual style and narrative content that is coded as modern and sophisticated' (79). But becoming modern and sophisticated doesn't mean copying Western or American cinema. For cool doesn't travel in a linear fashion from one cultural context to another. Rather, as this three-way exchange between Hong Kong, Hollywood and Bollywood shows, cool can be performed and re-performed in different contexts via a process of translation. After all, Hong Kong, Hollywood and Bollywood, three of the most popular film industries in the world, are not actually engaged in a Mexican stand-off. While they try to claim international cinematic superiority, they are always involved in imitating, contesting, and recirculating. Transnational remakes demonstrate this exchange most openly; they enable us to break with the old paradigm of original versus copy and explore how cinematic cultures simultaneously borrow from and oppose each other.

References

Aufderheide, Patricia (1998), 'Made in Hong Kong: Translation and Transmutation', in Andrew Horton and Stuart Y. McDougal (eds), *Play It Again, Sam: Retakes on Remakes*, Berkeley: University of California Press, pp. 191–9.

Baltrusch, Burghard (2010), 'Translation as Aesthetic Resistance: Paratranslating Walter Benjamin', *Cosmos and History: The Journal of Natural and Social Philosophy* 6, pp. 113–29.

Belzer, Thomas (2000), 'Dogs in Hell: *No Exit* Revisited', *Senses of Cinema* 6: no pag., <http://sensesofcinema.com/2000/feature-articles/dogs/> (last accessed 11 June 2015).

Benjamin, Walter (1969), 'The Task of the Translator', in Hannah Arendt (ed.), Harry Zohn (trans.), *Illuminations: Essays and Reflections*, New York: Schoken, pp. 69–82.

Bernard, Jami (2008), 'Reservoir Dogs (1992)', in David Sterritt and John Anderson (eds), *The B List: The National Society of Film Critics on the Low-Budget Beauties, Genre-Bending Mavericks, and the Cult Classics We Love*, Cambridge: Da Capo, pp. 31–4.

City on Fire (1987), film, directed by Ringo Lam. Hong Kong: Cinema City.

Dawson, Jeffrey (1995), *Quentin Tarantino: The Cinema of Cool*. New York: Applause Books.

De Man, Paul (1986), *The Resistance to Theory*, Minneapolis: University of Minnesota Press.

Desser, David (2005), 'Hong Kong Film and the New Cinephilia', in Meaghan Morris, Siu Leung Li, and Stephen Chan Ching-kiu (eds), *Hong Kong Connections: Transnational Imagination in Action Cinema*, Durham, NC: Duke University Press, pp. 205–21.

Fang, Karen (2004), *John Woo's A Better Tomorrow*, Hong Kong: Hong Kong University Press.

Ganti, Tejaswini (2012), *Producing Bollywood: Inside the Contemporary Hindi Film Industry*, Durham, NC: Duke University Press.

Gopal, Sangita (2011), *Conjugations: Marriage and Form in New Bollywood Cinema*, Chicago: University of Chicago Press.

Govil, Nitin (2015), *Orienting Bollywood: A Century of Film Culture between Los Angeles and Bombay*, New York: New York University Press.

Kaante (2002), film, directed by Sanjay Gupta. India: White Feather Films.

Leitch, Thomas M (2002), 'Twice-Told Tales: The Rhetoric of the Remake', in Jennifer Forrest and Leonard R. Koos (eds), *Dead Ringers: The Remake in Theory and Practice*, Albany, NY: State University of New York Press, pp. 37–62.

Mazdon, Lucy (2000), *Encore Hollywood: Remaking French Cinema*, London: BFI.

Mennel, Barbara (2008), *Cities and Cinema*, London: Routledge.

Pountain, Dick and David Robins (2000), *Cool Rules: Anatomy of an Attitude*, London: Reaktion Books.

Reservoir Dogs (1992), film, directed by Quentin Tarantino. USA: Miramax Films.

Stam, Robert (2000), 'Beyond Fidelity: The Dialogics of Adaptation', in James Naremore (ed.), *Film Adaptation*, New Brunswick, NJ: Rutgers University Press, pp. 54–76.

Stokes, Lisa Odham and Michael Hoover (1999), *City on Fire: Hong Kong Cinema*, London: Verso.

Tyrell, Heather (1999), 'Bollywood versus Hollywood: Battle of the Dream Factories', in Tracey Skelton and Tim Allen (eds), *Culture and Global Change*, New York: Routledge, pp. 265–81.

Verevis, Constantine (2006), *Film Remakes*, Edinburgh: Edinburgh University Press.

Wright, Neelam Sidhar (2009), '"Tom Cruise? Tarantino? E.T.? . . . Indian!": Innovation through Imitation in the Cross-Cultural Bollywood Remake', in Iain Robert Smith (ed.), *Cultural Borrowings: Appropriation, Reworking, Transformation*, Scope e-book, pp. 194–210.

8. TRADING PLACES: *DAS DOPPELTE LOTTCHEN* AND *THE PARENT TRAP*

Constantine Verevis

In 1961, Walt Disney Productions released *The Parent Trap*, a story of identical thirteen-year-old twins, Susan Evers and Sharon McKendrick, who meet for the first time at a summer camp and gradually realise they are sisters (separated at birth) whose divorced parents took custody of one child each. Curious and eager to meet each other's parent, the girls decide to trade places – Susan goes to Boston masquerading as Sharon, Sharon goes to Carmel (California) pretending to be Susan – whereupon the twins devise a plan to reconcile their estranged parents and re-create an ideal family unit. With Hayley Mills starring in the dual role of twins, *The Parent Trap* was a huge popular and commercial success for the Disney studio: it was theatrically reissued in 1968, and subsequently extended through two television sequels, *The Parent Trap* II and III (1986, 1989). Moreover, it was remade (by Disney) in 1998, 'introducing' Lindsay Lohan in the twin role (in this case) of Annie James and Hallie Parker, raised respectively in London and California. Perhaps less well known is that Disney's 1961 version of *The Parent Trap* was itself already a remake of German, Japanese and British versions – *Das doppelte Lottchen* (1950), *Hibari no komoriuta* (1951) and *Twice Upon a Time* (1953) – each in turn derived from Erich Kästner's 1949 novel *Das doppelte Lottchen* (published in English translation as *Lottie and Lisa*). While the cultural production does not end here – with subsequent versions reported in India, Iran and Korea, and animated and live-action remakes in Germany and Japan – this chapter inquires into the transnational connections between Kästner's novel and the American and German versions (originals and remakes). While the doppelgänger is a familiar figure in German fiction, this chapter extends its analysis beyond Kästner's twin figures of Lotte and Luise to chart not only a cartography of transnational flows – a political economy of textual production and reception – but also indicate the way in which the exchange of twins – Lotte (Lottie) and Luise (Lisa), Susan and Sharon, Charlotte and Louise, Annie and Hallie – is symptomatic of that between original and remake.

First published in German as *Das doppelte Lottchen* (1949), Erich Kästner's children's novel – 'Ein Roman für Kinder', as it is described on the title page – was translated into English as *Lottie and Lisa* in the following year.[1] The English translation tells the story of two nine-year-old girls – Lisa Palfy (in Kästner's original, Luise Palfy) from Vienna and Lottie Horn (Lotte Körner) from Munich – who meet on a summer camp at a small village on Lake Bohren. Lisa has curly hair and Lottie wears braids, but aside from these cosmetic differences their likeness is uncanny. The girls have never seen each other before, but upon matching one another's birth dates they realise that they are identical twins, separated as infants at the time of their parents' divorce. At the end of camp, they decide to trade places: Lisa (as 'Lottie') braids her hair and joins her mother Lisalotte Horn, who works for a Munich illustrator and lives modestly as a single mother. Lottie (as 'Lisa') curls hers, and joins her father, the composer-conductor Arnold Palfy, who lives by more comfortable means in a spacious apartment, and with a housekeeper. The girls correspond, but when Lottie finds out that her father is planning to remarry a fashionable woman of leisure, Miss Irene Gerlach, she becomes ill and stops writing to her sister in Munich. Meanwhile, Lottie's mother comes across a picture of the two girls that was taken while they were at summer camp, and confronts Lisa, who tells her the entire story. When Lisalotte calls Arnold to tell him what has happened and learns why Lottie has stopped writing she immediately travels, with Lisa, to Vienna. Reunited, the family has occasion to celebrate the twins' tenth birthdays, whereupon the girls tell their parents that they do not ever need birthday presents again so long as they don't have to be separated. The parents talk it over, realise that they still have feelings for one another, and decide to remarry.

A popular success, Kästner's novel was adapted to film the following year – *Das doppelte Lottchen* (Josef von Baky 1950) – with the author himself preparing the screenplay. In consultation with the film's director, Hungarian-born Josef von Baky, Kästner auditioned hundreds of pairs of twins for the lead roles, eventually choosing real-life twins Jutta and Isa Günther as the perfect expression of the fictional Luise and Lottie. Kästner's screenplay follows the book with precision, not only retaining all the key plot elements – situations, characters and locations – but also lifting large passages of dialogue and finding inspiration in the book's many illustrations, drawn by Walter Trier. Moreover, the novel's lively, omniscient third-person narration – which (in

English translation) opens with the following lines, 'Do you happen to know Bohrlaken? ... That's where the story begins ... It's a rather complicated story ... Complicated and pretty thrilling' (Kästner 1950: 1–2) – is imported wholesale as a voice-over by Kästner himself, who appears at the opening of the film in a direct address to the camera.

Kästner's close involvement led some commentators to describe the film version as a 'cinematic illustrated history' (Critchfield 2004: 238), but the film's director, Baky, does in fact manage to creatively visualise some passages from the book. For instance, the brief recounting of the parents' separation and divorce shows the temperamental artist Arnold Palfy (Peter Mosbacher) driven to a state of creative desperation by 'the little twins [who] howled day and night in the flat' (Kästner 1950: 61), comically rendering the incident in a sped-up, two-shot sequence: Palfy in shirtsleeves at the piano, tearing at his hair for the twins' distraction, and (next) Palfy in overcoat preparing to leave as removalists carry his piano to another flat. Similarly, the excursion of Lottie (dressed as Lisa) with her father, who is conducting *Hänsel and Gretel* at the Vienna Opera House, is also her first encounter with Irene Gerlach (Senta Wengraf), a figure whom Lottie immediately recognises as a witch, albeit 'a more beautiful witch than the one on the stage' (74). The episode leads to Lottie's nightmare (75–81), rendered in the film as a distorted, expressionistic dream sequence. The segment – which draws upon Trier's illustration, 'Lottie had a dream' (77) – begins in the family flat where the twins – exiled by the father – are magically transported, first to a dark forest and from there, at the command of the wicked witch (embodied by the fiancée, Gerlach), on further to a sunny meadow and gingerbread house where the twins are ultimately separated – literally cut in half – by their quite deranged father.

Despite objections to the film's perceived technical weakness and overt sentimentality, the film version of *Das doppelte Lottchen* went on to become a popular success and winner of several film prizes (including the 1951 German Film Prize in the categories of Best Picture, Best Director and Best Screenplay) and was theatrically reissued in 1979 (Holloway 1994: 7). Commenting on this success, Anne Critchfield writes that it is 'exceedingly tempting' to understand *Das doppelte Lottchen*'s story of separated twins as a metaphor for the division of Germany after World War II (2004: 234). Such an assumption is reinforced by the near-proximity of the 1994 German remake to the beginning of German reunification in 1990, but Critchfield more generally describes the dream of reunification – the discovery of someone or something thought to be long since lost – as a parable for the resumption of normal life after war-related faults and disjunctions. That is, rather than bind the narrative invention of *Das doppelte Lottchen* to a specific political and geographical situation, Critchfield identifies the book and film's longing for familial reconciliation as a broader, more universal theme, and one that more likely accounts for the popularity of the work and is reason for the international reach and multiple retellings of the story.

Further abstracted to the figure of the doppelgänger, the twin nature of the protagonists in *Das doppelte Lottchen* can be traced through literature and folklore (worldwide) to symbolise the duality of the self. In this case, the ultimate reunification of Lotte and Luise can be understood as an expression of the reconciliation of that fractured self, estranged in and through the broken family situation (Broad 1995: 123, 127). It is this 'universal' appeal that in all likelihood further accounts for the multiple versions – historical and regional – of the Kästner property. Critchfield (2004: 239) notes eleven film/television versions derived from (and in varying degrees, credited to) Kästner's novel. These include: Emeric Pressburger's authorised adaptation, *Twice Upon a Time* (1953); live-action film and animated television versions from Japan – *Hibari no komoriuta* (*The Lullaby of Hibari*, Koji Shima, 1951) and *Watashi to Watashi: Futari no Lotte* (*I and Myself: The Two Lottes*, 1991); the German remake, *Charlie and Louise: Das doppelte Lottchen* (Joseph Vilsmaier, 1994) and animated version, *Das doppelte Lottchen* (Toby Genkel, 2007); and *It Takes Two* (Andy Tennant, 1995) – a version with the Olsen twins, Mary-Kate and Ashley – widely recognised as an unofficial remake. Versions (not noted by Crtichfield) include *Double Trouble* (2007), a thirteen-episode children's television drama series, produced by the Central Australian Aboriginal Media Association, but the most widely known and distributed of all these adaptations is Walt Disney's *The Parent Trap* (David Swift, 1961) and its 1998 remake (directed by Nancy Meyers).

The material that was to become Disney production # 2136 – *Das doppelte Lottchen* – was uncovered by a reader in Disney's story department, shortly after the publication of the English-language edition. The discovery of the story – a tale of nine-year-old twin girls, separated as infants, who meet at summer camp, trade places, and subsequently bring the family unit together – meshed with an image that represented the Disney company as an upstanding moral organisation, one with an express commitment to middle-class family values, and to the welfare of children (Giroux and Pollock 2010: 25). Despite its resolutely commercial orientation, Disney had worked to situate itself as an icon of American culture and of family values, all delivered through 'the promise of making . . . dreams come true through the pleasures of wholesome entertainment' (27). Accordingly, Disney Studios had established itself not just as a provider of entertainment but also as a political force, one devoted to the development of models of instruction that would inform how young people were to be educated (27). This work – which was seen to contribute to, and naturalise, a dominant, 'middle-class patriarchal [and] heterosexual paradigm' (Griffin 2000: 38) – was especially evident in the period following World War II, during which a gradual adoption of a conservative aesthetic and underlying ideology resulted, by the beginning of the 1950s, in the consolidation of a new and massively successful Walt Disney Company. This was enabled not only through the ongoing investment in feature-length animated versions of famous children's tales – *Alice in Wonderland* (1951), *Peter Pan* (1953) and *Sleeping Beauty* (1959) – but also through its diversification into live-action feature films, wildlife documentaries, television programmes and – pre-eminently – its Disneyland theme park, which opened in the summer of 1955. The latter provided the Disney Company with a regular source of income, and the family-friendly image of the theme park coalesced in the kindly paternal figure of Walt Disney himself, who had entered the nation's living rooms in and through his hosting of the studio's weekly television anthology programme, initially entitled *Disneyland* (1955–7) and later *Walt Disney Presents* (1958–61). First broadcast on the ABC network, the anthology series went through a further change of title at the end of 1961, when it was moved to NBC in order to take advantage of the network's ability to broadcast in colour. Rebadged *Walt Disney's Wonderful World of Color*, it retained that title until 1969 when it became simply *The Wonderful World of Disney* (Gillan 2015: 215). By the time of Disney's death (in 1966) the studio had perfected its fashioning of a wholesome image, and 'the company had taken on the mantle of upholding traditional American values and was encouraged to find popularity and profit . . . through teaching these values to others' (Griffin 2000: 47).

The late 1950s and early 1960s also signalled Disney's move towards the embrace of 'tween-inclusive' live-action family comedy (Gillan 2015: 215): films that were – as Neal Gabler describes in his expansive Disney biography – 'broad, simple, and clearly child-oriented' (2007: 586).[2] Although still (in the main) profitable, Disney animations of the 1950s had typically enjoyed a lower profit margin than live-action films and the studio had scaled back production, with only three animated features – *101 Dalmatians* (1961), *Sword in the Stone* (1963) and *The Jungle Book* (1967) – produced in the decade following the poor performance of *Sleeping Beauty* (Schickel 1985: 295–316; Gabler 2007: 585). In place of these features, the emphasis had shifted towards live-action films, which were faster and cheaper to produce: typically, live features cost at least a million less than the minimum for an animated feature (Schickel 1985: 299). Specifically, Disney had experienced a surprise box-office success with its first venture into live-action comedy, *The Shaggy Dog* (1959), a film about a boy who turns into a sheepdog, which had earned nine times its production cost of slightly more than one million dollars (299). Additionally, at a time when other studios were shedding contract players, Disney was actively recruiting a repertory company, and *The Shaggy Dog* led to an ongoing relationship with Hollywood star and television actor Fred MacMurray, one that was extended through subsequent features such as *The Absent Minded Professor* (1961) and its sequel, *Son of Flubber* (1963).

A second, more important (and more lucrative) partnership was established with Hayley Mills, the British child-star who (at age thirteen) had taken the title role in Disney's *Pollyanna* (David Swift, 1960), and someone who Walt Disney had described as the greatest movie find in a quarter century: a 'model child . . . attractive, athletic, and middle-class' (*The Parent Trap* 1961: 4). Following the huge success of *Pollyanna* – a film for which Mills had earned an Honorary Academy Award – the actor was signed to a long-term, picture-a-year deal with Disney. Looking for a suitable vehicle for his new contract player, Disney ordered that the recently purchased Kästner property be tailored for Mills, lifting the age of the twins from nine-going-on-ten to thirteen-going-on-fourteen, not only to accommodate Mills but also to further open up the property's 'tween-appeal'. Even more significant was the decision to double Disney's investment in the star (that is, to have Mills take the role of each twin), a shift that distinguishes the Disney version/s from others, which (like the Kästner/Baky film) typically employ real-life twins. The undertaking to cast Mills in a dual role was also informed by the studio's reputation for technical innovation, specifically its development of a patented travelling matte (or double exposure) technique which meant that Mills could embody each of the twins, without sole (or substantial) reliance on a double. Although it was a time-consuming and expensive process, when Disney – who had by this time disengaged from issues connected with the theme park and reasserted control over the Burbank studio – saw how seamlessly the optical shots were able to fit together, he ordered that the script be further adjusted to include more intensive use of the special effect (supplemented with split screen shots and the use of Mills' uncredited double, Susan Hennig-Schutte). Finally, the task of helming the production was assigned to David Swift, the writer-director of *Pollyanna*, who would later use the opening summer camp sequences of *The Parent Trap* as basis for the creation of a television series, *Camp Runamuck* (1965–6).

The initial working title for the Disney production of *Das doppelte Lottchen* was that of the English translation ('Lottie and Lisa'), with the release title – 'The Parent Trap' – determined somewhat later by a competition and a one hundred dollar prize draw that selected it from five shortlisted entries. Disney himself had apparently favoured the title 'His and Hers', but this was dropped when it became known that it had already been secured for another studio's production (*His and Hers*, released in 1961). As Critchfield (2004: 243) points out, Disney's preference is evidence of an adaptation strategy that is contrary to Kästner's book and screenplay: namely, that the children (in the Disney version) be regarded as possessions – his and hers – of the parents. Moreover, in the Kästner/Baky version, the twins – Lotte and Luise – exchange places in order to meet and learn something about each twin's previously unknown parent, and therefore act principally in their own interests.[3] That is, the twins do not deliberately set out to bring the parents together and complete the family unit. The presence and actions of the children may well contribute to a growing awareness in the parents, but their decision to come together – along with Palfy's statement in the final pages of the book: 'we owe every second of our new happiness . . . to our two children' (Kästner 1950: 153) – comes too quickly and only further contributes to charges of sentimentality.

The 'trap' of the refigured Disney title shows a second and perhaps more drastic difference between the Kästner/Baky film and Disney's translation. Specifically, the shift in focus – from the children to the parents – and the attendant plan to set a 'trap' and so bring the family unit together are also symptomatic of a strategy through which to build a substantially larger target audience. This *commercialist* agenda effects, then, a generic shift in the remake, amplifying the wry humour of the German version to create a domestic (sometimes romantic) comedy – one complete with slapstick, musical numbers and star performers – and so ring up profits at the box office. The result is an uneven film (generically speaking) that wavers between broad physical comedy and more subtle humour in an attempt to appeal, simultaneously, to younger and more mature viewers. The former is most evident in the opening portion at summer camp where – prior to realising they are sisters – the twins play a series of practical jokes upon each other, culminating in a free-for-all at a Saturday night inter-camp dance in which the directress of the girls' camp, Miss Inch (Ruth McDevitt), gets a chocolate cake in the face and her opposite from the boys' camp is doused with a full bowl of punch. There is a reprise of these high jinks towards the end of the film when the twins harness their combined resources to antagonise, ridicule and expose father Mitch's (Brian Keith's) gold-digging fiancée Vicky Robinson (Joanna Barnes) during a camping trip. This is contrasted with other, somewhat risqué sequences, such as that in which the church minister Rev. Dr Mosby (Leo G. Carroll), visiting the ranch home to discuss details of the upcoming marriage between Mitch and Vicky, is not shocked – but rather merrily amused – by the unannounced appearance on the scene of mother (and ex-wife) Maggie McKendrick (Maureen O'Hara) suggestively dressed in one of Mitch's bathrobes (see Maltin 1973: 188).

If this generic shift suggests that the first agenda of the remake is one of commercialisation then this strategy is more than evident from Disney's *The Parent Trap* Press Book (1961).[4] With overt reference to the studio's diversification strategy, the press book announces: 'Walt Disney's hilarious motion picture *The Parent Trap* starring Hayley Mills as completely identical twins represents another seven-league step along the Burbank producers road to ever greater diversification in filmed entertainment . . . [It is] packed with all the goodies of entertainment – drama, humor, love, and even a fair amount of good old-fashioned slapstick' (1961: 2). Declaring the result a comedy hit, the press book continues: 'Walt Disney's Technicolor feature *The Parent Trap* is obviously dedicated to the proposition that all people are created equally hilarious' (5), and 'in a day when many a motion picture labeled "for adults only" is drawing the ire and fire of the public and press, Walt Disney continues to produce family fare of the highest order with a generous quantity of laughter mixed in. His latest Technicolor feature *The Parent Trap* is his funniest and familyest and could be labeled "For Everyone Only"' (5). Such comments are a paraphrase of contemporaneous opinions, such as those of nationally syndicated, conservative writer-educator Dr Max Rafferty, who wrote (sensationally), in the context of the post-War dissolution of the Hollywood Production Code Administration: '[Disney's] live movies have become lone sanctuaries of decency and health in the jungle of sex and sadism created by the Hollywood producers of pornography' (quoted in Gabler 2007: 586).

Disney's clean dream world and view of social realities – including high divorce rates in the post-war period – is offered in this big screen version of *Das doppelte Lottchen* as a solution to the alarming break-up of the family unit. At the service of this was an exhaustive Disney advertising and marketing strategy that included not only typical industry-wide practices – a standard deluxe Technicolor trailer, teaser trailers, lobby cards, 1-sheet and 3-sheet posters, and so on – but an invitation (extended to exhibitors) to 'DOUBLE your exploitation: *The Parent Trap* offers twice the opportunities' by offering up a range of promotional strategies, such as 'Top Twin Trick' in which theatres would 'invite twins to [their] town to submit a report on an interesting trick they have pulled in confusing people of their true identities' and thereby arrange a competition and merchandising tie-in (*The Parent Trap* 1961: 10–11). The property was additionally serialised and multiplied through such strategies as a thirteen-week Sunday colour-comic series, published coast to coast in fifty-five major cities (starting in July 1961), a ten-cent comic-book version of the story, and even (for the 1968 reissue) a novelisation of Swift's screenplay (Crume 1968).[5] Most important of all, though, were 'the rocking rhythms and bright ballads' of Disney's music campaign, which included a Vista Long-Play Album which headlined Annette Funicello and Tommy Sands – 'the favorites of the teen set' – singing their versions of two songs from the film, 'The Parent Trap' and 'Let's Get Together', and a further Vista seven-inch single on which 'Hayley Mills and Hayley Mills' sing 'Let's Get Together' (*The Parent Trap* 1961: 8).

The songs from *The Parent Trap* are key to the film's awareness and maintenance campaigns, and are further exploited through a broadcast television strategy of 'trailerising', a term that the trade magazine *Variety* had applied (in September 1957) to all of Disney's anthology programmes, especially those instances in which an episode's promotion of studio products was not effectively counterbalanced by original entertainment content (Gillan 2015: 214). Specifically, the trailerising of *The Parent Trap* occurs in 'The Title Makers', a June 1961 episode of *Walt Disney Presents* (the final episode broadcast in black-and-white at ABC) that focuses on the creation of the title sequence and song for *The Parent Trap* (217). As described by Jennifer Gillan, 'The Title Makers' is an example of a 'creative way' in which the Disney studios used episodes of the anthology series as 'long form trailers embedded within some original content' to create a 'content promotion hybrid', one that simultaneously functioned as:

> 1. a television episode; 2. an 'educational-informational' short on creating title sequences; 3. a 'company voice' advertisement for Walt Disney; 4. a grouping of 'behind-the-scenes' interstitials about Disney television and film studios and its production workers; and, most predominantly, 5. a hosted lead-in to the trailer for *The Parent Trap*. (2015: 217)

The latter – which includes a bonus preview of a song from another live-action Disney film in production – *Babes in Toyland* (1961) – looks in on a studio recording session in which the title song that will play over the credits for *The Parent Trap* is being performed by Annette Funicello and Tommy Sands. When the two performers take a break from recording, a mysterious voice speaks to them, asking to know details of the film. Funicello and Sands proceed to explain the story – of separated twins who meet for the first time and scheme to get their divorced parents back together – in and through the presentation of clips from – an extended trailerising of – *The Parent Trap*. Just before the denouement is revealed, Funicello and Sands become aware of the source of the voice, which turns out to be that of Walt Disney himself, disguised (*Wizard of Oz*-style) through special audio effects.

'The Title Makers' clearly contributes to the commercialisation of the Kästner property, but – as Gillan is quick to point out – the existence in 1961 of such a complex paratext is not nearly as surprising as 'the remarkable consistency of the [*alternative*] ideological messaging about "togetherness"' expressed in *The Parent Trap*, and that is more generally found throughout mid-twentieth-century Walt Disney programming (Gillan 2015: 217). Accordingly, 'The Title Makers' provides an opportunity to interrogate not only the remake's commercialist agenda but also its *culturalist* one. As previously stated, Disney values are typically assumed to be traditional and *The Parent Trap* appears to adopt an overtly anti-divorce position, with Susan (from California) declaring early in the film: 'It's scary the way nobody stays together anymore these days. Pretty soon there's going to be more divorces than marriages!' *The Parent Trap* is presented as a family-oriented situation comedy and, predictably enough, the 'trap' of the title is effective and the parents are reconciled: 'the romantic plot triumphs over divorce, class and geographical differences' (Broad 1995: 126). But as Gillan and (elsewhere) Douglas Brode (2004: xi) point out, in contrast to the kind of conservative

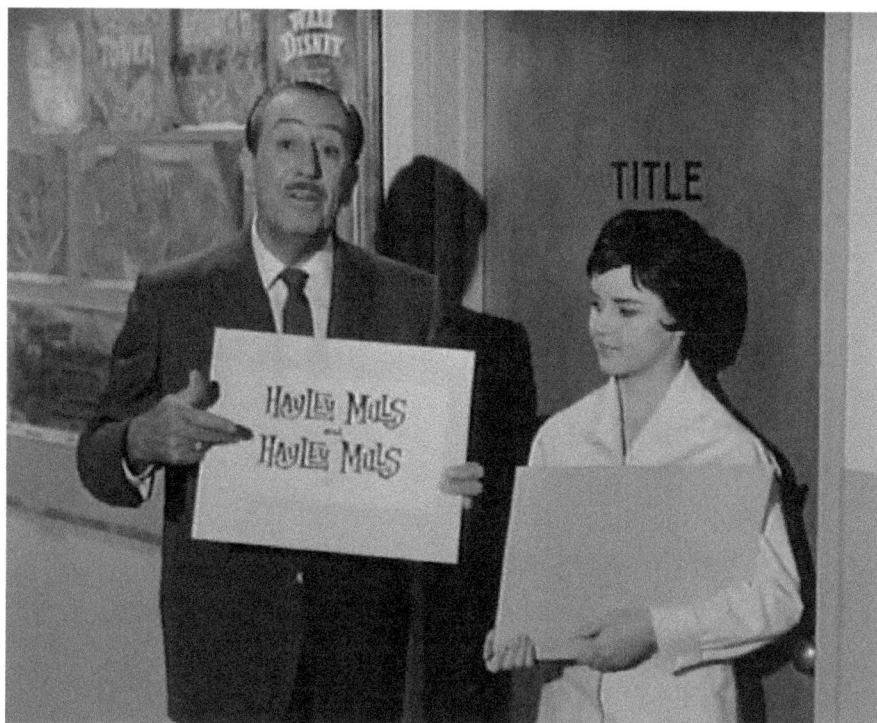

Figure 8.1 'The Title Makers', *Walt Disney Presents* (1961)

1950s discourse found in television sitcoms – for example, *The Parent Trap* spin-off *The Patty Duke Show* (1963–6) – *The Parent Trap*, along with 'The Title Makers', features several elements that are socially critical of, or at least ambivalent about, a 1950s ideology of the nuclear family and of that social formation's supposedly positive impact on children.

The contention that Disney films contain 'socio-political daring' (Brode 2004: xi) is especially evident in the title sequence for *The Parent Trap*, a segment that stands *mise en abyme* for the film as a whole. Specifically, *The Parent Trap* opens with an animated image of a well-known and old-fashioned saying, but with one word added: 'Bless Our – *Broken* – Home'. In the animated title sequence, two Cupids attempt to repair the aforementioned saying by eliminating the errant word. And across the course of the film, Susan and Sharon assume the Cupids' places, and the sign is literally 'made good' by the time of the film's end credits, where it reads 'Bless Our *Happy* Home'. The film's title song – performed by Funicello and Sands and played over the credits – comments on (as Disney describes it in 'The Title Makers') an unfolding 'melodrama in miniature': namely, the hostile antics of two animated figures in the estranged ('average') married couple of 'John' and 'Marsha'. More particularly, the lyrics instruct the twins, Sharon and Susan, and also teenagers in the audience, that the preservation of parental marriage – an institution evidently being eroded by selfish and 'immature' adults – is ultimately the responsibility of the children. As the lyrics of the song have it:

> If their love's on skids/
> Treat your folks like kids/
> Or your family tree's gonna snap/
> So to make them dig/
> First you gotta rig/
> The parent trap
> [. . .]
> If they lose that zing/
> And they just won't swing/
> Then the problem falls in your lap/
> When your folks are square/
> Then you must prepare/
> The parent trap
> [. . .]
> Straighten up their mess/
> With togetherness/
> Togetherness!/
> The parent trap

In evidence in the lyrics of this song – and *The Parent Trap* as a whole – is something ambivalent and – again – something quite foreign to the Kästner/Baky version: namely, the way in which (to recontextualise Scott Bukatman's description of the ambivalently defined futures of Tomorrowland) Disney culture is 'simultaneously reactionary and progressive, nostalgic and challenging' (Bukatman 1991: 58). That is, on the one hand, it is clear enough that childhood innocence and family togetherness is crucial to Disney's success (Giroux and Pollock 2010: 32). In this assessment, the specific appeal of Disney entertainment – not only films, but also other products and attractions, including the theme park – comes from its relentless quest for images of innocence, and this in turn is harnessed as a strategy to co-opt a productive market of children *and* adults, and to fuel company profits. But, on the other hand, in place of the unstable nuclear family which, even in 1961, is depicted as something so easily dissolved through divorce, Disney's *The Parent Trap* offers a different type of 'togetherness': specifically the lasting bonds of sisterhood, and close friendship, depicted in and through the twin characters of Susan and Sharon. In this case, the allure is that of a teen dream: the fantasy – or phantasy – of discovering another (more unified) self.

Figure 8.2 'Let's Get Together', *The Parent Trap* (1961)

This message – that a long-lasting, inter-generational friendship is more likely to sustain one through the upheavals that may well occur in cross-generational family life (Gillan 2015: 219) – is set up in the title sequence (and 'The Title Makers') and in turn reinforced in and through the film's signature teen tune, 'Let's Get Together'. Performed towards the end of the film, the number begins with one Hayley Mills (Sharon) dressed in a frock and seated at a piano on a makeshift stage playing Beethoven's Fifth Symphony before the other (Susan), more casually dressed in jeans and equipped with guitar, marches in and invites the twin to join her in a duet: 'You gotta get the new sound', Susan tells Sharon. 'Come on now, let's compromise. You give a little. I'll give a little. Let's get together.' In an assessment of this sequence that recalls the (aforementioned) notion of the duality of the self, Sean Griffin writes that the performance 'embodies a number of both gay and lesbian teen desires to be able to be two different people, one butch and the other feminine, and shows how people can act out both parts' (2000: 84). At the very least, the sequence demonstrates that 'togetherness is flexible enough to reference the standard cultural orthodoxy about nuclear family togetherness [but also draw out] a new myth story about friendship as [an alternative] mode of togetherness' (Gillan 2015: 219). In the context of the translation of Kästner's *Das doppelte Lottchen*, the main point is that 'togetherness' becomes a key figure in and through which to understand not just *The Parent Trap*'s (vertically integrated) commercial strategies of convergence, but also its methods of cultural transformation.

To conclude, although the performance of 'Let's Get Together' is a key segment for Disney's *The Parent Trap*, it is not in itself enough to rekindle romance for the twins' estranged parents and to re-create the 'ideal' family unit. Now that the twins have met, the proposed solution is that they spend part of each year, separately, first with one and then the other parent. This is an unhappy outcome to which the twins respond by adopting an identical deportment, frustrating their parents' ability to distinguish between them, and forcing the camping trip expedition that exposes Vicky's true nature and ultimately enables the desired reunion. The interchangeability of the twins at this point – a little ahead of the contrived ending which, like that of the Baky version, seems too abrupt – perhaps has something to say about the *multiple* versions of Kästner's story: the way that 'premakes' and remakes, originals and copies, do not simply follow – first one, and then the other – but coexist and *reflect* one another. *The Parent Trap* transforms, but also doubles, *Das doppelte Lottchen* just as Lindsay Lohan (and Lindsay Lohan) doubles Hayley Mills (and Hayley Mills), who sings a line from 'Let's Get Together' before going on to reunite (in the 1998 remake) the transatlantic (US–UK) parent couple, Nick Parker (Dennis Quaid) and Elizabeth James (Natasha Richardson).[6] At the end, the multiple versions of Kästner's work – *Das doppelte Lottchen* and *The Parent Trap* (1961), *The Parent Trap* (1998) and *Charlie and Louise: Das doppelte Lottchen* (1994), and a number of others – demonstrate that, for all the specificity of a particular version, the multiple versions of *Das doppelte Lottchen* – like the transnational film remake – are ultimately characterised by twin notions: those of proximity and reflection.

NOTES

1. Trans. Cyrus Brooks. Illustr. Walter Trier. London: Jonathan Cape, 1950.
2. This coincided with the cancellation of Disney's principal 'tween-address' television series, *The Mickey Mouse Club* (1955–9), which was dropped when the studio's contract with ABC ended and the anthology series was moved to NBC (see Gillan 2015: 215).
3. Upon discovering that their parents divorced and separated them, the twins do, however, express their solidarity and disapproval. Luise begins: '"Fine parents we've got . . . Just wait till we tell them a few home truths. That'll make them sit up!" "We couldn't do that" said Lottie timidly. "We're only children." "*Only!*" exclaimed Lisa, and threw back her head' (41).
4. Thanks to Kathleen Loock, who kindly provided *The Parent Trap* press book resource.
5. The inscription page of the 112-page novelisation of *The Parent Trap* describes it as an 'Adaptation by Vic Crume, Based on the screenplay' and 'Written for the Screen and Directed by David Swift. Based on a book by Erich Kästner.'
6. An account of the 'rom-com' transformations of the later Disney version requires a chapter of its own.

REFERENCES

Broad, David A. (1995), '*The Parent Trap*: A Myth of the Reunited Self', *Popular Culture Review*, 6: 1, pp. 121–31.

Brode, Douglas (2004), *From Walt to Woodstock: How Disney Created the Counterculture*, Austin: University of Texas Press.

Bukatman, Scott (1991), 'There's Always Tomorrowland: Disney and the Hyper-cinematic Experience', *October*, 57 (Summer), pp. 55–78.

Charlie and Louise: Das doppelte Lottchen (1994), Dir. Joseph Vilsmaier, Bavaria Filmverleih und Producktions GmbH.

Critchfield, Anne L. (2004), 'The Parent Trap: Hollywoods Verfilmungen von *Das doppelte Lottchen*', *Erich Kästner Jahrbuch*, 4, pp. 237–46.

Crume, Vic (1968), *The Parent Trap*, New York: Scholastic.

Das doppelte Lottchen (1950), Dir. Josef von Baky. Carlton Film.

Gabler, Neal (2007), *Walt Disney: The Triumph of the American Imagination*, New York: Alfred A. Knopf.

Gillan, Jennifer (2015), *Television Brandcasting: The Return of the Content-Promotion Hybrid*, New York: Routledge.

Giroux, Henry A. and Grace Pollock (2010), *The Mouse that Roared: Disney and the End of Innocence*, Lanham, MD: Rowman & Littlefield.

Griffin, Sean (2000), *Tinker Belles and Evil Queens: The Walt Disney Company from the Inside Out*, New York: New York University Press.

Holloway, Ron (1994), '*Charlie and Louise: Das doppelte Lottchen*', *Kino* 54 (May), pp. 7–8.

Kästner, Erich (1949), *Das doppelte Lottchen*, Wein: Verlag Carl Ueberreuter.

Kästner, Erich (1950), *Lottie and Lisa*, Trans. Cyrus Brooks, London: Jonathan Cape.

The Parent Trap (1961), Dir. David Swift, Walt Disney.

The Parent Trap (1961), Press Book, Walt Disney Company.

The Parent Trap (1998), Dir. Nancy Meyers, Walt Disney Pictures.

Maltin, Leonard (1973), *The Disney Films*, New York: Crown.

Schickel, Richard (1985), *The Disney Version: The Life, Times, Art and Commerce of Walt Disney*, New York: Simon & Schuster.

'The Title Makers' (1961), *Walt Disney Presents*, ABC, 11 June.

PART III

AUTEURS AND CRITICS

9. A TALE OF TWO BALLOONS: INTERCULTURAL CINEMA AND TRANSNATIONAL NOSTALGIA IN *LE VOYAGE DU BALLON ROUGE*

David Scott Diffrient and Carl R. Burgchardt

> Intercultural cinema moves through space, gathering up histories and memories that are lost or covered over in the movement of displacement, and producing new knowledges out of the condition of being between cultures.
>
> (Marks 2000: 78)

A brief, seemingly inconsequential encounter between two anthropomorphised objects – one red, the other blue – occurs in Albert Lamorisse's *Le ballon rouge* (*The Red Balloon*, 1956). That meeting, which has generally been overlooked by critics writing about this French classic of pre-New Wave cinema, occurs after the mid-point of the narrative, in the moments leading up to the film's initially tragic, eventually transcendent, ending. The camera, which has been tracking the street-to-street wanderings of a Parisian schoolboy named Pascal (who has befriended an inquisitive, mischievous balloon), suddenly pans from left to right to pick up the movement of a young girl and her own magically endowed balloon as they pass by the protagonist going in the opposite direction. Pascal turns on his feet and sees that his helium-filled companion has momentarily left him, drifting towards the other balloon much like it had sidled up to its own mirror-reflected image in an earlier scene set in an outdoor antiques market. The boy quickly fetches the red balloon by its string, an action that recalls his first encounter with it (climbing a streetlamp where it was stuck and descending with the thing in tow). Separated from its new 'friend', the girl's blue balloon pursues the red one, a paradoxically animated inanimate object whose mysterious driftings through Paris have thus far gone unexplained. Repeating Pascal's earlier action, the girl chases after her balloon, retrieving it and whisking it away, never to be seen again.

This strange convergence, where red and blue, boy and girl, action and reaction, come together in the calm interlude that precedes the film's penultimate scene (showing the titular object being chased and eventually destroyed by a gang of street urchins), stands out for a number of reasons. In addition to suggesting a 'shadow movie' of sorts, one that follows not the young boy and his red balloon but rather *the young girl and her blue balloon* (an alternative story tucked away in the folds of Lamorrise's film, one whose outcome can only be imagined by the spectator), this encounter materialises an otherwise immaterial idea. Although they appear only fleetingly in the film, walking out of the frame once the two balloons have been separated after a flash of gravitational attraction, the girl and her travelling companion might remind audiences that similarity as well as difference, friendliness as well as opposition, are dialectically aligned and prone to slippage in those moments when the physical gives way to the metaphysical. Paradoxically, though, it is the *materiality* of this scene – the fleshy latex 'proof' of the two balloons' physical existence – that facilitates philosophical inquiries into the nature of one's attraction to that most seemingly 'immaterial' of things: the cinematic image. For what more evocative conjuring trick can a filmmaker offer than this magical moment when two forces meet, if only momentarily, bringing with them a host of nostalgically imbued associations tied to our own spectatorial desire to reclaim a lost moment from an imagined past and see ourselves in the faces of others?

By the end of *Le ballon rouge*, after Pascal's balloon has been 'killed' by a group of his poverty-stricken, rock-throwing peers (one of the most heartrending 'death' scenes in the history of cinema), viewers will have witnessed several other moments of convergence and separation, ownership and loss. But it is this image of two airborne objects crossing paths that most reminds us of the need to reflexively position ourselves as momentary 'possessors' of the balloons, metaphorically chasing after them – or rather, what they represent – in much the same way that the children of Paris seem preternaturally drawn to these ineffable things. At once firmly within, yet forever beyond, our grasp, the cinematic image oscillates between ontological registers as a physically present yet elusive fetish object, something to be lovingly attended to even as it attends to *our* desires as emotionally stimulated, embodied subjects before the screen.

As media scholar Laura Marks remarks, 'All cinema has a fetishistic relationship to its object' (2000: 93). In her Deleuzian study of intercultural cinema and the physical memories of smell, taste and touch, Marks argues that an object in film 'is a particular sort of recollection-image that calls up different pasts for different people' (77–8). Millions of movie lovers around the world have experienced a range of emotions upon viewing Lamorrise's *Le ballon rouge*. As evidenced in the fan discourses surrounding it, many of the most adulatory responses have been triggered by the cultural associations and personal recollections generated by the bright red object that lends the film its title. One such fan is the English filmmaker Terence Davies, whose 2011 film *The Deep Blue Sea* has been interpreted 'as an adult translation' of the writer-director's 'own reading of *The Red Balloon*' (Walker 2012: 43). As Davies has stated in an interview, Lamorrise's film 'shows that you can overcome disaster. What happens to the balloon is a disaster for the child – which is also what it feels like watching it. I think the film symbolizes the ecstasy and terror of childhood and of life, but the end also signifies hope' (Walker 2012: 43). Moreover, in the years since the original theatrical release of that nearly dialogue-free, 34-minute fable, several filmmakers have made their collective fascination with it known through their individual works, motion pictures that reverentially bow down to that children's classic and, in some cases, gently spoof it. Perhaps no motion picture has demonstrated this more clearly than Taiwanese director Hou Hsiao-hsien's *Le voyage du ballon rouge* (*Flight of the Red Balloon*, 2007), a work of tremendous depth and complexity that pays homage to *Le ballon rouge* yet, in keeping with its title, puts greater emphasis on the *movement* of the object, which metaphorically represents the intercultural transit of the border-crossing film itself.

Although lacking the fantastical interludes of the earlier film (which culminates with an enormous bouquet of similarly sentient balloons sweeping Pascal up and away from the city) and filled with fewer flaneurial excursions through the alleyways of Paris, Hou's feature-length work is no less compelling as a series of quotidian scenes concerning the interwoven themes of companionship, loneliness, memory, and the restorative power of art. Set primarily inside the cluttered apartment of another young boy, Simon, and his harried mother, Suzanne, this film might appear to be claustrophobically tied to the interior lives of these characters, particularly to the single mother's attempts to balance her personal relationships (with a daughter now living abroad in Brussels, as well as with her layabout tenants downstairs) and her professional responsibilities (as a vocal performer at local puppet shows). But the Taiwanese director opens up the hermeneutic boundaries of this companion piece, injecting self-reflexive levity (as well as a childlike curiosity attentive to the magic of mundane things) by dropping a film student named Song into the proceedings. Paying for her studies through her employment as Simon's nanny, the cinephilic Chinese woman aspires to make her own tribute to *Le ballon rouge*, going so far as to restage scenes from the original film with Simon in the role of Pascal. Such internal 'mirroring' within *Le voyage du ballon rouge*, metaphorically suggested by a shot of the titular object pausing to 'gaze' at its own image (painted as part of a mural on a building), reflects Hou's own desire to memorialise a French classic, while extending its main themes into new, transnational territories. In *Le voyage du ballon rouge*, intercultural contact and the act of looking both *inward* and *outward* become the operative means of traversing social divisions and 'gaps' in one's memory. Drawing upon the work of Marks and other media scholars who have offered up phenomenological and memory-based studies of intercultural cinema, this essay explores the relationship between *recollections, references* and *reflections*, ultimately aiming to transnationalise (or 'uproot') nostalgia and show how twenty-first-century cinephilia performs a similar cultural function to the remaking process.

Reflecting on Remakes; Remakes as 'Reflections'

Before venturing into an assessment of *Le voyage du ballon rouge*'s formal complexity, intertextual references, and overarching themes, it will be helpful to first clarify and perhaps complicate the film's status vis-à-vis the work that inspired it (*Le ballon rouge*). This is done not to delimit the range of mutually impacting meanings engendered by either text, but rather to underscore Hou's deftness in deflecting conventional complaints or misapprehensions about remakes away from his film. The presumed status of this unusual motion picture – as a transnational remake produced by a French media company (Canal+), shot in Paris, directed by a Taiwanese filmmaker, and ostensibly beholden to a work of art produced half a century earlier – should be questioned, as should the classificatory impetus discernible within contemporary critical discourse. In other words, the impulse *to classify* – to set territorial limits – that is so pervasive within the literature of 'remake studies' should be leveraged against the boundary-dissolving functions of intercultural films like *Le voyage du ballon rouge*, if only to account for instances of cinematic output and reception that do not fit conveniently into established sub-categories (for example, the 'acknowledged, close remake', the 'acknowledged, transformed remake', the 'unacknowledged, disguised remake', and so on). Ultimately, one of our main concerns in this chapter is the binding concept of *intertextuality*, which joins together disparate theoretical models as well as the films themselves in a pact of reciprocal, transformative interplay.

With roots in Julia Kristeva's pioneering work on intertextuality (1980) as well as Gérard Genette's book *Palimpsests* (1992), the field of remake studies has spread to encompass a range of critical and theoretical positions that attest to its maturity and legitimacy as an area of evolving research and academic inquiry. Even before Genette set out to provide operational definitions for a range of intertextual (re)tracings, the former Hollywood screenwriter Michael Druxman wrote the first historical survey of movie remakes in the English language. Entitled *Make It Again, Sam* (a pun on a famous line spoken by Humphrey Bogart's character, Rick Blaine, in the 1942 classic *Casablanca*), this 1975 volume remains a somewhat controversial text today, as subsequent generations of film scholars continue to test and challenge Druxman's preliminary taxonomy. Believed to be 'sketchy' by some theorists, but also referred to as 'the most comprehensive investigation of Hollywood remaking practice' (Greenberg 1998: 126, n.1), this much-debated opening salvo in remake studies is both expansive and limited, focusing broadly (but exclusively) on films that share common literary sources (novels, poems, plays, screenplays, and so on). Obviously, were it necessary for a motion picture to meet this condition in order to claim the status of 'remake', then Hou's *Le voyage du ballon rouge* would fall short in the eyes of Druxman and other scholars. Unlike many other examples of remakes, neither this 2007 production, which was commissioned by the Musée d'Orsay to celebrate the Parisian art institution's twentieth anniversary, nor the 1956 film that inspired it is based on literary texts (Penz 2012; Lim 2014). Here the words of David Carter are worth quoting: 'While it is true that most film remakes are based on literary texts, as defined by Druxman, this limitation would exclude from consideration as a remake any film made by a director who arranged for a screenplay to be written based solely on viewings or even just memories of an earlier film' (Carter 2010: 7). As we will explain, references to *Le ballon rouge* in the Taiwanese director's film are literally *framed* as examples of cinema's built-in capacity to enshrine the past, to treat previous instances of cinephilic wistfulness or longing as a latent characteristic of the medium.

In the years since the 1975 publication of Druxman's book, several scholars have sought to bring greater theoretical rigour to the subject (see, for instance, Horton and McDougal 1998, Mazdon 2000, Forrest and Koos 2002, Verevis 2006). Foremost among them is Thomas Leitch, whose essay 'Twice-Told Tales: The Rhetoric of the Remake' (1990) provides a typology that distinguishes between 're-adaptations', 'updates', 'homages' and 'true remakes'. While the first two of those types 'primarily engage the filmic remake's relation to a classic literary text' (and thus do not offer useful lenses through which to perceive *Le voyage du ballon rouge*'s complex intertextual connections to *Le ballon rouge*), the latter two deserve consideration in light of Hou's resistance to what Salomé Aguilera Skvirsky calls the 'enabling paradox' of remakes (2008: 92). A paradoxical facet of many remakes, according to Skvirsky, is their tendency to solidify the 'classic' status of earlier cinematic texts even as they proclaim themselves to be 'better' than the originals. This is something that 'true remakes' are thought to do. Conversely, a homage is said to treat its filmic precursor as a superior text, a long-valorised classic that nevertheless is 'in danger of being ignored or forgotten' (Leitch 1990: 144). A noteworthy example of cinematic homage from a Taiwanese director is Tsai Ming-liang's *Goodbye, Dragon Inn* (*Bu San*, 2003). This low-key, minimalist film is set entirely in and around a Taipei movie theatre about to close its doors permanently, a cultural space that is showing the *wuxia* classic *Dragon Inn* (*Lóng*

Mén Kè Zhàn, 1967) to a small, mixed group of audience members. Unlike this martial arts film directed by King Hu, there is little chance that Lamorrise's *Le ballon rouge* will slip into the cracks of history and be forgotten, given the frequency with which it continues to be programmed as part of theatrical retrospectives and festivals. Nor is it likely that Hou's work will 'replace' the former, as some remakes are said to do. *Le voyage du ballon rouge* is neither 'better' nor 'worse' than its predecessor, and indeed such evaluative language adds little to an understanding of the persistent themes in Hou's increasingly transnational body of work, which in recent years has begun to encompass a range of geographically dispersed national/regional settings and languages. As the director of *Café Lumière* (*Kōhī Jikō?*, 2003), a Japanese-language tribute to Ozu Yasujiro's *Tokyo Story* (*Tōkyō Monogatari*, 1954), as well as *The Assassin* (*Nièyǐnniáng*, 2015), a multinational co-production that reflects the director's unique take on the Chinese martial arts genre known as *wuxia*, Hou – an art-house auteur once associated with quiet, contemplative dramas set in Taipei or other Taiwanese locales – is as mobile as the border-crossing balloon that stars in his 2007 film.

A simple way to frame the transnational remake is to refer to it as a film 'made in one cultural context and then remade in another' (Herbert 2009: 143). However, that description, while serviceable, hints at a slippage between two productions that might in fact be separated by a significant historical gap in addition to geographical distance. Moreover, it fails to convey both the movement and mixture of labour and resources required to bring such works to fruition. Daniel Herbert adds nuance to the above definition, arguing that English-language remakes such as *Insomnia* (2002) and *The Grudge* (2004) 'demonstrate the transnational mobility and cultural flexibility of the cinema', becoming, in his words, 'their own allegories'. These films, which foreground characters' 'psycho-spatial dislocations', allegorically register 'the rearrangement of space as a category of human experience and geography as a category of social practice' (2009: 143). This idea, which echoes Lucy Mazdon's claim that the remake 'can be seen to cross both spatial (national) and temporal (historical) boundaries' (2000: 3), is engrained in the ontology of moving images (3). For, just as the remake 'is as old as cinema itself', according to Herbert, so too has the medium been shaped by global cultural flows since its origins as a peepshow novelty and technological wonder in the 1890s.

In a sense, *Le voyage du ballon rouge* takes viewers back to cinema's embryonic state, its origins as a turn-of-the-century cultural form beholden to earlier storytelling and performative traditions, thanks to its inclusion of a puppet show for which Suzanne, Simon's mother, rehearses. One of the film's first scenes, coming after a lengthy pre-title sequence that depicts the boy's initial encounters with the red balloon (which floats above the ornate Bastille Métro entrance and nearby streets), takes place at a rehearsal space where hand puppetry is being performed. Tellingly, we follow the movement of Song, a young Chinese woman, who steps off a city bus and hesitantly enters that darkened venue, where she and we are granted a chance to watch puppeteers ply their trade. Audiences who are unsure of this theatrical performance's meaning might identify with Song, an onlooker/outsider who appears somewhat perplexed. However, given her background (as a cultural insider), it is likely that she is able to discern the connotations of that embedded story, a French-language version of *Zhang Sheng Zhu Hai* (*Master Zhang Boils the Sea*) that bears fruit in terms of deepening this film's intertextual meanings. A few details of this Yuan Dynasty-era variety-opera (written by the thirteenth-century playwright Li Haogu) emerge during the scene, including its central conceit that the title character has fallen in love with the daughter of the Dragon King. The latter character, because he opposes their marriage, has imprisoned his child in the ocean. In order to reach his sequestered bride-to-be, Zhang proclaims that he will boil every drop of the sea (Lim 2014: 69). Or, rather, Suzanne makes this proclamation in her role as vocal performer, lending voice to the play's French-speaking Chinese characters while accompanied by the sonic stylings of a bassoonist (whose instrument, one might note, is often associated with children's musical entertainment).

This scene is noteworthy for many reasons, not least for its suggestion that cultural appropriation – the French performers' adoption/adaptation of a centuries-old Chinese folktale – is a form of 'mimicry' for which the human voice and body are the main vehicles. But its foregrounding of puppetry as a storytelling form ushers forth the notion that cinema itself can be used for mimetic purposes, 'imitating' that which historically preceded it just as remakes are said to do. Scholars of mimesis have noted that this Platonic ideal, which infuses literature as well as image-based cultural productions (such as motion pictures), is an art of 'reflection' (see, for instance, Hutson 2007). With that in mind, and at the risk of clogging the already crowded list of sub-categories comprising cinematic remakes, we wish to introduce another conceptual orientation: that of the *remake as reflection*. The term 'reflection' contains multiple meanings, not only gesturing towards the mimetic relationship between art and nature but also connoting both external and internal engagements with the *self*. That is, a person confronts an image of himself or herself in the presence of a reflective surface, such as a mirror, but can also be said 'to reflect' when afforded a moment to meditate, to ponder, to think. A person is therefore metaphorically 'outside' himself or herself when he or she is positioned before a mirror (or mirror-like surface), whereas the process of reflecting on past experiences, feelings, and so on, necessitates an inward turn. *Le voyage du ballon rouge* makes this combined sense of outwardness and inwardness an experiential part of its cinephilic project, particularly during those moments when Song is shooting and completing her own homage to Lamorrise's *Le ballon rouge*.

Figure 9.1 The titular object floats up alongside a white building, next to another red balloon (part of a painted mural), *Le voyage du ballon rouge* (*Flight of the Red Balloon*, 2007)

Approximately two-thirds of the way through *Le voyage du ballon rouge*, we see Simon's Chinese caretaker editing her short film on a laptop. Simon has been cast in a role that he inherits from Pascal in the original film, that of temporary possessor of the balloon. This film-within-the-film first shows Simon at a train station where, firmly grasping his beloved red object, he ascends a stairway leading out to Rue Benjamin Franklin. Reminiscent of the stairs that Pascal is frequently shown climbing in Lamorisse's 1956 film, this diegetic yet real-world space (located in the sixteenth arrondissement) is one among many reminders that ascendancy or elevation as well as movement are part of the remake's intertextual dynamics, its tendency to place itself 'above' that which preceded it (that is, the 'original' film). However, this conventional idea is complicated by the fact that the balloon, when released by Simon, floats up alongside a white building only to stop at the sight of a mural. Painted on the side of the building, the mural depicts *another* red balloon, and this representational icon becomes, at least for a moment, a kind of mirroring device, allowing the titular object to 'recognise' itself before departing on the wind.

Here we are reminded of Gilles Deleuze's notion of the 'powers of the false', which Marks summarises as the point at which nothing 'can be referred to as real or true' (2000: 65). That is, what looks to be an 'actual' balloon, whose 'realness' or material solidity is accentuated when positioned opposite its 'mirror' image (which is painted on the building), is in fact little more than a virtual construct. Not coincidentally, *nostalgia* – which, along with repetition, fuels cinephilia (according to Elsaesser 2005: 35) – has often been criticised by sociologists as a 'false consciousness', a mystification of the past that is 'fundamentally fake' and thus deserving of scepticism (Wilson 2013: 158; see also Outka 2013: 259). However, Marks argues that nostalgia 'need not mean an immobilizing longing for a lost past: it can also mean the ability of past experiences to transform the present' (2000: 201). And what distinguishes transnational nostalgia? According to Margaret Hillenbrand, it is 'a retreat from precisely the place from where "true" nostalgia is supposed to spring: the remembered past and, most particularly, the past as home'. Quoting Andreas Huyssen, who noted that 'nostalgic longing for a past is always also a longing *for another place*' (italics added), Hillenbrand makes the case that nostalgic desire necessarily links temporality and spatiality. And yet, 'nostalgia is nothing but a floating simulacrum unless it is bedded down in ground that feels like home; but a sense of place, too, must inspire feelings of nostalgia if it is to seed itself in memory' (2010: 390, 398). The wind-tossed balloon might very well be that 'floating simulacrum' that is forever beyond one's grasp, an image of an image that begins to evaporate with each cinematic homage/remake that, ironically, seeks to solidify an earlier film's place in history. What *Le voyage du ballon rouge* registers is a longing for what the cinematically fetishised Paris of Lamorisse's film once was (or was thought to be); a memory, in other words, as faded as the weather-beaten painting of a red balloon on the side of a white building.

By presenting Song's film internally, on a laptop whose rectangular borders are visibly contained within the cinematic frame (and thus doubly distanced from the spectator), Hou foregrounds his own film's constructedness, its status not as an unmediated reality but rather as a cultural artefact beholden to another, 'external' work: Lamorrise's *Le ballon rouge*. Interestingly, Marks adopts 'reflective' language when describing Deleuze's aforementioned 'powers of the false', stating that 'the original point at which actual and virtual image reflect each other produces, in turn, a widening circuit of actual and virtual images like a hall of mirrors. When a film reflects upon its own production process, its obstacles, and the very cost of its making, it acts as [a] sort of catalytic crystal, reflecting the film-that-could-have-been in the complex of its virtual images' (2000: 63). Significantly, the shot described above, which recalls a moment in *Le ballon rouge* when the balloon seems to be regarding itself in a mirror situated among other objects in a flea market, is immediately followed by an image of Simon seated inside a bus, pushing his face against a glass window and studying his own reflection in close-up.

An earlier instance of people confronted by their own reflections, cast by the mirror-like surface of a moving vehicle's window, occurs at the film's fifty-minute mark, when Suzanne and Song take a train-ride home. Seated beside Song is an older Chinese man named Ah Zhang, who has been giving

Figure 9.2   Seated inside a bus, Simon pushes his face against a glass window and studies his own reflection in close-up, *Le voyage du ballon rouge* (*Flight of the Red Balloon*, 2007)

guest lectures in Paris as a master puppeteer. The scene preceding this one had indeed established the old man's mastery as an artist capable of transporting his spellbound audience into another time and place (much like the celebrated Taiwanese performer Li Tian-lu does in Hou's 1993 film *The Puppetmaster* [*Xì mèng rénshēng*]). Suzanne, who translated Ah Zhang's dialogue during his performance, now sits opposite him on the train, where she verbally recalls the experience of having witnessed and participated in that master-class. She also offers him a postcard that she has kept in her possession since childhood, one that bears a long-cherished image that strikes her as being 'profoundly Chinese'. Two pasts – one immediate, fresh in the mind, and shared by others, the other a personal part of Suzanne's adolescence – are brought together in this scene, which further suggests that this melancholy character's relationship to the world is and has always been mediated by art. For Suzanne, memory and art are intertwined, and her act of reflecting on previous experiences is visually complemented by Hong's framing of the shot, which captures both Suzanne and her image reflected in the window of the train.

Old and worn, the black-and-white postcard that Suzanne gifts to the Chinese puppeteer is like the red balloon insofar as it provokes nostalgic sentiments. And this mechanically reproduced image of an Asian musical instrument is no less transnational than the balloon, for it was procured long ago not in Paris but in London, specifically at the British Museum, which Suzanne had visited while working abroad as an au pair. This bit of information, besides suggesting that the French woman shares something in common with Song (who, like an au pair, is a domestic assistant from a foreign country), also emphasises the theme of border-crossing movement that finds its visual correlative in the blurry images seen through the window as the train speeds towards its destination. Turning her attention from Ah Zhang to the landscape that passes by outside, Suzanne (who is normally quite antic and frazzled) appears to be lost in thought as this scene concludes. But her reflected image, superimposed atop that blurry background, is what lingers in the mind as a sign of this film's overriding concern with internal and external expressions of sentimental longing – a feeling tied to childhood and the search for one's lost or nearly forgotten 'origins'.

Not coincidentally, the title of Song's student film, made when she was studying production back in China, is *Origins*. An early scene in *Le voyage du ballon rouge* features a brief conversation between the two characters in which Suzanne expresses interest in Song's first film, an abstract short that she calls 'touching'. 'It reminded me of childhood', the older woman tells her, before indicating that the appropriately titled *Origins* brought back memories of living with her parents (events that she had 'almost forgotten'). It is evident, even from the subtle hints that she drops into this conversation, that Suzanne had a troubled life as an adolescent, and the largely suppressed pain or 'darkness' of having grown up in a house filled with hostility or resentment is similar to the sentiment that the Chinese puppeteer Ah Zhang later expresses during his performance. During that master-class, he acts out the role of Zhang Yu, a character in the aforementioned *Master Zhang Boils the Sea*, who lost both parents as a child and has remained 'engulfed in a dark cloud', according to Suzanne's translation. Although her son Simon is not an only child, he too appears to be lonely, prone to drift (much like the balloon), in part because his absentee father has absconded to Montreal to write a book. Moreover, like Zhang Yu, who distracts himself from his pain by playing the *guqin* lute, Simon is taking musical lessons, learning to play the piano (an instrument that provides this film's lyrical, elegiac soundtrack). One can argue that he has inherited his mother's reliance on artistic activity as a way to ease feelings of urban isolation and familial separation.

This internal/external 'mirroring' between a thirteenth-century play from China and a modern-day film set in Paris is a sign of Hou's commitment to transnational meaning-making, a process that necessitates cinephilic recollections and reflections on the part of audiences, who are asked to look towards a past threatened by obsolescence in search of a motion picture's intertextual 'origins'. Not just intertextual but also intercultural, *Le voyage du ballon rouge*'s referential ties to previous productions include the director's aforementioned film *The Puppetmaster*, which demonstrates Hou's interest in theatrical traditions as well as the historical circumstances that either curtail or support artists' rights (for example, Japanese colonialism, in the case of the 1993 production). It is significant that *The Puppetmaster* begins with a scene in which the celebrated performer Li Tien-lu, recounting 'how his last name, shared by his maternal side of the family, was given to him through a careful series of arrangements between his father and grandfather', grapples with his own origins as a colonised islander, a 'third-class citizen'. As Nick Schager argues, the fact that the ageing puppeteer 'ascribes his origins to a set of legal provisions immediately connects him to his occupied homeland – a disempowered territory now defined by the rules and regulations of a foreign party – just as his age-old profession ties him to the ancestral traditions of Taiwanese culture' (2005). The fact that Suzanne's profession likewise bears the influence of her father and grandfather (as former puppeteers) indicates that her commitment to the artistry and craft of this ancient form of storytelling (originating over 2,000 years ago in Asian contexts, such as India, China and Japan) is linked to her desire to keep a familial legacy intact despite having endured a difficult, loneliness-filled adolescence.

We learn about Suzanne's grandfather through the inclusion of yet another film-within-the-film, this time a home movie that features the white-bearded man entertaining Simon's now-estranged sister Louise while holding a hand puppet. Because Song has transferred this silent 8mm film to video disc, Simon is able to watch it (but not hear it) while seated in a moving van, one that is equipped with a small monitor on the dashboard. On a reduced scale (that is, at the local level), such mobile spectatorship gels with *Le voyage du ballon rouge*'s thematic preoccupation with international travel. Moreover, because the nostalgically imbued home movie lacks audio, Suzanne once again employs her skills as a voice actor, adding a humorous soundtrack to its quotidian scenes of familial contentment. When her son asks her about the voices, Suzanne replies 'I make it up'. This line runs counter to an earlier comment made by Ah Zhang, the ageing puppeteer visiting Paris, who explained that classic Chinese theatre has little room for improvisation. Only a true master, the old man suggests, would attempt any unscripted departures from the traditional formula. One wonders if Hou, a filmmaker universally recognised as a 'master' of the highest order, is slyly commenting on himself (or the auteurist myths surrounding his public persona), since most of the dialogue in *Le voyage du ballon rouge* was improvised, spoken 'in the moment' of collaborative conception by Juliette Binoche, Simon Iteanu, Fang Song and other actors. Regardless, one can see in this scene that, for Suzanne and possibly other characters, manipulating reality or the appearance of things is much easier in theatre (and, by extension, film) than in one's actual, day-to-day encounters with others. This is partially due to the unpredictability of the latter, which lacks the 'scripted' or structurally contained (and oft-repeated) mechanisms of genre productions, be they theatrical plays or cinematic remakes.

CINEPHILIC RECOLLECTION AND THE MUSEUM OF (MOVIE) MEMORIES

In their recently published study of film remakes, Scott A. Lukas and John Marmysz refer to a dialectical interplay that partially defines the genre: that between *recollection* and *repetition*. The former, they argue, is a 'backward movement', while the latter is a 'forward movement'. More specifically, when an individual recollects something, he or she consigns that thing to the past, whereas the desire to repeat something speaks to the need to 'bring it to actuality in the present' (2010: 10). As such,

> while recollection makes us unhappy, repetition makes us happy. Recollection is a symptom of longing for something that is no longer with us. It is tinged with melancholy and sadness for things lost. Repetition, on the other hand, is an expression of our power to recreate something anew, again and again. It is a positive expression of our will toward the future. (2010: 10)

Lukas and Marmysz further explain this seemingly self-cancelling drive in the cinematic remake by way of references to both Sigmund Freud and Søren Kierkegaard. After gesturing towards the Austrian psychoanalyst's notion of 'repetition compulsion' (a tendency in organisms to 'restore an earlier state of things which the living entity has been obliged to abandon under the pressure of external disturbing forces'), the authors summarise the Danish philosopher's belief that life itself becomes a 'series of transitory moments' without either recollection or repetition, dissolving into 'empty, meaningless noise' (10). This idea hints at the distinction between mimetic representation and the *thing* – the reality – that it signifies or references.

Having already invoked Marks's belief that 'all cinema has a fetishistic relationship to its object', we now wish to offer a slightly different perspective on what constitutes the 'thing' that serves as cinephilic fetish. This necessitates seeing beyond the red balloon's material existence or presence in the text as a physical object, and perceiving it along the lines that James Tweedie prescribes: as an *image* and *mirage*, as the tantalising possibility for recovering another lost object – Lamorrise's *Le ballon rouge* – even if it too exists less as an actual film than as a virtual thing, a cinephilic memory (2013: 176). It is true that the cinephilic spectator sees the film medium itself as a fetish object, a means by which desire is not only visualised (according to the logic of psychoanalytic theory) but also lent material substance. And yet, the film image can be said to 'repress' the medium's materiality, privileging visual representation over the physical properties and technological tools through which the signifying process is partially achieved. Cinephilia, then, rescues or, to borrow Christian Keathley's word, *reanimates* the inherently material dimensions of cinematic discourse while simultaneously transforming 'selected films into historical fetishes' (2005: 53). This, according to Mikhail Iampolski, furthermore functions to cultivate those films' 'museum value' (1997: 37), enhaloing canonical or cultic works as being worthy of ritualistic devotion – a practice that ironically risks turning the animated, physical thing into a metaphysical ideal (that is, an untouchable perfection or auratic abstraction kept at a respectful distance even as it is figuratively embraced by fans). A cinephilic ritual, Iampolski concludes, is 'a ritual of a restoration of aura through an imposition of museum value by distantiation' (37).

It is worth pointing out that an actual museum appears in *Le voyage du ballon rouge*. Near the end of the film, Simon and a group of children are learning from their teacher how to critically interpret a work of art housed inside the Musée d'Orsay, a famous museum on the left bank of the Seine, situated in the heart of Paris. The oil painting that captures their attention is Félix Vallotton's *Le ballon*, a post-impressionist masterpiece from 1899. The teacher points out to her students the various hermeneutic possibilities of the painting, a high-angle, sunlit landscape depicting a child with blond hair in pursuit of the titular object (tellingly, a bright red ball). Chasing after the thing, the boy in the painting allegorically represents the children's collective search for meaning. Simon, absorbed by his peers' conversation, has spent the better part of the film's preceding sections looking for security and companionship (in the absence of his sister and father). Because of that, his status as a personification of the nostalgic impulses experienced by the cinephilic viewer, who might recall Lamorrise's 1956 film while watching this 2007 feature, is accentuated by virtue of this painting, this embedded representation-within-a-representation that has been sacralised and sanctified owing to its cultural enthronement within the Musée d'Orsay, a former railway station dating back to the early twentieth century that was itself transformed into a place of 'worship' for art connoisseurs and acolytes in the 1980s.

Like Hou's film, Vallotton's artwork is a study in contrasts – its deep, mysterious shadows offset by a bright burst of sunlight that engulfs the child and makes the red ball stand out against the browns and greens of the park setting. The painting is both 'happy' and 'sad', the teacher announces, and that tonal slippage – that coexistence of the two extremes that we referenced earlier, with regard to 'recollection' and 'repetition' – also characterises *Le voyage du ballon rouge*, a film that exudes melancholia but hints at the optimistic possibility of transcendence. Literal and figurative buoyancy is suggested by the presence of the balloon, which returns in this penultimate scene and can be seen hovering outside one of the museum's glass skylights, as if it were a voyeuristic spectator gazing at the cultural edification of the children inside. Only Simon, who shifts his attention from the painting to the nearby window, appears to notice the object bouncing to and fro, and this combination of attentiveness and distraction, immersion and distance, conjures the spectatorial snag that audiences sometimes face as they too shift from one extreme to another, particularly when watching motion pictures that invite cinephilic or nostalgic recollections of past productions.

With this being the first time that Simon has actually *seen* the balloon (in 'reality', that is, apart from its presence in Song's video-recorded homage) since *Le voyage du ballon rouge*'s opening scene, it seems appropriate to piggyback on Tweedie's notion that a 'pedagogy of the image' asserts itself upon the children in the film's penultimate scene (2013). In a way, the young protagonist and his classmates are taught by their instructor how to regard Vallotton's painting, but to do so openly, inquisitively, with an unfettered arsenal of hermeneutic possibilities at their disposal. Notably, when the artwork first appears on screen, it is out of focus, its glass protection reflecting the children as their adult supervisor instructs them to sit on the floor to better see the painting. At this precise moment, Hou's cinematographer, Pin Bing Lee, racks focus to show the object of their collective fascination. And yet, even with the blond-haired child and the bright red ball of the painting now in focus, the hazy reflections of the young museum patrons remain visible, as if they too are a part of *Le ballon*. It would seem, then, that any attempt to deconstruct the artwork's meanings is a bid for self-realisation, a means of understanding one's own creative potential. Simon in particular seems content in this moment of self-realisation, brought about by the simultaneity of speaking with his peers about the painting and seeing the balloon through the window before it ascends into the heavens.

As the object floats away from the Musée d'Orsay, vistas of the Parisian skyline fill the frame – touristic images (including a shot of the Sacré-Coeur) that are accompanied by the song 'Chin-Chin'. The lyrics of that song conclude with a dedication, 'To you, my red balloon', which, sung over the final shot before it fades to black, suggests that Hou's film is both a homage and a memorialisation, one that is steeped in 'sheer love and reverence' for an earlier production that is deserving of valorisation (Ng 2005: 68). However, *Le voyage du ballon rouge* is not simply a companion piece to the 1956 film, an adulatory homage or respectful remake that merely enhances the latter's status as a post-war classic (through a kind of reverential referencing of it). It is, rather, a critical intervention in the nostalgic framing of *Le ballon rouge* as an evocation of adolescent longing. Such longing, diegetically expressed via the young boy's desire for companionship, speaks to certain audiences' extradiegetic yearning for intercultural connection – a desire, hinted at in the final scene of Lamorisse's film (showing a 'rainbow cluster' of balloons sweeping Pascal away from the city), which necessarily transcends geographical barriers and which is only fully realised in Hou's border-crossing film. Despite their many tonal and stylistic dissimilarities as cultural productions from different eras, in both films we witness balloons leaving the city, an event that resonates with Hillenbrand's definition of transnational nostalgia, which she describes as 'a spatial and temporal *flight from the city of recent recall*' (2010: 384, italics added).

Unlike other commentators who have stressed the 'near irrelevance of the titular red balloon' in Hou Hsiao-hsien's film, 'especially in comparison with the original story by Lamorisse' (Tweedie 2013: 175), we wish to emphasise its importance in making 'visible the invisible', to borrow Adrian J. Ivakhiv's words (2013: 124). On one level, Hou's film is dedicated to an 'exploration of interior and exterior spaces, homes and parks, windows and walls and the images that adorn them' (Tweedie 2013: 175). More profoundly, the Taiwanese director provides contemporary audiences with a new way of 'seeing' the 1956 motion picture, which is retroactively transformed in the process of serving as a transnational film's source material. According to Yiman Wang, a cinematic remake allows a filmmaker to 'critically engage in dialog' with an earlier motion picture, 'with the goal of producing a new vision through reversioning' (2013: 14). As stated earlier, *Le voyage du ballon rouge* builds towards the aforementioned revelatory moment inside the Musée d'Orsay, where Simon and a group of children are learning how to bring their already sophisticated interpretative skills to a work of art (Vallotton's painting *Le ballon*). That richly evocative, strategically placed scene illuminates the intercultural linkage and dialectical interplay of two mutually enriching texts – one a French classic of the 1950s, the other a multinational co-production of the new millennium – whose 'partnership' is greater than the sum of their parts.

REFERENCES

Carter, David (2010), 'Remakes – And Why They Are Worth Studying', *Splice*, 5: 1, Autumn/Winter, p. 7.

Druxman, Michael (1975), *Make It Again, Sam: A Survey of Movie Remakes*, Cranbury, NJ: A. S. Barnes.

Elsaesser, Thomas (2005), 'Cinephilia or the Uses of Disenchantment', in Marijke de Valck and Malte Hagener (eds), *Cinephilia: Movies, Love and Memory*, Amsterdam: Amsterdam University Press, pp. 27–44.

Forrest, Jennifer and Leonard R. Koos (eds) (2002), *Dead Ringers: The Remake in Theory and Practice*, Albany, NY: State University of New York Press.

Genette, Gérard (1997), *Palimpsests: Literature in the Second Degree*, Lincoln, NE: University of Nebraska Press.

Greenberg, Harvey R. (1998), 'Raiders of the Lost Text: Remaking as Contested Homage in *Always*', in Andrew Horton and Stuart Y. McDougal (eds), *Play it Again, Sam: Retakes on Remakes*, Los Angeles, CA: University of California Press, pp. 115–30.

Herbert, Daniel (2009), 'Trading Spaces: Transnational Dislocations in *Insomnia/Insomnia* and *Ju-on/The Grudge*', in Scott A. Lukas and John Marmysz (eds), *Fear, Cultural Anxiety, and Transformation: Horror, Science Fiction, and Fantasy Films Remade*, Lanham, MD: Lexington Books, pp. 143–64.

Hillenbrand, Margaret (2010), 'Nostalgia, Place, and Making Peace with Modernity in East Asia', *Postcolonial Studies*, 13: 4, pp. 383–401.

Horton, Andrew and Stuart Y. McDougal (eds) (1998), *Play It Again, Sam: Retakes on Remakes*, Berkeley: University of California Press.

Hutson, Lorna (2007), *The Invention of Suspicion: Law and Mimesis in Shakespeare and Renaissance Drama*, Oxford: Oxford University Press.

Iampolski, Mikhail (1997), 'Translating Images . . .', *RES: Anthropology and Aesthetics*, 32, Autumn 1997, pp. 37–42.

Ivakhiv, Adrian J. (2013), *Ecologies of the Moving Image: Cinema, Affect, Nature*, Ontario: Wilfrid Laurier University Press.

Keathley, Christian (2005), *Cinephilia and History, or The Wind in the Trees*, Bloomington, IN: Indiana University Press.

Kristeva, Julia (1980), *Desire in Language: A Semiotic Approach to Literature and Art*, New York: Columbia University Press.

Leitch, Thomas M. (1990), 'Twice-Told Tales: The Rhetoric of the Remake', *Literature/ Film Quarterly*, 18: 3, pp. 138–49.

Lim, Song Hwee (2014), 'The Voice of the Sinophone', in Audrey Yue and Olivia Khoo (eds), *Sinophone Cinemas*, Basingstoke: Palgrave Macmillan, pp. 62–76.

Lukas, Scott A. and John Marmysz (eds) (2010), 'Horror, Science Fiction, and Fantasy Films Remade', in *Fear, Cultural Anxiety, and Transformation: Horror, Science Fiction, and Fantasy Films Remade*, Lanham, MD: Rowman & Littlefield, pp. 1–20.

Marks, Laura (2000), *The Skin of the Film: Intercultural Cinema, Embodiment, and the Senses*, Durham, NC: Duke University Press.

Mazdon, Lucy (2000), *Encore Hollywood: Remaking French Cinema*, London: British Film Institute.

Ng, Jenna (2005), 'Love in the Time of Transcultural Fusion: Cinephilia, Homage, and *Kill Bill*', in Marijke de Valck and Malte Hagener (eds), *Cinephilia: Movies, Love and Memory*, Amsterdam: Amsterdam University Press, pp. 65–81.

Outka, Elizabeth (2013), 'Afterword: Nostalgia and Modernist Anxiety', in Tammy Clewell (ed.), *Modernism and Nostalgia: Bodies, Locations, Aesthetics*, Basingstoke: Palgrave Macmillan, pp. 252–61.

Penz, François (2012), 'Museums as Laboratories of Change: The Case for the Moving Image', in Angela Dalle Vacche (ed.), *Film, Art, New Media: Museum Without Walls?* Basingstoke: Palgrave Macmillan, pp. 278–300.

Schager, Nick (2005), 'The Puppetmaster', *Slant*, 18 September, <http://www.slant-magazine.com/film/review/the-puppetmaster> (last accessed 22 September 2015).

Skvirsky, Salomé Aguilera (2008), 'The Price of Heaven: Remaking Politics in *All that Heaven Allows, Ali: Fear Eats the Soul*, and *Far from Heaven*', *Cinema Journal*, 47: 3, Spring, pp. 90–121.

Tweedie, James (2013), *The Age of New Waves: Art Cinema and the Staging of Globalization*, Oxford: Oxford University Press.

Verevis, Constantine (2006), *Film Remakes*, Edinburgh: Edinburgh University Press.

Walker, Elsie (2012), 'Editorial: A Reflection on Forty Years', *Literature/Film Quarterly*, 40: 4, pp. 243.

Wang, Yiman (2013), *Remaking Chinese Cinema: Through the Prism of Shanghai, Hong Kong, and Hollywood*, Hong Kong: Hong Kong University Press.

Wilson, Janelle L. (2013), *Nostalgia: Sanctuary of Meaning*, Cranbury, NJ: Bucknell University Press.

10. 'CRAZED HEAT': NAKAHIRA KO AND THE TRANSNATIONAL SELF-REMAKE

David Desser

We might think of remakes as taking place along four axes. The two most familiar of these would be the remake within national circumstances, as for instance with Hollywood often remaking earlier American films, or the transnational remake, again with Hollywood frequently remaking foreign films. This is not to say that other cinemas do not remake their own films (Hong Kong is particularly prone to this), or that we cannot find transnational remakes across other national cinemas, for example from Korea to Japan, or to Bollywood from Hong Kong, and so on. Another, somewhat familiar, axis would be instances of directors remaking their own film within the same broad national context. These are cases that move beyond the typical auteur who persistently works in the same idiom or with the same motifs. Of course, remaking one's own film is an attractive option for directors who do, in fact, continually rework their own devices. Howard Hawks, for instance, certainly was one who was given to authorial repetitions. Still, there is the clear remake *Ball of Fire* (1941) into *A Song Is Born* (1948). Raoul Walsh undertook *The Strawberry Blonde* in 1941 and turned it back into *One Sunday Afternoon* in 1948 (the name of the original film version done in 1933 by Stephen Roberts). John Ford, another powerful auteur given to repetitions and variations, more closely remade, say, his *Judge Priest* (1934) into *The Sun Shines Bright* (1953). And then there are surely the least familiar, and certainly the least studied (if perhaps because the most rare), instances of directors remaking their own films in different national contexts. We could point to Denmark's Ole Bornedal, who remade his Danish original *Nattevagten* (1994) into the American

Nightwatch in 1997. Shimizu Takashi made *Ju-On* (aka *Ju-On: The Grudge*) in 2002; in 2004 he was tempted by Hollywood into remaking his own film, again in Japan but with an American cast, as *The Grudge*.

Each type of remake, as I have encapsulated them here, involves changes in both text and context. Even the auteur directors who remade their own films do not stand outside this duad. In the case of the Hawks and Walsh films mentioned above, the context shifts from pre-war to post-war; another context is genre – the shift from comedy to musical; another is aesthetic in the shift from black-and-white to colour. A change in casting can be crucial to a film's text. In the case of Hawks, what does it mean to substitute Danny Kaye for Gary Cooper, or Virginia Mayo for Barbara Stanwyck? For Walsh, we find Dennis Morgan in lieu of James Cagney. In every instance there is a shift in understanding the differing films – no matter how similar.

The transnational remake by the same director presents, generally speaking, the most radical shift in context and thus might be the most interesting test case for issues of remakes and remaking. This essay will deal with one such case study, that of a move from Japan to Hong Kong: specifically *Crazed Fruit (Kurutta kajitsu*, 1956) / *Summer Heat (Kuang lian shi*, 1968). In fact, a number of early instances of this sort of transnational remake can be found in the Hong Kong cinema of the 1960s. In its attempts to modernise its product and capture a young, restless audience, Hong Kong hired a handful of Japanese directors. One such director was Inoue Umetsugu, who remade a small number of his films at the start of his career in Hong Kong at the newly dominant Shaw Brothers studio. His *Hong Kong Nocturne (Xiang jiang hua yue ye)* of 1967 was a remake of his Japanese *The Night I Want to Dance (Odoritai yoru*, 1963) made at Shochiku's famed Ofuna Studio. His equally popular *Hong Kong Rhapsody (Hua yue liang xia)* in 1968 was a remake of *Jazz on Parade 1954 nen: Tokyo Cinderalla musume* (1954) for Shin Toho. Inoue's most important Japanese film was undoubtedly *Man Who Causes a Storm (Arashi o yobu otoko*, 1957), made in the wake of the *taiyozoku* (sun tribe) films at Nikkatsu, and it is no surprise that it was remade in Hong Kong, this time as *King Drummer (Qing chun gu wang*, 1967). In all, Inoue made seventeen films at Shaws, by far the most of any Japanese director.

Another Japanese director lured to Hong Kong was Nakahira Ko. Though hardly as significant as Inoue in Japan, he had directed *Crazed Fruit (Kurutta kajitsu)* in 1956, an immediate sensation, part of Nikkatsu's *taiyozoku* cycle and a vehicle for emerging youth superstar Ishihara Yujiro. Nakahira would stay at Nikkatsu over the next decade, making basically programme pictures with Nikkatsu stars like Japanese-Hawaiian comedian Frankie Sakai or Watari Tetsuya, the last of Nikkatsu's 'Diamond Line' of male stars. But it was certainly *Crazed Fruit* which made his reputation and which, seen today, is both the quintessential and most entertaining of the *taiyozoku* films. Characterised as containing 'jazz, sex, dancing, fast cars, cool clothes and indifference to parents, teachers and the law' (Davis and Yeh 2003: 260), the sun tribe films were meant to both outrage the older generation and chastise the younger. *Crazed Fruit* star Ishihara Yujiro shot to fame in the film that lent its name to the *taiyozoku* cycle: *Season of the Sun* (*Taiyo no kisetsu*, 1956). *Season* was released in May of 1956; *Crazed Fruit*, already in production, was released a mere two months later and allowed the sun tribe cycle to enter the history books.

It is common to say that Ishihara Yujiro was often likened to Elvis Presley and James Dean. Maybe so. Yet Presley did not break out of his regional stardom until early in 1956; his famous appearance on the *Ed Sullivan Show* was in September of that year, when both *Season* and *Crazed Fruit* had already been released. Similarly, Presley's film debut *Love Me Tender* was released in November of 1956. Even his singles like 'Hound Dog' and 'Heartbreak Hotel' that shot to the top of the charts appeared in 1956. Though Presley was certainly famous before 1956, it is unlikely that *Season of the Sun* and *Crazed Fruit* author Ishihara Shintaro had Elvis in mind for his model *taiyozoku* youths or that Nikkatsu modelled Ishihara Yujiro on him. As for James Dean, his *Rebel Without a Cause* appeared in the USA in October 1955, while *East of Eden* had appeared the previous spring. It is true that Dean became a cult figure in Japan in 1956 and that Ishihara was compared to him and Marlon Brando (see Raine n.d.). For Isolde Standish, the sibling rivalry of *Crazed Fruit* is derived from *East of Eden* (Standish 2005: 228). (How much actual influence Steinbeck's 1952 novel, translated into Japanese in 1955, could have had on Ishihara Shintaro is debatable.) Though Ishihara Yujiro was compared to the American rebel-icons of Dean and Brando at the time of the release of *Crazed Fruit*, it is a comparison that is more *retrospectively* applied. In other words, with *Season of the Sun* and *Crazed Fruit* already in release, critics could slot the new star into a global pattern of rebellious youth. His status as an iconic youth-rebel figure comparable to Elvis Presley came shortly after the *taiyozoku* films. These facts render Ishihara's rebellious youth as specifically Japanese at that moment of the film's release, and only later would Nikkatsu attempt to parlay his particular looks and persona into comparison with the American stars.

America occupies, as it were, a kind of pride of place in the film itself; if not necessarily a major one, then certainly one not to be ignored. As Yiman Wang has it, 'The fact that the wealthy Frank, who is also the only character with an English name due to his mixed heritage (an allusion to the American occupation of the postwar Japan), lends his house as the Taiyozoku gathering place crystallizes the ambivalent US–Japan relationship in the Cold War era' (2010: 83). Frank's mixed heritage may perhaps be an allusion to the American Occupation, but the twenty-one-year-old actor, Okada Masumi, who plays him was obviously born before both the Occupation and the war.

He was, in fact, of Japanese and Danish heritage, born in Paris in 1935. His character here is indeed bi-racial: his mother is American. And American allusions are clear: his friends joke with him at one point, 'Yankee Go Home!' At another, a waiter in a Yokohama nightclub mistakes him for an American and addresses him in English (which Frank speaks on a number of occasions). But it is Eri's (Kitahara Mie's) American husband (Harold Conway) who most clearly highlights the burgeoning resentment of America after the Occupation – a resentment that novelist Ishihara Shintaro would carry forward into the 1980s, most significantly with his famous 1989 essay 'The Japan That Can Say No: Why Japan Will Be First Among Equals' ('*No' to ieru Nihon*) and also his political career as a leading conservative. We never learn why Eri married this older, white American, nor when. We imagine an economic underpinning to the marriage: he has a car and a rather luxurious two-storey home. We also see another young woman and an older, white man with Eri and her husband at one point. Of course there is an irony here: the sun tribe brothers Natsuhisa (Ishihara Yujiro) and Haruji (Tsugawa Masahiko) are also quite well-to-do, or, at least their parents are. So it isn't economic competition that they resent, but rather, the man's being an American and, perhaps, in this early instance of the generation gap, older.

For all that, the film is not precisely political, and whatever its politics they are rather inchoate. More than its politics, then, the film marks a real break with traditional Japanese cinematic culture in its style, seen particularly nicely in one of the moments where its 'politics' meets its form. The sequence within the first scene in Frank's home begins with an extreme close-up of Natsuhisa as he proclaims: 'Fancy words and old ways don't cut it now.' Then a close-up of another youth: 'Listen to our professors, always spouting the same drivel.' This is followed by a close-up of another boy rejecting the teaching of a famous economics professor, concluding: 'Chasing rainbows with the Soviets and Red China next door.' Natsuhisa, then, 'Look what the older generation tries to sell us. You find anything exciting in that?' The second youth then exclaims: 'I've given up trying. We'll find our own way to live.' Haruji is unconvinced by their vague arguments, saying, 'You guys have no idea what you want to do. They call people like you the Sun Tribe. I'm not gonna live like that.' But when questioned by his brother, Haruji has no alternative to suggest. When Frank's new girlfriend, Michiko, exclaims 'We live in boring times', Natsuhisa agrees and says they make boredom their credo.

In this slightly more than one-minute interlude, with an average shot length of 4.5 seconds (about half that of a typical Japanese film of the period and a little bit faster than the rest of the film itself) Nakahira breaks down the leisurely and picturesque style so common in Japanese cinema. The ragged editing combines interestingly with a kind of noir lighting, with the youths' faces partly in shadow and filmed from slightly canted angles. This overt announcement of the youths' boredom and alienation does seem to recall *Rebel Without a Cause* (released in Japan in 1956), but is a far cry from the Technicolor and cinemascope of the high-budget American production. Indeed, as Michael Raine notes, the entire film utilises an impressionistic, elliptical style that takes advantage of location shooting and perhaps recalls Ingmar Bergman's controversial *Summer with Monika* (1953) with its style and theme of youthful sexual desire (Raine n.d.).

Also recalling noir, at least for some, is the idea that Eri is something of a femme fatale. Standish calls her a 'sultry, noir-like heroine' (2005: 228). Standish relates the film's ambiguous image of Eri to the granting of political and legal autonomy to women under the aegis of the post-war constitution. Eri's marriage and her affairs with both brothers is clearly a transgression of established gender boundaries (228). Indeed, Eri is first seen some three and a half minutes into the film when, in a reversal of typical male chivalry, Haruji drops his handkerchief and she picks it up and hands it to him. Haruji is clearly immediately smitten, but Eri walks out of frame at the ticket-taker's turnstile. Haruji talks about her as the boys ride in the motorboat (which is named, in English, 'Sun-Season', recalling both *taiyozoku*/sun tribe and the earlier Nikkatsu *taiyozoku* film, *Season of the Sun*), thus reminding us of her and hinting at her later importance. Of course, the later importance of the speedboat is also noteworthy.

Eri is next seen some eleven minutes later, swimming far out in the bay, in a moment which foreshadows the film's ending: Eri swimming far out at sea and Haruji in the motorboat. It turns out that Eri, whose name the boys do not yet know, is a bit of a thrill-seeker herself, choosing to swim far from shore. Her sexuality is immediately apparent when she takes off her swimming cap and shakes out her long hair as she climbs into the boat. She is also very vague about where she lives, thus imbuing her with an air of mystery.

Haruji next sees Eri very briefly at the Kamakura train station in the company of a much older American man along with another couple featuring an older American man and a young Japanese woman. It is perhaps needless to say that both of the young women are dressed in Western clothing: no kimonos in this film. Eri does not board the train with the other three, telling Haruji that those people were a friend, her husband, and his friend. Of course, as it turns out she is lying to him, the first instance of her duplicity. As with a classic femme fatale, we wonder if she is telling the truth when she claims to Natsuhisa that Haruji makes her feel innocent again; and that at age twenty, though she is already married, she is only now having her 'flings' (though Haruji is no fling). She gets something wicked and dark in her eyes when she is with Natsuhisa and at those moments the young and beautiful Kitahara Mie – who would retire from acting in 1960 upon her marriage to Ishihara Yujiro – does indeed seem the duplicitous deadly woman.

If we have concentrated on Eri, more than the brothers, that should not disguise the fact that it is unquestionably the case that the film belongs to the two brothers, and for most commentators Ishihara's character of Natsuhisa, in particular. Raine interestingly notes that it was Ishihara Shintaro, author of the early *taiyozoku* novels on which the films were based, who came to represent a new image of masculinity, a specifically post-war masculinity that included a sportsman's athletic body, a love of thrills and a hairstyle that became all the rage. And it was Ishihara Yujiro who completely embodied this image in the film. Again, it is because of Yujiro's subsequent superstardom – embodying an image closer to Elvis Presley than Brando or Dean – that readings of the film concentrate on him. In fact, the real centre of the film – its moral compass, albeit one that ultimately goes off course – is Tsugawa Masahiko's Haruji.

Tsugawa is certainly the most prolific star in post-war Japanese cinema (over two hundred film and television appearances) and among the most respected. He would go on to work with directors such as Kinoshita Keisuke, Oshima Nagisa, Yoshida Yoshishige, Makino Masahiro and Yamamoto Satsuo, all the way to Itami Juzo in the contemporary era. Yet he never achieved the role of icon. Nevertheless, it is a mistake to read the film through the lens of Ishihara Yujiro, for that misses an essential conservatism in the film's image of its raw youth. Though the film, along with others of the short-lived *taiyozoku* cycle, was a *succès de scandale*, its subscription to Japanese mainstream ideals of monogamy should not be forgotten. Even Natsuhisa falls in love with Eri and asks her to forsake both her husband and Haruji in favour of him. Haruji's killing of Eri and Natsuhisa, running them over with the Sun-Season motorboat, is like some kind of moral retribution recalling the old Hays Code of Classical Hollywood. Thus, for all its notoriety, we must acknowledge that it is the film's experimental, raw style and the stylings of Ishihara Yujiro that make it so memorable and so powerful, less so its image of the sun tribe.

The brilliance of *Crazed Fruit* belies the ordinariness of Nakahira's other films, and perhaps it was this career dead-end that led him to Hong Kong. Although the modernisation process which Shaws imported Japanese and other foreign talent to undertake mostly revolved around technical issues like colour and cinemascope photography, as well as production practices that were more budget-conscious (see Davis and Yeh 2003: 258–9), Nakahira also brought a more modern sensibility to the action film. Indeed, his first effort at Shaws was *Inter-Pol* (1967), a deliberate knock-off of James Bond-style thrillers (the film's Chinese title translates as *Special Agent 009*). Indeed three of his four films for Shaws, all under the name of Yeung Shu-hei, and all with cinematography by the Japanese Nishimoto Tadashi under the pseudonym of He Lanshan, are slick, stylish and satisfying entertainments, very much like his programme efforts at Nikkatsu. His one attempt to break out of the genre mode was with *Summer Heat* (*Kuang lian shi*) in 1968, his remake of *Crazed*

Fruit, called by Chuck Stephens a 'long-forgotten potboiler ... starring Shaw Eurasian ingénue Jenny Hu' (Stephens n.d.).

To understand the significant differences between the two films one could undertake a scene-by-scene or even shot-by-shot analysis. Such an endeavour would not be without interest, given the number of scenes, amount of dialogue and even individual shots that are virtually the same. With that in mind it is interesting how thoroughly inferior the Hong Kong version is. Wang chalks this up to a lack of socio-political context, unlike the Japanese original which grounded itself in the *taiyozoku* phenomenon. She notes that it has been argued that many of the Japanese directors imported by Shaws tended to recycle their Japanese productions without showing explicit interest in localising them in Hong Kong. Consequently, their remakes bear few identifiable traces of Hong Kong specificity (2010: 71). Instead,

> from the Hong Kong producer's perspective, a film like *Crazed Fruit* could be distilled into just an entertaining film about the luxurious, wild life of a group of nihilist and self-destructive young people – a sensational story that could be set in any post-war 'modern' city. As a result, the temporal-geographical specificity of Japan was inadvertently or deliberately dropped, without being replaced by or transferred into certain Hong Kong-specific qualities. (75–6)

For Wang this is at the crux of the film's problems, since in 1968, when the film was made, Hong Kong was experiencing intense political turbulence owing to the expansion of the Cultural Revolution in mainland China. She asks:

> What is the connection, if any, between the invisible historical and political background and the apparently apolitical film? How did the film manage to occlude that significant background? How do we understand the negative inscription of politics? First, it is important to note that depoliticization was not an exception, but a norm in Hong Kong cinema from that era. In this sense, *Summer Heat*'s omission of political turmoil in its immediate context is exemplary of the overall cultural politics of filmmaking in the late 1960s Hong Kong. (85)

It is indeed the case that Hong Kong cinema in this period (and well into the 1980s) was distinctly apolitical, or at least, overtly apolitical. One could argue that all those wonderful Ming vs Qing stories in the martial arts films have an allegorical dimension to them regarding legitimate leadership as regards both the Communists and the Colonialists. Still, it is the case that the modern stories had even less obvious politics underlying them than the period action spectaculars. This apolitical dimension to Hong Kong cinema was one of the few interventions made by the British colonial administration. As Jing Jing Chang notes, the colonial administration did not forbid any one particular genre, but rather content that criticised the colonial regime or pitted one party against the other (that is, KMT vs CCP) on screen (2011: 106).

I do not ascribe the failure of *Summer Heat* to its lack of politics or concrete context, but to its portrayals of the characters and to certain structural weaknesses. But before enumerating upon those, it is worth returning to the contexts in which the film was made, if only to see how it does, at least in part, highlight important social issues of the moment while at the same time pulling back from them.

Unlike in Japan, where the fact that few youths were born into the luxuries of the *taiyozoku* did not lead to social protests (or a lack of box office for the films of the cycle), Hong Kong had serious social problems that often spilled out into the streets. From the mid-1950s onward, the colonial authorities worried about social discord. As Jing Jing Chang puts it, 'despite Hong Kong's urban development, youths born and raised in the colony continued to be disenfranchised and did not all reap the benefits of Hong Kong's modernized growth' (2011: 133). For historian Poshek Fu:

> The advent of industrial capitalism gave rise to a 'revolution of expectations' among the masses, who became increasingly captivated by the wider availability and spectacular display (in department stores and advertisements) of consumer goods, by the dazzling circulation of images and bodies in shopping areas, and by the marketplace of new ideas (through the popular press, radio broadcasts and the new medium of television). (2000: 74)

Unequal access to consumer goods and rising prices often led to intense demonstrations and labour unrest. For instance, in April 1966 peaceful demonstrations turned to rioting over the proposed increase in the fare for the Star Ferry. And just before *Summer Heat* went into production there were riots that were sparked by a labour dispute in April 1967 at the Hong Kong Artificial Flower Works factory in San Po Kong, Kowloon, owned by the entrepreneur Li Ka-shing (now one of Hong Kong's richest men). The dispute broke out into riots in May 1967, egged on by local Communists who supported the Cultural Revolution on the mainland. These riots and ongoing demonstrations lasted eight months, and led to fifty-one deaths, 800 injuries, the arrests of 5,000 people, and millions of dollars' worth of damage to property and economic damage (Chang 2011: 150–1).

Led primarily by young people, the riots worried the British and their Chinese supporters, who couched the demonstrations as the work of Communists or lazy, misguided youth. Kenneth Fung Ping-fan (who would be knighted by the

Queen in 1971), son of the founder of the Bank of East Asia and a prominent businessman and government adviser, understood the youth problem as a generation gap. He was quoted as saying, 'unlike their hard-working, war-weary parents, [youth are] alienated, restless, antisocial, melancholic, spoiled and weak-willed' (Fu 2000: 76). It was at this time that a 'problem-youth' genre arose in Hong Kong cinema. But it was not the product of the dominant, high-budget Mandarin-dialect cinema that latched on to problem youth. It was the low-budget, perpetually under-funded, female-dominated, youth-oriented Cantonese cinema.

The first of these Cantonese-dialect problem-youth films is often ascribed to director Wong Yiu, whose 1966 melodramatic romance *Girls Are Flowers* (*Goneung sap baat yat do fa*) was a huge box-office success (Fu 2000: 81). The film starred two of the Cantonese cinema's brightest young women, Connie Chan Po-Chu and Nancy Sit Ka-yin. Although Chan would continue to make martial arts films by the score, she interspersed them with a number of contemporary youth films, such as the drama *Forget Not Tonight* (1966), the rock 'n' roll musical *Colorful Youth* (1966) and the hybrid melodrama-musical *Waste Not our Youth* (1967). The latter film is often mentioned as part of the problem-youth cycle, and it clearly looks forward to a film like *Summer Heat* with its focus on upper-middle-class youth, starring Connie Chan as a spoiled rich brat whose antics lead to her amnesia. One critic, waxing both nostalgic and perceptive, writes of the youth movies: 'in the sixties, the cinema became young as if overnight. The women were no longer maternal but slick incarnations of lust' (Chang 1996: 87). This cycle of films would culminate in one of the truly great works of the Cantonese cinema, *The Teddy Girls* (*Fei lui jing chuen*), directed by the great Patrick Lung Kong in 1969, and featuring young superstar Josephine Siao Fong-fong along with Nancy Sit.

Though it is debatable just how much, if any, influence the Cantonese cinema exerted upon the more successful Mandarin industry, it is also probably not a coincidence that Shaws took up the mantle of 'youth' just at the time of the problem-youth films. It is probably a coincidence that the year 1966, which saw the release of *Girls are Flowers*, also saw the film debut of Jenny Hu Yan-ni (b. 1946). If so, it was a happy coincidence for Shaws. In their switch to younger female stars, then twenty-year-old Jenny Hu made her film debut in 1966 with the melodrama with music, *Till the End of Time*. They paired her with young, rising star Lily Ho Li-li (b. 1946, eleven months younger than Jenny Hu) and with their veteran male star Peter Chen Ho (1931–70). The film was a huge hit and Jenny an immediate sensation. With her exotic good looks and trim, yet full, figure Jenny represented a young, vibrant kind of beauty. She was the bi-racial offspring of a Chinese father and a German mother and this fact was part of her brand. She followed her debut the next year with *Madam Slender Plum*, a remake of *Mildred Pierce* (1945) in which

Jenny played, against type, the spoiled, wicked older daughter. *Black Falcon*, a James Bond-style adventure with Jenny as 'the Bond girl', and *Four Sisters*, which co-starred Essie Lin Cha (b. 1947) and, unusually, Patrina Fung Bo-bo (b. 1953), one of the Seven Princesses of the Cantonese Cinema (along with other stars like Connie Chan, Josephine Siao and Nancy Sit), followed quickly apace. Of course, Shaws were also developing a new generation of young male stars at this same time. These young men – like Jimmy Wang Yu, Lo Lieh, David Chiang, Chen Kuan-tai and Ti Lung – would come to dominate the box office for the next decade and a half with the exception of new, young female star Cheng Pei-pei (b. 1946). It was also at this time that Shaws, in their effort to lock up the Hong Kong market and further expand throughout the rest of Asia and, it was hoped, into the USA and Europe, brought in the Japanese directors, who would include Nakahira Ko.

In *Summer Heat* we are presented with a colour and cinemascope version of the black-and-white, academy ratio *Crazed Fruit*. Wang notes the homology between the nearness of the bay/ocean to Tokyo and Hong Kong. Much of *Crazed Fruit* was shot in Hayama, a bedroom community to Tokyo and Yokohama, the prefectural capital of Kanagawa where Hayama is located. In turn, *Summer Heat* takes place in Stanley, located on Hong Kong Island's south coast. But as Wang discovered, some of *Summer Heat* was actually shot in Hayama, probably much of the swimming and boating scenes given the calmer waters off Japan's east coast (2010: 73). Simply put: 'the fact that both Japan and Hong Kong sit on the edge of the Asian landmass makes the decision to remake the island-and-ocean-based film in Hong Kong a felicitous and natural move' (74).

Structurally the films are similar as well: older brother David is the film's equivalent to Natsuhisa; younger brother Xiaochun mirrors Haruji; Judy (Jenny Hu) is the femme fatale equivalent of Eri; the brothers come from a well-to-do family; Judy is married to an older man; and Peter does the honours of mirroring Frank, his home and sailboat central to the film's action. Other similarities concern the party scene where David sings a song and dances with Judy, goes to Judy's home to have sex with her, and intercepts the letter to Xiaochun and takes off with her in the sailboat. Judy, like Eri, is hardly present throughout the first third of the film, but when she begins her affair with Xiaochun she becomes increasingly important. And, of course, there is the murderous, apocalyptic ending. No doubt it was more than mere entertainment value that inspired Shaws and Nakahira to remake *Crazed Fruit*.

Given, then, the basic similarities between *Crazed Fruit* and *Summer Heat*, it seems hard to argue that some of the problem-youth context is absent from the Hong Kong version. The boys in the Chinese film gamble, waste time, chase girls, go to nightclubs and parties, drive motorboats and sailboats and engage in premarital sex, all to the horrors of the older generation. Sexual laxity is what brings about the similarly apocalyptic ending of the Hong Kong film.

There are two moments in the film when the social context seems clearly about to appear. The first is when Xiaochun, like Haruji before him, questions why his brother and his friends don't spend their time more profitably. 'You could do something else', he exclaims. 'You're just idling away.' When his brother begins to defend their lifestyle, we think we are in for a repeat of that wonderful, perceptive montage: that litany of complaints and castigations. Instead, the young woman says immediately after that that she is hungry, and the scene cuts to a dinner. For Wang this (drastic) alteration of the equivalent scene in the Hong Kong film 'reiterates the youth ennui without contextualizing it'. As a result, youth ennui is figured as a categorical concept independent of socio-cultural and political conditions, which implies that young people indulge in boredom out of inexplicable compulsion (2010: 84). To audiences at the time, however, the boredom of youth and their rebelliousness, seen in recent demonstrations and riots, may have been one of those extra-textual dimensions unnecessary to be made explicit in the film. This failure to reproduce the Japanese scene in its entirety may also have something to do with the more conservative Shaw Brothers and the Confucian ideology which appears in so many of their films. An important component in the Japanese original was the lack of respect for the older generation, in particular their economics professor and, implicitly, their parents. No such disrespect could quite be permitted at Shaws.

Another moment in the film when the social context comes to the fore is more subtle, but here one has to rely not on the subtitles (mediocre at best throughout the film) but on the actual dialogue. Xiaochun's mother warns him not to be like his brother or his brother's friends, claiming, as the subtitles have it, that they are 'hooligans'. This is a reasonable translation, but it is important to note that what she actually says in the dialogue is not to act like 'Ah Fei'. (The Chinese character 'Fei' is the same one as is used in the Chinese title of The Teddy Girls.) The term 'Ah Fei' first came into use in Shanghai in the early twentieth century to describe hooligans or bullies. It developed a different layer of meaning in the later Hong Kong context when massive numbers of Mainland Chinese, among whom were many Shanghainese, flooded Hong Kong in the late 1940s and took the word with them to describe a young man who is rebellious, restless, or even anti-establishment. The 'Ah' has no specific meaning but is often prefixed to a monosyllabic first name to make it a diminutive or to substitute for the first character in a two-character name. More than that, 'Ah Fei' grounds its historical moment. This is why, for instance, Wong Kar-wai can use the title Ah Fei zing zyun (The True Story of Ah Fei) for his 1960-set film known in English as Days of Being Wild (1990). If we lose 'Ah Fei' in the subtitles then we lose a bit of the 1960s context and the specifically Hong Kong terminology.

There are other changes that impact on the film's effectiveness as drama. For instance, the subtle role-reversal when Eri picks up Haruji's handkerchief and returns it to him in her introductory scene is completely absent from the remake. Instead, Xiaochun glimpses Judy walking through a restaurant in a quite bucolic Sha Tin (a far cry from this shopping and transportation hub of the New Territories today). She gets into her car and, smitten by her beauty, Xiaochun, along with his brother David, follows her in their car. This makes Xiaochun a kind of aggressor, taking an active role in pursuit, instead of the more passive Haruji of the original. More than that, every instance of David's sexual relations with Judy are close to, if not outright, sexual assault. (By today's standards his actions would certainly and unambiguously qualify as rape.) Judy, on the other hand, is far less the femme fatale. It is true that she tells David that she has had affairs before, but there is nothing of that wicked glint in her eyes when she is with him. It is even questionable if she has real feelings for David.

Also changed, and for the worse, is the racial dimension of both Judy's husband and the character of Peter (the counterpart of Frank). Eri's older husband is a white American; Judy's older husband is a Chinese-American. Frank is bi-racial: half American. Peter is Hong Kong Chinese. The bi-racial character is Judy herself, though nothing is made of that in the film. Even as an extra-textual element, her bi-racial background carries no symbolic weight. With both Peter and Judy's husband having been made Chinese, the anti-American implications of the original have no counterpart. Here, too, it would have been near-impossible to create such an equivalence. Judy would have had to be married not only to an older white man, but to a Brit. Then an implication of the colonisation of Chinese Hong Kong by the British via the white man 'colonising' the Chinese woman could have had some dramatic impact. But no such symbolic imagery could have taken place. Hong Kong cinema of the 1950s and 1960s is notable for the absence of British characters, certainly major ones, let alone negatively symbolic ones. In the universe of the Shaw Brothers it is as if Hong Kong existed in some purely and imaginary Chinese world of its own.

Perhaps the film deserves to be a long-forgotten potboiler as Chuck Stephens claimed. With too many moments cut off before they can properly play out, and the mishandling of certain scenes (for example, we do not see Judy with her husband on the ferry, she only mentions she is with him to Xiaochun), the film fails as drama. Its revelations of problem youth have little vitality or immediacy. This is to say that we can reclaim something of the film's social context, its historical moment, but, unlike with *Crazed Fruit*, little of it bleeds onto the screen. The strictures against criticism of the colonial government and the solidly Confucian ideals of the Shaw Brothers cinema work against whatever politics Nakahira Ko brought to his Nikkatsu *taiyozoku* exposé.

The importance of *Crazed Fruit* to the history of post-war Japanese cinema is in inverse proportion to the little-known remake that is *Summer Heat*. We could simply wonder if self-remakes tend always to be inferior or less significant than their originals. Certainly that is the case with the Ford, Hawks and Walsh films mentioned above. Yet it is also true that a couple of the Umetsugu films he made in Hong Kong are undoubtedly superior and more important for their respective cinemas than their Japanese progenitors. So, too, Nakahira Ko turned his little-known *Hunter's Diary* (*Ryojin nikki*, 1964) into the deliriously stylish *Diary of a Lady Killer* in 1969. As a tentative solution to the problem of the transnational self-remake, we should merely insist that films be taken on a case-by-case basis.

REFERENCES

Chang, Bryan (1996), 'Waste Not Our Youth: My World of Sixties Cantonese Movies', in *The Restless Breed: Cantonese Stars of the Sixties*, The 20th Hong Kong International Film Festival, Hong Kong: Urban Council, pp. 86–8.

Chang, Jing Jing (2011), 'Towards a Local Community: Colonial Politics and Postwar Hong Kong Cinema', Unpublished Ph.D. thesis, University of Illinois.

Davis, D.W. and Emilie Yeh Yueh-yu (2003), 'Inoue at Shaws: The Wellspring of Youth', in Wong Ain-ling (ed.), *The Shaw Screen: A Preliminary Study*, Hong Kong: Hong Kong Film Archive, pp. 255–71.

Fu, Poshek (2000), 'The 1960s: Modernity, Youth Culture and Hong Kong Cantonese Cinema', in Poshek Fu and David Desser (eds), *The Cinema of Hong Kong: History, Arts, Identity*, New York: Cambridge University Press, pp. 71–89.

Raine, Michael (n.d.), 'Imagining a New Japan: The *Taiyozoku* Films', Booklet Criterion Collection DVD *Crazed Fruit* (n.p.).

Standish, Isolde (2005), *A New History of Japanese Cinema: A Century of Narrative Film*, New York: Continuum.

Stephens, Chuck (n.d.), 'Heat Stroke! Japanese Cinema's Season in the Sun', Booklet Criterion Collection DVD *Crazed Fruit* (n.p.).

Wang, Yiman (2010), 'City of Youth, Ocean of Death: Taiyozoku on the Edge of an Island', in James Tweedie and Yomi Braester (eds), *Cinema at the City's Edge: Film and Urban Networks in East Asia*, Hong Kong: Hong Kong University Press, pp. 69–87.

11. REMAKING *FUNNY GAMES*: MICHAEL HANEKE'S CROSS-CULTURAL EXPERIMENT

Kathleen Loock

Over the past decades, Austrian director and screenwriter Michael Haneke has become internationally known for disturbing films that raise questions of morality and seek to systematically undermine viewers' expectations while holding them responsible for the crimes and violence playing out on screen. Haneke scholar Catherine Wheatley has observed that

> the numerous awards and critical acclaim garnered by *La Pianiste* [*The Piano Teacher*, 2001], and ... *Caché* [*Hidden*, 2005], have cemented Haneke's status as one of a new generation of *auteurs* currently leading European cinema, alongside (among others) the Dardenne brothers, Catherine Breillat, Lars von Trier, Gaspar Noé and François Ozon, all of whom have been known to offer dismal – even nihilistic – perspectives on the current state of society. (2009: 14)

Haneke's most recent films, *Das weiße Band* (*The White Ribbon*, 2009) and *Amour* (2012), have earned him an unprecedented number of nominations and awards, among them not only two Palmes d'Or at the Cannes Film Festival and various other European film prizes but, for the first time in his career, also two Golden Globes and one Academy Award for Best Foreign Language Film from juries in the USA. His status as European auteur has been sealed by the overwhelming critical success of *Das weiße Band* and *Amour*, which are, like most Haneke films, transnationally funded and executed projects.

Das weiße Band, a German-language film set in rural Protestant Germany in the years leading up to World War I, deals with a specifically German theme, was shot in Germany, and had a German cast and crew; but it is also a co-production between Germany, Austria, France and Italy. *Amour*, on the other hand, is a French-language film that tells the story of an elderly couple struggling to cope with the slow, agonising death of the wife. Filmed in France, it stars French actors Jean-Louis Trintignant, Emmanuelle Riva and Isabelle Huppert, and has a Franco-German-Austrian production context. Many films made outside the USA (or more precisely: Hollywood) are, of course, transnational co-productions. Unable to compete with Hollywood's high budgets and marketing machine, national film industries in Europe 'pool finances, government subsidies, labour and talent' (Baltruschat 2013: 11) for projects that gain immediate access to the different national markets involved.

Against this background, Haneke's films stand out not only because they move freely between different languages and national cinemas, but also because their narratives often transcend borders despite their local settings and national elements to take on universal meanings. And yet, they can never fully erase questions of national identity and cultural specificity – when prestigious awards are involved, for example. The Austrian Film Commission voiced its discontent that Germany had submitted *Das weiße Band* to the Academy Award competition, and later entered *Amour* into the contest despite its French dialogue (cf. Walker 2009; O'Neil 2012).[1] Haneke himself, who was born in Munich, raised in Austria and is now dividing his time between Vienna and Paris, has made it clear that he is weary of such national appropriations of his work: 'I am not an Austrian director and I am not a French director. I am a director for myself, and anyone who gives me money and lets me do serious work, can claim me for himself – I couldn't care less' (quoted in Müller 2014: 16, my translation). Regardless of Haneke's opinion voiced in interviews, which form part of his eloquent self-fashioning and subtle strategies to channel 'Haneke reception' among scholars and critics (cf. Sannwald 2011: 11),[2] the content of his films and their transnational production contexts complicate their attribution to an Austrian, German or French national cinema, making it, in effect, difficult to describe Haneke's films as any kind of national auteur cinema (Müller 2014: 18).

If debates about nationality (and nationalism) surround Haneke's decidedly transnational director persona as well as his work, which in turn makes pretence at universal validity, they become particularly intriguing in the case of Haneke's film remake *Funny Games US* (2007). The original *Funny Games*, written and directed by Haneke, premiered at the Cannes Film Festival in 1997. After thirty-five years, it was the first Austrian entry to the competition, and brought Haneke international attention. At the same time, the film would be his last exclusively Austrian production to date: as producer Veit Heiduschka told the press at the time, potential foreign partners had backed out because they had found the project too daring (Müller 2014: 152). At the Cannes Film Festival, *Funny Games* shocked and polarised the film-critical community.

The film tells the story of a middle-class couple and their son, who drive with the family dog to their lakeside house. Upon arrival, two seemingly polite young men dressed in shorts, canvas shoes, white sweaters and white gloves show up at their doorstep politely asking for some eggs. But once inside the house, they hold the family hostage, and proceed to terrorise, torture and murder them. Disguised as a commercial family-in-peril horror-thriller, *Funny Games* quickly reveals itself to be a highly manipulative film that departs from familiar generic formulas and conventions. As the perfect holiday turns into the family's worst nightmare, viewers are not only denied graphic scenes of gore and violence (these happen largely off screen) but also a cathartic relief from the tension that builds up as the film progresses. The effects have been widely discussed and analysed by film critics and scholars, as has the fact that Haneke frequently pronounced in interviews that he had intended to address an entirely different – an American – audience when he made the film. He claimed this to be the reason why he decided to direct the shot-by-shot remake *Funny Games US*:

> The first film didn't reach the public I think really ought to see this film . . . So I decided to make it again . . . The original was in German, and English-speaking audiences don't often see subtitled films. When I first envisioned *Funny Games* in the mid-1990s, it was my intention to have an American audience watch the movie. It is a reaction to a certain American cinema, its violence, its naivety, the way American cinema toys with human beings. In many American films, violence is made consumable. But because I made *Funny Games* in German with actors not familiar to US audiences, it didn't get through to the people who most needed to see it. (quoted in Jeffries 2008)

Although he made concessions concerning the language, location and cast of actors in the remake, Haneke meticulously re-created settings and props, and repeated almost every single shot and line of his original film. Yet the critical reception of both films has differed considerably. While 'many European and English-language critics expressed mild forms of outrage along with admiration' for the original *Funny Games* (Koehler 2008: 56), US film critics found the remake 'ugly and pretentious' (Richard Roeper quoted in Price 2010: 43), or they described it as 'a cool, intellectual exercise, as devoid of character and motivation as the two psychos themselves' (Elley 2007: 39), as 'less an experiment than an act of arrogance' (Croce 2008), and as 'even more pointless' than the original film (Elley 2007: 31).

The perceived failure of *Funny Games US* notwithstanding, the film remains an interesting and rare case for inquiries into the processes and workings of film remaking because it qualifies at once as transnational remake, auto-remake, and shot-by-shot remake. As such a multifaceted object of investigation, it not only raises broad theoretical questions surrounding the film remake's position in a wider culture of cinematic recycling and repetition, but also challenges notions of national identity constructions and cultural exchange, of national, transnational and global cinemas, of possible modes of revision and the director's role as auteur. Along these lines, this chapter extends the idea that *Funny Games* is founded on the programmatic subversion of genre conventions and ingrained responses to the mechanisms of remaking a film in a different cultural context, arguing that Haneke experimented with the meaning of the transnational remake itself.

Against the common allegation that US remakes of foreign films are a form of cultural imperialism, Haneke used Hollywood connections in order to have a wider distribution and to position his art-house film within the US entertainment culture. At the same time, he did not adapt *Funny Games* to the American cultural context, as is typically expected of transnational remakes, but placed virtually the same film into a different cultural environment. This refusal distinguishes Haneke from other European directors like George Sluizer, for example, who remade his own Dutch film *Spoorloos* (1988) according to Hollywood demands. Haneke was instead compared to Alfred Hitchcock, an auteur filmmaker obsessed with revising his earlier work, including his 1934 thriller *The Man Who Knew Too Much*, which he remade as a Hollywood movie in 1956, and to Gus Van Sant, whose painstakingly exact shot-by-shot remake of *Psycho* (1960) was met with hostility by Hitchcock fans, critics and academics upon its release in 1998.

TRANSNATIONAL REMAKES AND HOLLYWOOD ENDINGS

Lucy Mazdon has observed that 'however precarious definitions of the "nation" and of "national cinemas" may be, films can be seen to emerge from, and to enter into debate with, specific national constructions' (2000: 68–9). Transnational film remakes circulate in a global film industry which takes for granted that 'different cinemas establish particular cultural identities via narrative and subject matter, genre and form, stars, industrial conventions and so on' (2000: 69). Such discursive constructions of national identities, cinematic traditions and film cultures have routinely served film critics to condemn Hollywood remakes as artistically inferior copies, products of America's unrestrained commercialism and cultural imperialism. It has also enabled them to compile an 'informal set of import rules' (Edelstein 2001: 20) that sheds light on the transformations generally associated with American makeovers of European films.

In a search for a good story with universal appeal and potential in the global marketplace, Hollywood has repeatedly turned to artistically and commercially successful European films. Transnational remakes are attractive because they are cost-effective: the rights to the story are often available for a modest sum, and there is no need for lengthy and costly script development. Unlike old Hollywood movies that are also remade on a regular basis, even recently released European films are often unknown to audiences in the USA (or countries outside the original home market). As Audrey Farolino put it in the *New York Post*, film studios 'figure nobody saw [these movies], and, relatively speaking, they are right' (1993: 27). Foreign films have limited distribution, and when they reach US cinemas they are generally associated with art house and subtitles – two things the average American moviegoer is said to avoid when looking for entertainment (27). Yet, 'the fact that it's foreign in its origin does not necessarily mean that it's a foreign concept', ICM's Ken Kamins explains (quoted in Lyons 2002: 24).

In theory, then, remakes based on successful European films, featuring well-known American stars and profiting from the efficiency of Hollywood's marketing machine and global distribution practices, promise to be sure-fire hits at the box office. Yet more than one transnational remake cycle has proven that the commercial potential of a remade foreign film remains unpredictable – unlike that of a sequel to a US original, for instance (cf. Williams and Mørk 1993: 8). Some critics have referred to this state of uncertainty as Hollywood's 'foreign-lingo bingo' (Lyons 2002: 24); others have attributed failures to the studios' tendency to ignore cultural differences. Films like *Profumo di donna* (1974, remade as *Scent of a Woman*, 1992), *La femme Nikita* (1990; remade as *Point of No Return*, 1993), *Spoorloos* (1988; remade as *The Vanishing*, 1993), *Der Himmel über Berlin* (1987; remade as *City of Angels*, 1998), *Abre los ojos* (1997; remade as *Vanilla Sky*, 2001) or *Insomnia* (1997; remade in 2002) 'have a way of getting garbled in the translation', as Farolino puts it (1993: 27).

Foreign films generally undergo a substantial makeover when they are remade in Hollywood and adapted to appeal to US audiences and their specific viewing habits. Ginette Vincendeau has therefore argued that transnational remakes 'throw into relief the notion of national identity in cinema. What constitutes a story, how stars are framed and how gender is constructed all undergo considerable change as they cross the Atlantic – despite a seeming similarity of plot' (1993: 23). According to her, US cinematic tradition privileges 'clear-cut motivation, both of causality (no loose ends) and character (good *or* evil)', whereas European auteur cinema favours 'ambiguity' (23). Hence, narratives are usually streamlined and 'morally recalibrated' (Price 2010: 43) in the remaking process; the films are also shot and edited differently, opting for shot/reverse shot constructions and the build-up of scenes from general shot to close-up, as well as faster pacing and continuity editing that prevents the viewers' temporal disorientation (cf. Vincendeau 1993: 24; Edelstein 2001: 20).[3] Most notably, open endings of European predecessors are often eliminated in the remakes, and 'Hollywood screenwriters [are] engaged in rewriting foreign films to cross every t and dot every i, filling in the blanks of a character's back story and making sure his actions are overtly motivated' (Stuart 2002: D18). This kind of clarity and direct storytelling appeals to American audiences, while it is harder for them to relate to more experimental European films that refuse to spell everything out (cf. Beale 1992: 61). Yet, ultimately, Hollywood's 'concern for thoroughness also results in movies that are generally more bloated and prolix than the originals', as Jan Stuart notes (2002: D18).

Thus, *Point of No Return* not only provides more background information about its heroine (Jane Fonda), but also changes the ending of the French original, in which junkie turned government-sponsored assassin Nikita (Anne Parillaud) simply disappears. Because 'the last third of the original seemed confusing, and featured an open-ended finale [considered] a no-no in American films', screenwriter Robert Getchell, who worked for Warner on the US version, changed the script into a 'really seamless story' (Beale 1992: 61). Similarly, *The Vanishing* streamlines its source material and resolves questions that were left unanswered in the Franco-Dutch original *Spoorloos*. The US version of the thriller about the disappearance of a young woman and her partner's obsessive search for her, which finally brings him face to face with the abductor, restructures the narrative of the entire film for the sake of temporal linearity, cuts a symbol-laden dream sequence which anticipates the doom that befalls the couple, and adds an upbeat ending in which the main character, after being buried alive, is now saved by his new girlfriend and the killer no longer goes unpunished. Even though critics regarded *The Vanishing* as 'a textbook case of Hollywood ruining an excellent picture by stomping on its subtlety' (Farolino 1993: 27), it might in fact come across as 'the more emotionally gratifying of the two [films]' or as 'more complete' (Stuart 2002: D18) – just like the US version of the psychological thriller *Insomnia* about sleep-deprived detective Will Dormer (Al Pacino), who is sent to a small Alaskan town to investigate the murder of a teenage girl. Where police inspector Jonas Engström (Stellan Skarsgård) in the Norwegian original commits a number of moral transgressions and gets away with them after the case is closed, the remake tones down the cop's disturbing anti-heroism, presents palpable reasons for his shocking behaviour, and lets him die in the end. 'True to the penitential bylaws that have governed the Hollywood ending since time immemorial', Stuart writes, 'Dormer redeems himself and pays for his sins, all in the closing seconds' (D18).

In contrast to these examples, *Funny Game US* resists most of the changes that European films tend to undergo when they get the Hollywood treatment. According to the quotation above, Haneke was well aware that English-speaking audiences would be less likely to see the German-language original, set in Austria and starring Susanne Lothar (Anna) and Ulrich Mühe (Georg), than the remake, set in the USA and featuring familiar actors Naomi Watts (Ann) and Tim Roth (George). In that sense, then, Haneke did play by Hollywood's 'import rules' (Edelstein 2001: 20) when he made concessions concerning the remake's language, location and cast of actors. Yet these remain the most striking changes, whereas the bleak finale of the original is still the same in *Funny Games US* and not replaced by a Hollywood ending.

Once the two strangers, who call themselves Peter and Paul, are inside the family's lakeside house, they bet whether Ann/a, Georg/e and their son Georgie will still be alive by 9.00 a.m. the next morning, and start to 'play' sadistic versions of children's games with them – in the name of entertainment, as they stress repeatedly. First, Ann/a has to find the body of the family dog the two have killed with Georg/e's golf club in a game of hot-and-cold. Then, Georgie escapes to the neighbours' house, only to find that Peter and Paul had been there earlier and murdered the entire family. Paul follows Georgie pretending to play hide-and-seek and brings him back, and Peter finally shoots him after he is 'it' in a counting-out rhyme. At one point, Ann/a manages to grab the shotgun and kill Peter. But this cathartic moment of bloodlust and vengeful satisfaction which Haneke has so cannily provoked is immediately taken away from the viewers when Paul picks up a remote control to rewind and replay the scene, this time preventing Ann/a from reaching the gun. Ann/a's attempt to flee from the house and look for help fails, and in the end Peter and Paul kill Georg/e, take Ann/a bound and gagged out on the family boat to almost casually push her off the side and let her drown in the water. In the final scene, the two murderers stop at another lakeside house, get out of the boat, knock at the door and ask for eggs, apparently continuing their horrible killing spree without hindrance.[4]

What is so disheartening about the remake is that it does not even remotely engage with the conventions of US filmmaking and the Hollywood ending in particular. In the same manner in which Haneke 'cheats' his audience by simply rewinding and replaying the table-turning shotgun scene, he deliberately undermines viewer expectations when ignoring the industry-wide promoted need for US-style redemption as well as the fact that it 'is a very American impulse . . . to have questions resolved in a tidy, rational manner – particularly grey-area questions like why bad things happen to good people' (Stuart 2002: D18). There is no discernible motivation behind Peter and Paul's torturous games – the characters even ridicule this notion by giving all kinds of reasons (divorced parents, homosexuality, drug addiction, incest, etc.) and immediately revealing everything they say to be lies – and, unlike in *The Vanishing*, for instance, the ending is nowhere close to 'how we wished that the original had turned out' (Edelstein 2001: 20). Haneke's refusal to play by the rules outraged many critics who had seen the original; they found their initial frustration with the film and their feeling of having been manipulated by the director amplified after watching the remake. 'Michael Haneke is a clever guy', Fernando F. Croce wrote in *Slant Magazine*. 'I promised myself I'd never revisit his 1997 film *Funny Games*, yet he's tricked me into doing just that by remaking it, shot by agonizing shot' (2008).

Considering the history of transnational remakes and Hollywood's preference for the 'unrealistically happy, upbeat, and optimistic [ending, which] ultimately upholds the social order', Leland Monk argues that 'it is quite remarkable that the film actually got made, as . . . Haneke (like Peter and Paul with the golf club, shotgun and sailboat) expertly wields the expensive equipment of the Hollywood players, those producers of the Hollywood state-of-mind, against them' (2010: 433). This was, in fact, Haneke's declared intention: *Funny Games* was conceived as an assault on spectacles of violence, exposing (just like other Haneke films) the complicit role of the film industry and mass media in transforming violence into a commodity. By denying his audience graphic scenes of gore and violence and focusing on the prolonged suffering of the victims, Haneke makes the involuntary complicity of the viewers with the perpetrators transparent. As Croce (2008) puts it, 'our own supposed hunger for brutal thrills is somehow responsible for willing the monsters into being', which in turn foregrounds Haneke's argument that violence can never (or rather should never) be made consumable. That *Funny Games US* is a 'carbon copy' of the original arguably strengthens Haneke's point; that the film was released without the typical changes made to foreign fare was only possible because Haneke himself directed the US version as a virtually identical, shot-by-shot remake and because he succeeded in asserting authorial control over the final product.

Auto-remakes and Authorial Control

Steven Jay Schneider has pointed out that 'it is quite unusual for a director to remake his own film', and that 'it is even more unusual for a non-American director to remake his own foreign film in the States, the second time as a Hollywood production' (2002). For film studios, transnational remaking means to transform a foreign movie into something that will appeal to US (and in extension, global) audiences. Accordingly, foreign filmmakers are not the first choice to direct the remake because they are thought to come from a different cinematic tradition that will somehow show in their work. As Schneider has correctly observed, however, 'the most part of the films in question are already so laden with the conventions of mainstream Hollywood cinema that there is little risk of foreign "contamination". If anything, getting an outsider to direct the latest studio-conceived thriller, action flick etc. is thought to add something of an "edge" to the production' (2002).

To be sure, a studio's decision to collaborate with a foreign director is often tied to the ownership of remake rights and the degree of authorial control the filmmaker demands. In this context, Vincendeau has remarked that transatlantic contracts are, above all, concerned with defining 'what constitutes the auteur of a film, and what rights he/she has over the product' (1993: 25). While foreign filmmakers might be flattered when Hollywood calls with an offer for them to direct a remake of their own film, they are also wary, and – like French directors Luc Besson (*La femme Nikita*, 1990) or Coline Serreau (*Trois hommes et un couffin*, 1983) – may eventually pull out of directing the US version (cf. Vincendeau 1993: 25; Williams and Mørk 1993: 8). With hindsight, French director, screenwriter and producer Francis Veber found filming the Hollywood remake *Three Fugitives* (1989), based on his hit comedy *Les trois fugitifs* (1986), 'a sobering experience' (Williams and Mørk 1993: 8). In an interview, he said he had thought that directing the remake would give him an opportunity to improve on the French original for the American market, but that was not the case. Like other European directors, he felt 'that some studios overlook key cultural differences in their rush for a quick translation' (Williams and Mørk 1993: 20). According to Veber, 'There's a difference between Europe and America which is very hard to define ... It's as if the studios take a foie gras and add chantilly cream to make the film richer. This is not a recipe that always works' (20).

In the case of the auto-remake *The Vanishing* (1993), which was a critical and financial failure despite its acclaimed original, director George Sluizer owned the rights to *Spoorloos* and Dutch author Tim Krabbé's novel *Het gouden ei* (*The Golden Egg*) on which the film was based. He agreed to remake it for Twentieth Century Fox under the condition that he could direct the remake with only minor alterations (cf. Schneider 2002). Whether the film's radical makeover was studio-dictated or not is not certain, but in the end, Hollywood screenwriter Todd Graff left only around 60 per cent of the original script unchanged and added the upbeat ending described earlier (cf. Schneider 2002). For Monk, 'the tacked-on climax of Sluizer's remake is a travesty of every psychological, aesthetic, and cinematic principle that made the film so compelling and unsettling; and it speaks volumes about what qualifies as a proper Hollywood ending' (2010: 426).

In an interview with *The Guardian*, Haneke claimed that he was well aware of this and other failed auto-remakes like Hideo Nakata's *The Ring Two* (2005) or Takashi Shimizu's *The Grudge* (2004):

> 'But I was convinced that I could hold on to control of my film in the way that many of these directors did not'. How, then, has he found the experience of working in the US? He struggles with his German translator for the right English word. 'Cumbersome', he finally offers. Why? 'Because

they always try to get to influence you. They don't listen. I say "No" but they ask me the same question the next day. I had to fight hard to get what I wanted, in a way I wasn't used to.' (Jeffries 2008)

What Haneke wanted was a faithful shot-by-shot remake. In an interview with a German newspaper, the director stressed that he was not willing to negotiate with his producers: 'I told them clearly from the outset that I will only do this if I have final cut. With the music, they tried to replace John Zorn with Marilyn Manson for publicity reasons. But they had no way of doing it. The contract says final cut and shot-by-shot remake' (quoted in 'Interview' 2008, my translation).

Reading these statements, it is important to remember that, whereas most transnational remakes are major studio productions with wide domestic and international releases and long theatrical runs, *Funny Games US* was distributed by Warner's specialty division Warner Independent, and that it ran for no longer than seven weeks in the USA, reaching only 288 theatres in its widest release (cf. boxofficemojo.com). In other words, Haneke never left the realm of art cinema when he remade *Funny Games* for its intended (supposedly mainstream) American audience (cf. Grundmann 2008). For Roy Grundmann, 'the low-risk American boutique treatment showed that the culture industry has sufficiently diversified to assimilate these types of subversive games' (2010: 29). It also meant that, unlike other foreign directors who remade their films as big-budget blockbusters, Haneke found himself in a position to enforce his authorial control: that is, to ignore Hollywood's rules for transnational remaking and to faithfully replicate his film with American actors in an American setting.

REVISION, REPETITION, AND THE SHOT-FOR-SHOT REMAKE

If it is unusual that directors remake their own films, then it is unheard of that they opt for a shot-by-shot remake the second time around. Haneke's *Funny Games US* remains, in fact, the only example to date. The case continues to puzzle critics, who cannot quite wrap their heads around the fact that Haneke chose not to revise his earlier work. Alfred Hitchcock is often evoked when it comes to the possible modes of updating and revision offered by the remaking process. More than twenty years after Hitchcock shot the black-and-white thriller *The Man Who Knew Too Much* for Gaumont British, he remade it in Hollywood with substantial changes, in widescreen and Technicolor. Considering both films, he told François Truffaut in an interview: 'the first version is the work of a talented amateur and the second was made by a professional' (quoted in McDougal 1998: 58). To a certain extent, the two renditions of *The Man Who Knew Too Much* document Hitchcock's development as an artist, and the films do so in a different manner from the 'continuous remaking of shots, sequences and themes' (53), which have established Hitchcock as an auteur figure and have lent an overall sense of cohesion to his entire oeuvre. It almost seems as if film critics and scholars had expected Haneke to display a Hitchcockian obsession with the details of filmmaking and penchant for revising his own work, and that *Funny Games US*, made a decade after the first film, disappointed in that respect, and could even be considered a step backwards in Haneke's career. 'After accomplished adult fare such as *The Piano Teacher* and *Hidden*', Mark Kermode remarked in *The Observer*, 'revisiting the postgraduate postmodern gimmicks of *Funny Games* (Look, it's a movie! Watch, I can rewind it!) seems at best regressive, while remaking a foreign-language cause célèbre in English just smacks of selling out' (2008).

Many critics found the remake a 'pointless exercise' or 'failed experiment', echoing labels that had marked the initial response to Gus Van Sant's shot-by-shot remake of Alfred Hitchcock's *Psycho*.[5] However, the fact that Haneke had remade his own film while Van Sant had chosen to replicate an untouchable classic directed by the 'Master of Suspense' made all the difference. Both films were regarded as superfluous, as affronts to audiences, but 'Haneke doing Haneke' frame by frame and shot for shot was largely perceived as 'an act of navel-gazing redundancy' (Lee 2008: 28).

And yet, *Funny Games US* remains the only transnational remake of its kind and as such has raised interest in processes of cultural translation, encouraging critics and academics to look more closely at both versions and to develop on their part an obsession with cinematic details, with the slight variations between scenes and their cultural meanings. Leland Monk, for instance, points to relatively minor changes in the remake and reads them convincingly against the cultural schemas of class and manhood prevalent in Austria and the USA. Although the family's leisure-time objects transformed into murder weapons by Peter and Paul are identical in both films, for example, the golf club, hunter's shotgun and sailboat carry very different meanings as status symbols. In the European context, Monk explains, they stand for class privilege and '"place" the couple as a very specific type of the upper-level bourgeoisie', while 'golf and sailing are more associated with the professional and managerial classes than the upper class' in the USA, 'and shotguns are used *primarily* to blow someone away' (Monk 2010: 421–2).

Similarly, Monk argues, Tim Roth's 'George, the American family man, has a much tougher model of manhood to live up to, or fall short of' than Ulrich Mühe's Georg in the Austrian version (424). Following this model, which is grounded in the tradition of the Western, 'the *pater familias in extremis* is obliged to (im)prove his manhood by dispelling the invasive threat to his family with a new-found virility that usually takes the form of a virulent violence' (424). While both men fail to protect their son and wife, George comes across

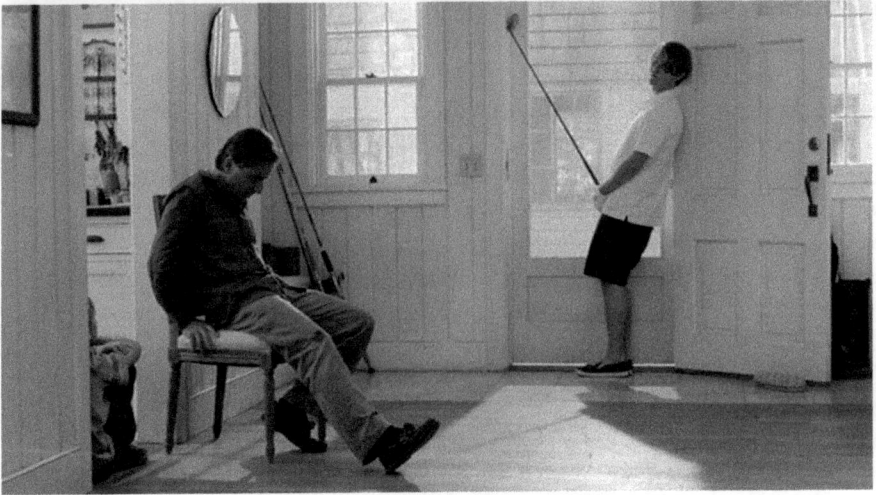

Figures 11.1 and 11.2   Michael Haneke's shot-by-shot remake of *Funny Games* (2007, 1997) has encouraged critics to examine cinematic details and analyse slight variations and their cultural meanings

as weaker than his Austrian counterpart Georg – because Mühe's performance is so much more powerful than Roth's, but also because the American cultural context demands different ideals of masculinity and self-reliance.

Apart from these (maybe unintended) side-effects of transnational remaking that result from different interpretations based on culturally specific schemas, Haneke's shot-by-shot reproduction makes very explicit concessions to the new American setting. In a conversation about the last vacations, Italy is replaced with Miami, and while Georg and Anna try to call a relative because neither of them can think of the emergency phone number, George and Ann immediately dial 911. Ten years after the original version, concessions had to be made to accommodate technological advances as well. Thus, when Ann's cellphone no longer works after Paul let it drop into the kitchen sink, George needs to explain that he left his phone in the car. In the original, there was just one cordless telephone in the house. While these details were changed in the otherwise faithfully translated script, the polite form of address common in German is entirely lost in the English version – and with it the unsettling quality of Georg and Anna's first outbursts of anger, in which they drop the formal 'Sie' and set the spiral of violence in motion.

More obvious changes concern the look of the two films. Although the lake house interior has been carefully re-created, for example, white and grey furniture dominates in the remake, which has further been digitally colour-graded to give it a cold, antiseptic look. The original, however, features wooden surfaces, shades of yellow and warm colours. The visual aesthetics of the first film thus stand in stark contrast to the cold, methodical violence executed by the two home invaders and amplify the disturbing effect of their actions. The remake's whiteish tinge, on the other hand, creates a cold and bleak horror film atmosphere that is in keeping not only with the film's narrative but also with the current colour-grading trend in Hollywood (see Hoad 2010). This change might, in fact, be one of Haneke's few concessions to Hollywood. The director has frequently been accused of making a US version that 'inched close to the sort of exploitational detail that it was supposed to abhor' (Lane 2008). More prominent (and controversial) examples are the CGI-enhanced shotgun scene, and long takes in which Naomi Watts wears nothing but a bra and panties (whereas Susanne Lothar wore a full slip in the original).[6]

Funny Games US repeats every single shot of the original film in order to create a copy of it, and still the two films – 'a pair of identical, staring twins' (Lane 2008) – are uncannily the same *and* different (if watched side by side) precisely because of the remake's new cast of actors, the 'transformational linguistic effect' (Koehler 2008: 56), the American setting and cultural context, and the many details that have changed in the process of transnational remaking. Stefan Hafner and Karin Hammer's short film *Funny Games Ghost* (2011), which layers footage from key scenes of Haneke's original and remake on top of each other, exposes such variations in an almost uncanny manner that affirms the independent existence of both films.[7] The short simultaneously draws attention to Haneke's precision, style, and authorial control, as the overlapping scenes reveal the actors' and film crew's formal confinement within the framework the director has both envisioned (for the remake) and already realised (with the original).

Conclusion

As the overwhelming hostility with which Van Sant's *Psycho* was once met upon its release in 1998 is slowly giving way to more moderate analyses and revisionist appreciation of the remake as a unique meta-commentary on American film history, the horror genre, and the practice of remaking,[8] it remains to be seen whether public and critical opinion will eventually come around and reconsider *Funny Games US* as well. For one thing, the remake serves as a powerful and provocative reminder of Haneke's still-timely critique directed at filmic representations of violence. He manipulatively appropriates and modifies codes of Hollywood's genre cinema in order to repeat the exact same critique in the exact same darkly parodic manner. In this sense, the decision to remake *Funny Games* shot by shot is also a statement 'that Haneke's faith in his erstwhile treatment of the topic remains unbroken' (Grundmann 2008).

The world around *Funny Games* might have changed with 9/11, the war on terror, and the torture and abuse of Iraqi detainees in the Abu Ghraib prison which was widely covered in the global media, but the film keeps repeating the same message. Following the release of the original in 1997, a new sub-genre of horror film, dubbed 'torture porn', had conquered Hollywood and instantly proven to be very successful at the domestic and worldwide box office. Films like *Saw* (James Wan, 2004) and *Hostel* (Eli Roth, 2005) show graphic scenes of violence, torture, nudity and mutilation. *Funny Games US*, which was released among this fare, is also about torture, but its 'violence is all imaginary, a factor of clever editing, precise camera placement, and the power of suggestion' (Hoberman 2008). Compared to this new kind of horror cinema, then, one critic found the remake 'downright nostalgic' (Buß 2008, my translation), but the context of its American release also changed its meaning in a different sense than merely framing it as outdated, or the odd one out among the many gory spectacles on the marquee. *Funny Games US* increased the urgency to critically reflect on cinematic representations of violence, and it also 'address[ed] questions of global consumption as it intersect[ed] with cultural and linguistic divides' (Messier 2014: 72).

Along these lines, Haneke's shot-by-shot remake must further be regarded as a cross-cultural experiment. As I have mentioned earlier, *Funny Games* only masquerades as a home-invasion thriller because Haneke repeatedly undermines audience expectations on the narrative and formal-aesthetic levels. The film provokes because it never delivers the cathartic release associated with the horror film, and in breaking this rule it lays bare how the genre typically manipulates its viewers. In a similar fashion, Haneke proceeded to subvert the industry-wide practice of transnational remaking with *Funny Games US*. Once more, he broke the rules – this time because he did not adapt

Funny Games to the American cultural context. In this regard, Vartan Messier has observed:

> The films underline the constructedness of cultural identity while simultaneously eliding cultural difference through the experience of cinematographic fidelity . . . Together, [they] suggest that unlike the vast majority of US remakes, the aesthetics do not need to be drastically reconfigured or transformed to *accommodate* or *respond* to the specific tastes and values of audiences purportedly predicated on notions of national or cultural consciousness. (2014: 72)

Both films pretend to lose their cultural specificity in a global consumer culture, and, like other Haneke films, claim to be valid for all Western capitalist societies. The original film already rejects specific national cinematic traditions (the Austrian *Heimatfilm*, for instance), and the remake, as we know, transgresses the codes of mainstream Hollywood production. And yet, the US version is no 'how-to' guide to a more balanced practice of transnational remaking in an increasingly globalised entertainment market, as Messier seems to be suggesting. Quite paradoxically, it foregrounds what is actually at stake when Hollywood executes its highly formalised processes of transnational remaking, and draws attention to the ways in which national cinemas and cultural exchange continue to inform the US film industry. Together, the production, distribution and reception of *Funny Games US* thus locate both films in the realm of global art-house cinema and ultimately confirm Haneke's status as a provocative European auteur.

NOTES

1. Academy rules used to dictate that films entered for the best foreign-language film category had to be in one of the official languages of the submitting country. In 2005, the Academy disqualified the Austrian submission of Haneke's French-language film *Caché* on the grounds that French is not an official language in Austria. The ensuing controversy prompted the foreign language committee to respond to the realities of transnational co-productions. They changed the rule the following year.
2. Sannwald argues that Haneke's willingness to talk about his films in interviews and to offer possible interpretations has led to rather strange consequences. Catchphrases like 'glaciation of feeling' ('Vergletscherung der Gefühle'), 'original sin of repression' ('Erbsünde Verdrängung'), and 'legitimate violence' ('legitimierte Gewalt') are Haneke's own creations, but they have been repeated, justified, and used in critical and academic Haneke discourse, and ultimately seem to have taken on lives of their own (2011: 11).
3. In her discussion of *Martin Guerre* (1982) and *Sommersby* (1993), Vincendeau explains that the French film uses longer takes, medium shots, two and three shots, and tableau scenes instead (1993: 24). On the different camerawork in European and Hollywood productions, see also Schneider (2002).
4. This ending suggests, of course, that the remake could as well have been a sequel

because the plot reveals that Peter and Paul have pulled their murderous prank before and that they will do so again and again, maybe ad infinitum. Viewers of the remake, who have also seen the original, are thus confronted with a new rendering that repeats the exact same narrative. Yet, this repetition is simultaneously part of the narrative, so that the murders in the remake could equally have happened before or after the original took place.

5. In his review of *Funny Games US*, Jim Emerson described Haneke's 'experiment' as follows: 'You (the lab rat) are placed in a Skinner box (the movie theater) and subjected to random negative stimuli (filmed violence, as a substitute for painful electrical jolts) . . . To pass the test, you must reject the false premise of the experiment itself (if only on the grounds of insufferable smugness) and walk out' (2008). Croce (2008), Elley (2007), Grundmann (2010), Lee (2008) and Monk 2010, among others, use the terms 'experiment' or 'exercise'. For a detailed discussion of *Funny Games US* side by side with Van Sant's *Psycho*, see Hantke 2010.

6. About the shotgun scene in the remake, Monk writes: 'Haneke turns up the visceral CGI wattage on this, the most cathartic moment in *Funny Games*, only to hollow out a larger void in the American moviegoer's sensational appetites' (2010: 425). For a discussion of Naomi Watts' controversial wardrobe change, see Elley (2007), Hoberman (2008) and Monk (2010: 430).

7. See also Müller (2014: 151). In 2014, Steven Soderbergh made a feature-length mash-up, in which he switches between scenes from Alfred Hitchcock's *Psycho* and Van Sant's shot-by-shot remake, occasionally splicing scenes from both films together. The mash-up is available on Soderbergh's website: <http://extension765.com/sdr/15-psychos>. In 2000, video artist Michael Olenick had already superimposed both versions in a live projection entitled *Psycho 2000* (Adams 2014).

8. See Vern (2013). Such re-evaluations and studies of the initial film-critical and academic reactions to Van Sant's *Psycho* remake can also be found in Hantke (2010), Kelleter (2015), Leitch (2003), Loock (2014) and Verevis (2006).

REFERENCES

Adams, Sam (2014), 'Watch Steven Soderbergh Mash Up *Psycho* with . . . *Psycho*?', *Indiewire.com*, 25 February, <http://blogs.indiewire.com/criticwire/watch-steven-soderbergh-mash-up-psycho-with-psycho> (last accessed 26 August 2015).

Baltruschat, Doris (2013), 'Co-Productions, Global Markets, and New Media Ecologies', in Manuel Palacio and Jörg Türschmann (eds), *Transnational Cinema in Europe*, Wien et al.: LIT Verlag, pp. 11–23.

Beale, Lewis (1992), 'Once Is Not Enough: Hollywood Filmmakers Are Looking to Translate Foreign Films Into Americanese', *New York Newsday*, 10 September, pp. 60–1.

Buß, Christian (2008), 'Sadismus für Nostalgiker', *Spiegel Online*, 28 May, <http://www.spiegel.de/kultur/kino/gewaltstudie-funny-games-u-s-sadismus-fuer-nostalgiker-a-556248.html> (last accessed 10 October 2013).

Croce, Fernando F. (2008), 'Funny Like a Crutch: *Funny Games U.S.*', *Slant Magazine*, 14 March, <http://www.slantmagazine.com/house/2008/14/funny-like-a-crutch-funny-games-us> (last accessed 10 October 2013).

Edelstein, David (2001), '"Remade in America": A Label to Avoid', *New York Times*, 4 November, pp. 3, 20.

Elley, Derek (2007), 'Haneke's Chilly Remake Plays Sadistic "Games"', *Variety*, 22 October, pp. 31, 39.

Emerson, Jim (2008), 'Funny Games', *RogerEbert.com*, 13 March, <http://www.rogerebert.com/reviews/funny-games-2008> (last accessed 25 August 2015).

Farolino, Audrey (1993), 'Make It Again, Sam!: H'wood Accent Is on $', *New York Post*, 12 April, p. 27.

Grundmann, Roy (2008), 'Michael Haneke's Subversive Games', *Chronicle of Higher Education*, 54: 25, pp. B14–B15. *Academic Search Premier*, <https://www.ebscohost.com> (last accessed 19 August 2015).

Grundmann, Roy (2010), 'Introduction: Haneke's Anachronism', in Roy Grundmann (ed.), *A Companion to Michael Haneke*, Oxford: Wiley-Blackwell, pp. 1–50.

Hantke, Steffen (2010), 'The Aesthetic of Affect in the Shot-by-Shot Remakes of *Psycho* and *Funny Games*', *English Language Notes*, 48: 1 (Spring/Summer), pp. 113–27.

Hoad, Phil (2010), 'Hollywood's New Colour Craze', *The Guardian*, 26 August, <http://www.theguardian.com/film/2010/aug/26/colour-grading-orange-teal-hollywood> (last accessed 26 August 2015).

Hoberman, J. (2008), 'Michael Haneke's *Funny Games*: One-Trick Phony', *The Village Voice*, 11 March, <http://www.villagevoice.com/2008-03-11/film/one-trick-phony/full/> (last accessed 11 October 2013).

'Interview: Die Leute fühlen sich an der Nase gepackt' (2008), *Der Tagesspiegel*, 29 May, <http://www.tagesspiegel.de/kultur/kino/interview-die-leute-fuehlen-sich-an-der-nase-gepackt/1244236.html> (last accessed 18 August 2015).

Jeffries, Stuart (2008), 'Master Manipulator', *The Guardian*, 31 March, <http://www.theguardian.com/film/2008/mar/31/austria> (last accessed 6 July 2015).

Kelleter, Frank (2015), 'Das Remake als Fetischkunst: Gus Van Sants *Psycho* und die absonderlichen Serialitäten des Hollywood-Kinos', in *Pop: Kultur und Kritik* 7, pp. 152–73.

Kermode, Mark (2008). 'Scare Us, Repulse Us, Just Don't Ever Lecture Us', *The Observer*, 30 March, <http://www.theguardian.com/film/2008/mar/30/features.horror> (last accessed 10 October 2013).

Koehler, Robert (2008), 'Funny Games', *Cineaste*, 33: 2, pp. 55–7.

Lane, Anthony (2008), 'Recurring Nightmare: *Funny Games*', *The New Yorker*, 17 March, <http://www.newyorker.com/arts/critics/cinema/2008/03/17/080317crci_cinema_lane?currentPage=all> (last accessed 11 October 2013).

Lee, Nathan (2008), 'The Return of the Return of the Repressed! Risen from the Grave and Brought Back to Bloody Life: Horror Remakes from *Psycho* to *Funny Games*', *Film Comment*, 44: 2 (March/April), pp. 24–8.

Leitch, Thomas (2003), 'Hitchcock without Hitchcock', *Literature/Film Quarterly*, 31: 4, pp. 248–59.

Loock, Kathleen (2014), '"The past is never really past": Serial Storytelling from *Psycho* to *Bates Motel*', in Kathleen Loock (ed.), *Serial Narratives*, special issue of *LWU: Literatur in Wissenschaft und Unterricht*, 47: 1–2, pp. 81–95.

Lyons, Charles (2002), 'Remakes Remodel Foreign Pix', *Variety*, 21–7 October, p. 24.

McDougal, Stuart Y. (1998), 'The Director Who Knew Too Much: Hitchcock Remakes Himself', in Andrew Horton and Stuart Y. McDougal (eds), *Play It Again Sam: Retakes on Remakes*, Berkeley: University of California Press, pp. 52–69.

Mazdon, Lucy (2000), *Encore Hollywood: Remaking French Cinema*, London: BFI.

Messier, Vartan (2014), 'Game over? The (Re)play of Horror in Michael Haneke's *Funny Games U.S.*', *New Cinemas* 12: 1–2, pp. 59–77, doi: 10.1386/ncin.12.1-2.59_1.

Monk, Leland (2010), 'Hollywood Endgames', in Roy Grundmann (ed.), *A Companion to Michael Haneke*, Oxford: Wiley-Blackwell, pp. 420–37.

Müller, Katharina (2014), *Haneke: Keine Biografie*, Bielefeld: Transcript Verlag.

O'Neil, Tom (2012), 'Video: Michael Haneke on *Amour*, Oscars, Cannes, Love and Horror', *GoldDerby*, 31 October, <http://www.goldderby.com/news/3542/michael-hanake-amour-entertainment-news-528174926.html> (last accessed 4 July 2015).

Price, Brian (2010), 'Pain and the Limits of Representation', in Brian Price and John D. Rhodes (eds), *On Michael Haneke*, Detroit: Wayne State University Press, 35–48.

Sannwald, Daniela (2011), 'Vorwort oder: Schwarz und Weiß. Ästhetik und Moral in Michael Hanekes Werk', in Daniela Sannwald (ed.), *Michael Haneke*, special issue of *Film-Konzepte* 21 (February), pp. 3–15.

Schneider, Steven Jay (2002), 'Repackaging Rage: *The Vanishing* and *Nightwatch*', *Kinema* 17, 1 April, pp. 24–66, <http://www.kinema.uwaterloo.ca/article.php?id=153&feature> (last accessed 2 June 2015).

Stuart, Jan (2002), 'Continental Divide', *Newsday*, 28 July, pp. D18, D20.

Verevis, Constantine (2006), 'For Ever Hitchcock: *Psycho* and Its Remakes', in David Boyd and R. Barton Palmer (eds), *After Hitchcock: Influence, Imitation, and Intertextuality*, Austin, TX: University of Texas Press, pp. 15–29.

Vern (2013), 'Gus Van Sant's *Psycho* Just Turned 15 – and Is More Fascinating than You Remember', *The Village Voice*, 4 December, http://www.villagevoice.com/film/gus-van-sants-psycho-just-turned-15-and-is-more-fascinating-than-you-remember-6440289> (last accessed 27 August 2015).

Vincendeau, Ginette (1993), 'Hijacked', *Sight & Sound* 3: 7 (July), pp. 22–5.

Walker, Tamsin (2009), 'Germany Picks Historical Film for Race to the Oscars', *DW.com*, 27 August, <http://dw.com/p/JJUT> (last accessed 4 July 2015).

Wheatley, Catherine (2009), *Michael Haneke's Cinema: The Ethic of the Image*, New York and Oxford: Berghahn Books.

Williams, Michael, and Christian Mørk (1993), 'Remake Stakes Are Up', *Variety*, 19 April, pp. 5, 8, 20.

12. REINTERPRETING REVENGE: AUTHORSHIP, EXCESS AND THE CRITICAL RECEPTION OF SPIKE LEE'S *OLDBOY*

Daniel Martin

> Let's get rid of the word 'remake', please, for this film at least.
> (Spike Lee, quoted in Roberts 2013)

Park Chan-wook's *Oldboy* (2003) achieved only moderate success on its initial release in its home country of South Korea, where the film's extreme violence and apparent anti-commercial personal style alienated many mainstream audiences. When the film found international distribution, however, it attained much greater notoriety, winning a major prize at Cannes and attracting an unusually passionate and positive critical consensus. *Oldboy* also came to serve as a symbol for the growing East Asian 'extreme' cinema cycle, generating attention and a degree of visibility rare for a foreign-language cult film.

Oldboy tells the gruesomely violent tale of a man inexplicably imprisoned in isolation for fifteen years, released to seek an explanation from his captor and horrified by the revelations that follow. The film's significant cultural impact, coupled with its irresistible high-concept plot hook and weighty examination of the 'universal' theme of revenge, led, inevitably, to talk of a Hollywood remake. Given the financial success and critical prestige of contemporaneous remakes of 'Asia Extreme' films, such as Gore Verbinski's blockbuster horror *The Ring* (2002, based on the 1998 Japanese original) and Martin Scorsese's Oscar-winning *The Departed* (2006, based on the 2002 Hong Kong film *Infernal Affairs*), an American *Oldboy* was seen as pregnant with potential. Initially mooted as a vehicle for director Steven Spielberg, the project ultimately fell to the much-celebrated but undeniably controversial auteur Spike Lee.

Spike Lee was in many ways an incongruous choice of director: for someone with a career characterised by authorial preoccupations with the African-American cultural experience and race relations in contemporary society, and a reputation for creative control and independence, a remake of a South Korean film struck many critics as odd. Yet Lee, in promoting the film through press interviews, exercised a strategy of claiming creative ownership, insisting his *Oldboy* was not a remake but a 'reinterpretation' (Hill 2013; Roberts 2013) and emphasising his personal investment in reshaping the material – a claim that would not endure rumours of creative conflict over the final cut of the film. Produced by Good Universe and distributed by FilmDistrict, on its domestic theatrical release in 2013 Lee's *Oldboy* became a notable failure: 'one of the bigger flops of the year' (Rosen 2013) in economic terms and a film largely dismissed by critics. In particular, critics found little of Lee's authorial voice in the film, and debated the inability of American cinema to equal the transgressive extremes of Korean film.

This chapter examines Lee's 'reinterpretation' in terms of its critical reception, and the way the film was framed by its director in press interviews and public discourse. The following sections offer analysis of the ways in which Lee attempted to escape the negative connotations of the 'remake' and brand his film as another entry in his own auteurist canon, despite the sceptical response from critics. While it is possible to detect some evidence of Lee's signature subtext in the film, the collective refusal of critics to acknowledge his *Oldboy* as the work of a committed auteur is telling. This chapter further analyses the critical reception of the film in terms of the ways in which critics address the spectacle of violence, notions of taste, and the assumed cultural differences between American and South Korean audiences. Reactions against the supposed 'Americanising' of the original run parallel to Orientalist celebrations of East Asian cinema as peerlessly explicit and immoral. The case of Lee's *Oldboy* thus offers the opportunity not only to examine the transformation of material from one director to another, but to interrogate broader debates over the intersection of the auteur as symbol/brand and the imagined (lack of) creative freedom afforded directors of remakes, as well as the persistence of Orientalism in critical discourses around East Asian cinema.

RECLAIMING *OLDBOY*: SPIKE LEE'S REINTERPRETATION

Spike Lee's cycle of promotional interviews conducted prior to the release of his *Oldboy* reflect a consistent rhetoric designed to project an image of a director in full creative command of his material. The director's repeated insistence that his *Oldboy* be dubbed a 'reinterpretation', rather than a 'remake', occurred at least once as part of a broader discussion of the nature of remakes. Speaking to the website *Collider*, Lee asked to 'get rid of the word "remake" please, for this film at least' (Roberts 2013). Citing numerous other remakes, Lee settled on Gus Van Sant's infamous shot-for-shot remake *Psycho* (1998, based on Alfred Hitchcock's 1960 film of the same title) as an exemplar of the approach he aimed to avoid, claiming 'why do that? Gus is a great filmmaker, but that's just something I wouldn't do. Here's the reason why you use reinterpretation instead of remake' (Roberts 2013). Lee's goal, rather than simple replication, was to 'know that you have something that's great, and then, in full respect of that source, just make it your own' (Roberts 2013; see also Verevis 2006: 132–7).

Lee's self-promotion and interviews demonstrated his firm commitment to establishing his ownership of – and creative contribution to – his version of *Oldboy*. In one interview, he reminded a journalist that he need not write a film to leave his creative stamp on it (Kastrenakes and Bishop 2013) and, in another, expressed confidence that his traditional (predominantly African-American) fan base would support his new film (Roberts 2013). Alongside his comments on the nature of his 'reinterpretation' many critics expressed their anticipation of the film in highly positive terms: almost a year before the film's release one journalist wrote that 'if anything can be assumed of a Spike Lee film, it's that it's definitely *not* going to be a commercial cash-in. Lee cares deeply about artistic integrity' (Chitwood 2012).

Lee's commentary thus influenced the popular press in precisely the way he desired. Ironically, Lee would use that same power of influence to distance himself from the project shortly before its release. One website reported conflicts between Lee and the studio over final cut and running time, describing the subsequent edit of the film as 'studio-led mangling' (Suebsaeng 2013), while star Josh Brolin was meanwhile quoted as preferring the 'original' three-hour cut of the film (Rodriguez 2013). These widely circulated reports of a superior director's cut had the dual effects of diminishing critical expectations, and allowing Lee to distance himself from culpability for what might transpire to be a poorly received film. Indeed, creative independence has been a hallmark of Lee's career: he is well known for (typically) retaining final cut privileges on any film he directs (Reid 1993: 93; Massood 2008: xxiv), has been praised for maintaining 'a resolutely independent presence' in the film industry (Sterritt 2013: 7), and, famously, successfully battled for creative control over his 1992 film *Malcolm X* (Everett 2008). A subtle but significant indicator of Lee's ultimate creative input was his final credit on the film: *Oldboy* was billed as a 'Spike Lee Film' rather than as a 'Spike Lee Joint' as his previous works were; the phrase is as strongly associated with Lee's authorship as the Windsor font in the opening credits of a Woody Allen film.

When reviewed by critics, *Oldboy* largely failed to impress; more significantly, though, critics addressed Lee's authorial input in mostly negative terms. *Time* magazine described Lee as simply a 'director for hire' (Corliss 2013) while *Variety* likewise called the film 'impersonal' and suggested Lee was 'on director-for-hire autopilot' (Chang 2013). Most damning was Stephanie Zacharek in the *Village Voice*, opining that the film 'doesn't even feel like a work-for-hire project, the kind of challenge Lee might take on because he happened to be free and could use the money. Colourless and soulless in the extreme, it bears no one's fingerprints at all' (2013). The critical response to the film, and to Lee's role as director, was not quite universally negative, with at least one critic persuaded by Lee's earlier insistence on creative ownership, arguing that Lee 'practically defines the slippery term auteur . . . This is very much a Spike Lee Joint' and describing the film as a 'reimagining' rather than a remake (Savlov 2013). These comments, both negative and positive, reinforce the notion, argued by Mark Jancovich (2002), that press and publicity materials and discourses have a direct observable effect on critical reviews.

When *Oldboy* was released in the USA, it represented an example of 'counter-programming' during a Thanksgiving weekend dominated by televised sports and family adventure movies. *Forbes*' analyst predicted that 'with lousy reviews [and] no buzz . . . *Oldboy* will probably get lost in the shuffle' (Mendelson 2013). This prediction proved correct, and the film earned a fraction more than $2 million on a production budget of $30 million, making the film an undeniable 'box office bomb' (Acuna 2013; Rosen 2013). A critical consensus emerged in the wake of the film's failure that it simply wasn't original or inventive enough to warrant attention. Far from the reinterpretation Lee had (initially) promised, critics argued that his film was a 'faithful' remake (Chang 2013; Corliss 2013; Staunton 2013), a 'facsimile' which 'pilfered wholesale' from Park's film (Brady 2013), and that Lee was guilty of 'uninspired fidelity' to the original (Chang 2013); in essence, as Mark Kermode argued, 'it's hard to see what Spike Lee has brought to the table' (2013).

The attack on Lee mounted by critics, based on assumptions of him working 'purely' for hire with little personal investment, is perhaps understandable given his *Oldboy*'s lack of obvious engagement with African-American social issues. If Lee's career could be summarised by a single theme, it would undoubtedly be Black America, and *Oldboy* contributes to this concept only in very minor ways. One direct reference is a framed portrait hanging, with dark irony, in the protagonist's motel-room prison, of a stereotypical black bellboy, accompanied by the text 'What can we do to improve your stay?'. This object of racist Americana recalls a similar collection of blackface souvenirs scathingly showcased in Lee's earlier *Bamboozled* (2000), but *Oldboy* is otherwise – at least on the surface – bereft of Lee's most distinctive authorial preoccupation.

However, a closer analysis of the film's subtext suggests a significant connection to Lee's traditional preoccupations. Perhaps critics were largely blinded by the vast number of similarities between the two films, and ascribed insufficient importance to the relatively few narrative deviations in Lee's film. Indeed, the basic plot structure of Lee's and Park's films is essentially identical: the central protagonist – Daesu Oh (Min-sik Choi) in the Korean version, Joe Ducett (Josh Brolin) in the remake – is initially depicted as an uninspiring and unsympathetic drunken, loutish oaf who neglects his family. Kidnapped by unknown and largely unseen forces, the protagonist spends the next fifteen years (twenty in Lee's version) imprisoned in a sparse motel room, with a television the only contact with the outside world. During this time, his wife is murdered, and he is cast as the prime suspect; while planning an escape, the protagonist is inexplicably released. Taunted by the man who imprisoned him, and aided by a kind young woman with whom he falls in love, the protagonist tracks down his former jailers and seeks clues to the identity of his nemesis. Both films climax with essentially the same twist in the narrative, as the intricate extent of the revenge the angry anti-hero has suffered is fully revealed when he learns he has been manipulated into consummating a loving relationship with his own estranged daughter.

What Lee inserts here is a new theme, weaving into the existing narrative a sub-plot exploring the power of the media to manipulate its audiences. Lee's film adds a new explanation to perhaps an obvious question posed (but not answered) by Park's Oldboy: why doesn't the protagonist recognise his own daughter? In the later film, the nature of the deceit engineered by the film's antagonist, Adrian Doyle Pryce, extends further than Joe could imagine, as it transpires that the 'true crime' television show Joe watched while imprisoned, which would occasionally feature the case of Joe's wife's murder and warmly chart the recovery and maturation of surviving daughter Mia, was in fact fabricated by Pryce. The woman Joe obsessively thinks of as his estranged daughter is simply an actress, and the show, as Pryce smugly informs Joe, 'only had one viewer'. Pryce has taken advantage of what he proves to be a simple truth: 'People just believe whatever they see on television'. The film's villain wields visual media as a deadly weapon: he records both the murder of Joe's wife and the lovemaking between Joe and his daughter – images that shock and sicken Joe for obvious reasons (it is worth noting, too, that in Park's film the equivalent moment of revelation was accompanied by only an audio recording of the sex, not a video). Joe's entire worldview has been built on his false trust in the accuracy of the media, and it is easy to see how this theme connects to Lee's frustration with (what he believes to be) 'inherently racist' representations of African-Americans in news shows and popular entertainment (Vest 2014: 185). Lee has been described as a 'deeply personal' filmmaker (Sterritt 2013: 4) and thus his attempt to 'reinterpret' Oldboy can certainly be read through the lens of an auteur's recurring preoccupations.

ADAPTING *OLDBOY*: THE STRUGGLE FOR CREDIBILITY

Perhaps because of the two films' many narrative parallels and similar scenes, Lee continually emphasised in press interviews his own directorial input, and made efforts to avoid the accusations of creative bankruptcy that often come with remakes. These comments went beyond his insistence on using the word 'reinterpretation' and extended to numerous references to the manga series (written by Garon Tsuchiya and illustrated by Nobuaki Minegishi, serialised in *Weekly Manga Action*, 1996–8) on which Park's *Oldboy* was based. As he told one interviewer, 'I always point that out, that the original source material was Japanese. I find it very interesting. We have three interpretations of it: The origin, the Japanese manga; next manifestation, whatever the word is, Korean; and now it's American' (Roberts 2013). Lee's strategy, of implying that his version of *Oldboy* is as much a new adaptation of the original manga as it is a remake of Park's film, attempts to diminish perceptions of the originality of Park's *Oldboy* and further distance this new film from expectations that it is a simple imitation.

It is worth briefly noting here that Lee's *Oldboy* was not the first remake of the South Korean film; it was merely the first *authorised* remake. In 2006, Bollywood filmmaker Sanjay Gupta directed *Zinda*, an unlicensed and officially unacknowledged (though utterly unmistakable) remake of Park's *Oldboy*. Despite its relatively ambitious goal of achieving a wider global audience than the majority of other Bollywood films (Smith 2013: 194), *Zinda* failed to make a significant impact in the West, or to impress even the niche audience who constitute the key 'Asia Extreme' demographic. The complete absence of *Zinda* in the critical discourse surrounding Lee's *Oldboy* is itself fascinating, and testament to the power of the structured narrative, put forward by Lee and the film's official press materials, of Lee's film as the only remake. Indeed, as Iain Robert Smith notes in his analysis of *Zinda*, the combination of elements from the manga and Park's film in the Bollywood remake make it less productive to regard the South Korean *Oldboy* as the 'original' text and instead focus on the 'intertextual exchanges and borrowings' that constitute the remake (2013: 189). Lee's desire to reposition his film as something other than a remake necessitates the same approach, hence his repeated comments on the manga.

Officially, according to its opening credits, Lee's film is 'Based on the Korean Motion Picture *Oldboy*' with no official acknowledgement of Tsuchiya and Minegishi's manga. A detailed comparison of the manga series and Lee's film reveals very little to support Lee's suggestions of a re-adaptation. Park's *Oldboy* made numerous significant changes to the narrative, and Lee's film preserves virtually all of them. The major theme of incest, the key plot point of a murdered wife, the significantly modified roles that the protagonist's lover, friend, and former teacher play were all additions of Park's film. Lee's film preserves parts of the manga discarded by Park in only minor ways: one example is the run-down bar that serves as Joe's temporary lodging and base of operations, recalling the tiny bar in which much of the manga is set, and changed in Park's film to a typical Korean internet café (or 'PC bang'). The only other significant connection between Lee's film and the manga – one absent in Park's film – is the theme of alcoholism. While Daesu is first seen drunk and disorderly in Park's film, Lee's Joe Ducett is a genuine alcoholic, rampant and self-destructive in his consumption of liquor (even as a school-boy, according to the flashback sequence), conquering his crippling addiction only with enormous effort. This plot thread recalls – though certainly does not precisely transfer – the boozy tone of the manga, which has its protagonist arrive at a major epiphany only after he decides to analyse his conundrum without the aid of alcohol, realising the value of a clear head and the disadvantages of constant drinking.

Lee's desire to brand his film as (at least partially) an adaptation rather than a remake is thus less a reflection of the truth and much more a powerful rhetorical gesture, drawing on the relative critical prestige attached to literary adaptations. This assertion is one way of distancing himself and his film from the crass commercial associations of the remake and, in concert with the repeated use of the word 'reinterpretation', positions Lee's *Oldboy* as a 'personal' project.

The 'Americanisation' of an Asia Extreme Classic

Jennifer Forrest and Leonard Koos argue that 'the existence of many critically acclaimed remakes hinders us from adopting as a general rule the widely accepted notion that all remakes are parasitical' (2002: 3), and suggest that the critical reception of remakes is becoming more sympathetic. This is a trend most certainly not evident in the case of *Oldboy*. In fact, a great deal of the critical backlash against *Oldboy* was rhetoric against the very notion of the remake; Lee's film was often a scapegoat within broader, well-rehearsed debates about crass, commercial Hollywood. Kermode asked 'why do we need an English-language remake of Park Chan-wook's prize-winning Korean thriller?' (2013), while Nigel Andrews of the *Financial Times* revealed he was predisposed to dislike the film, noting it was 'a sad day in cinematic Hell' when Lee chose to remake *Oldboy* (2013). These critics are reacting not against Lee's film itself, but against the very *idea* of a remake of *Oldboy*. Critics variously described the film as 'superfluous' (Andrews 2013; Bradshaw 2013) and 'pointless' (Bradshaw 2013; Brady 2013). This negative response to a remake is hardly unique to the case of *Oldboy*, yet the South Korean film has a quality that inspires a more intense level of debate.

The critical reception of Lee's *Oldboy* not only reflects the status of the remake, but also exhibits a rhetoric that simultaneously celebrates and Orientalises the original Korean film. Acknowledged by critics as a powerful and influential film of artistic accomplishment, Park's *Oldboy* is also seen as the unmistakable product of a more 'extreme' East Asia, in which transgressive depictions of sex and violence are more permissible. Within reviews of Lee's *Oldboy*, one critic praises the 'inventive brutality' of Park's film (Vance 2013), another describes it as a 'sick classic' (Corliss 2013), while yet another dubs it 'trashy material' (Andrews 2013). This discourse directly recalls the influential 'Asia Extreme' brand, the label founded by British distributor Tartan Films that distributed *Oldboy* and a slew of highly influential titles to American and UK audiences. Asia Extreme films were promoted precisely on their potential to shock and offend, attaining visibility if not widespread popularity by consolidating Orientalist assumptions about East Asian film and culture as inherently and peerlessly explicit (Martin 2015). The critical reception of *Oldboy* reveals a shared assumption that American cinema is simply incapable of reaching equivalent levels of extreme spectacle.

Park's film is described by one critic as 'a revered cult film' (Savlov 2013) and several reviews make passing reference to an assumed fan base of unusual devotion. The *San Diego Tribune* describes how *Oldboy*'s 'legions of fans were up in arms when they heard that it would be remade, in English, for American audiences' (Wright 2013), while *Film Comment* alludes to 'wildly loyal' fans taking issue with Lee (Robbins 2013). *Variety* describes the 'feverish grip on fanboy imaginations' (Chang 2013) exerted by Park's film, and, most scathingly, the *East Bay Express* identifies a 'possessive cult' of *Oldboy* fans and criticises the 'moaning' of these 'K-dazed fan boys' (Vance 2013). These comments serve to both acknowledge and dismiss the habitual consumer of cult film and Korean cinema, presenting the niche market as 'other', outside the mainstream and thus, ironically, seeming to indirectly justify Lee's more mainstream-friendly remake. Indeed, the notion of Lee's film as 'mainstream' is a key conceptual thread dominating various aspects of the critical discourse: as a 'mainstream' film, Lee's *Oldboy* is less personal and less provocative than the director's other work, while, simultaneously, the supposedly mainstream nature of the remake sets it apart from the strictly cult-audience original. In a particularly telling statement, *Time*'s critic compares Lee's *Oldboy* to Scorsese's *The Departed*, described as 'a bloated Americanizing of the Hong Kong cop movie' (Corliss 2013).

What does it mean to 'Americanise' an Asian film? The critical reception of *Oldboy* reveals that cultural differences are defined by film critics in terms of taste and transgression, and a selection of reviews suggests a clear essentialising of East Asian culture. Two reviews make almost identical points. *Variety* argues that Lee's film is 'several shades edgier than the average Hollywood thriller' yet still sees it 'falling short' of its predecessor's 'unhinged, balls-out delirium' (Chang 2013). And the *San Diego Union-Tribune* observes that the 'new version does not stack up to the Korean film, though it dares to get far more unsavoury than most American films' (Wright 2013). These comments suggest that even at its extreme limits of graphic content, American cinema fails to match the explicit and unusual nature of Korean film. Thus, when *Film Comment* calls Lee's film 'less gory and thus easier to stomach than Park's version', it isn't praise; the same review describes Park's film as 'magical and sickening' (Robbins 2013). *The Guardian*'s review laments the removal of the squid-devouring scene in Lee's film, assuming the reason is that 'cruelty to animals offends Hollywood correctness' (Bradshaw 2013), while Marc Savlov references the American body of film censorship (under the auspices of the Motion Picture Association of America), arguing 'Lee does right by the story, or as right as the MPAA allowed him' (2013).

The apparent 'Americanisation' of *Oldboy* is evident in a significant 'softening' of the film's key characters. Though just as violent, Lee's protagonist is a vastly more sympathetic and redeemable character than Park's anti-hero. While Daesu sought only revenge on his captor, Joe is motivated entirely by his love for his daughter. While incarcerated, Joe obsessively writes loving, confessional letters to his daughter, begging her forgiveness (knowing the letters can never be sent); Daesu only writes lists of the people he has wronged, trying to guess who might have orchestrated his imprisonment (Joe does this too, though his list is considerably shorter). Throughout the imprisonment sequence, Lee's *Oldboy* focuses on Joe's recovering sense of fatherhood, exemplified in a brief sequence that shows Joe befriending a mouse in his room; the mouse gives birth to several babies, and Joe is overcome with joy, nurturing the new life. Following a quick cut, the mice disappear and are delivered to Joe by his captors, dead and on a plate, in place of his dinner. Joe's anguish is severe. The brief sequence also functions as wickedly playful foreshadowing, essentially conveying the film's overall narrative: Joe's love of his 'babies' is a weakness to be exploited, the most effective way of hurting him.

Once released, Joe seeks out his captor not with the simple goal of revenge, but with the objective of proving his love for his daughter by finding the man who framed him; Joe is further motivated under the pretence that his nemesis now holds his daughter captive. This represents a significant change from Park's film, in which Daesu considers his estranged daughter only briefly, feeling a pang of painful emotion when he is told she has been adopted by overseas parents but then swiftly resuming his violent quest. Indeed, while Lee's film goes to efforts to paint Joe as a redeemed father, Park's touches on a theme of specific relevance in the South Korea context: adoption. Hye Seung Chung (2013) has argued that adoption has a particular social stigma in

Korea, and is thus addressed as a subject of national/personal guilt in several horror films. Park's protagonist thus neglects his parental responsibilities in a way that rings true to a painful social issue in contemporary Korea, resulting in a character truly single-minded and arguably beyond redemption. Joe, meanwhile, reflects the precise opposite, representing a complete character arc that charts the redemption of a flawed, selfish man by showing his transformation into an utterly selfless protector of his daughter, in myriad ways.

The profoundly ambiguous ending of Park's film, in which Daesu has selfishly attempted to erase his knowledge that his lover is his daughter through hypnosis, is likewise changed in Lee's *Oldboy*. Here, a repentant Joe, seemingly satisfied that his daughter will live a good life without him, voluntarily re-incarcerates himself in the same secret prison that held him for two decades. This moment recalls another Lee film, *He Got Game* (1998), which ends on a similar note: a father back in prison, at once reconnected to and disconnected from his estranged child. In both films the protagonist experiences an odd sense of satisfaction, though not necessarily a happy future.

The film's antagonist, Pryce, has also been modified to better explain his cruel behaviour and apparent psychosis. The equivalent character in Park's *Oldboy* sought revenge because Daesu witnessed an act of brother–sister incest and spread rumours; these rumours led to the shame-fuelled suicide of the antagonist's sister, leaving him heartbroken. The loss of his lover/sister spurs his elaborate and poetic scheme for revenge. Lee's *Oldboy*, however, transplants the brother/sister incest with a father/daughter coupling, and further reveals that the patriarch of the Pryce family sexually abused both of his children, Adrian included. Joe's nemesis, then, is depicted as a *victim* of incest, twisted by his upbringing. He is essentially a dark mirror of Joe's worst fears: a 'bad' person because of 'bad' parenting. The moral worldview of Lee's film neatly supplies an explanation for every act of wrongdoing in the film, eliminating much of the ethical ambiguity of the original. The key characters of Lee's film are thus gifted with greater sympathy on all sides, and Joe especially comes much closer to a typical Hollywood action film hero, driven by the desire to protect his loved ones against harm from his enemies.

The Orientalism of *Oldboy*: Translating an 'Alien' Experience

The appeal of the Hollywood remake is inherently contradictory (or, perhaps, uncanny), promising something at once familiar and unfamiliar, old and new (Lukas and Marmysz 2009). The original *Oldboy* achieved relatively wide visibility precisely because of its associations with Orientalism and transgression: concepts that Lee's film attempts to reproduce. Consequently, one of the notable features of Lee's film is a minor but significant depiction of East Asian influence, a number of references and representations that rely on Orientalist stereotypes. Indeed, Lee made it clear just how culturally distant he regarded South Korea, commenting to one journalist that 'most Americans don't go see foreign films, *especially* Korean foreign films' (emphasis added) and suggesting that the cultural remove between American audiences and the Korean *Oldboy* can be explained by the difficulty, for Americans, of identifying with such 'exotic people' (Roberts 2013). This is an especially disappointing perspective given Lee's passionate investment in representing racial inequality in American society, and in working to depict African-Americans in a much more nuanced and sympathetic light than much of mainstream Hollywood cinema.

The result is a collage of snippets of Oriental influence and imagery, with little cohesion or narrative justification. The film – shot in New Orleans but set in an unspecified and deliberately anonymous American city – shows the first phase of Joe's abduction taking place as he drunkenly stumbles through a Chinatown district, and buys a cheap souvenir from an ethnically Asian peddler speaking pidgin English. While imprisoned, Joe trains his body by watching old Hong Kong kung fu films on television. Both Lee's and Park's films include a visual gag involving elevator doors opening and unconscious hoodlums tumbling out, defeated by the weary protagonist left standing. In Lee's film, the moment includes a samurai sword protruding from the chest of one of the thugs. Finally, and most prominently, the antagonist's bodyguard/ sidekick character – an unremarkable man in Park's film – is here recast as a martial artist sex-bunny geisha (demonstrating lethal skills in hand-to-hand combat in some scenes, bathing her employer while wearing lingerie in another). It is difficult to imagine a more on-point depiction of the 'deadly China Doll' stereotype: dangerous, attractive, exotic, and eager to please (Funnell 2014: 115). The inclusion of these images may be intended to pay playful homage to the South Korean *Oldboy*, but the film ultimately reduces Asian culture to a handful of stereotypical images.

Beyond essentialist references to Asian culture, Lee's film is rife with obligatory allusions to the most iconic moments of Park's *Oldboy*, most obviously the sequences in which the protagonist fends off an army of thugs armed with nothing but a hammer and another in which he tracks his captors by sampling fried dumplings. Another major talking point surrounding Park's film was the scene in which Daesu eats a live squid, chomping on its body as its legs spasm and twist around his mouth and fingers; Lee's film contains only a playful reference to the scene, as Joe briefly observes a squid in a tank at a restaurant. Eager to avoid accusations of softening the brutal violence of Park's film, Lee showcases a variety of gruesome tortures, replacing a scene of horrifically amateur dentistry with an even more graphic sequence, as Joe slowly carves out small slivers of flesh from his enemy's neck, promising he will 'keep going till I can pull your head off with my bare hands'.

While many of these references to the original and reproductions of the film's most iconic scenes are tonally appropriate to Lee's film, some aspects of the Korean film have been transplanted to the American context in ways that seem ill-fitted. Take, for example, the above-mentioned hallway fight: the original film features Daesu in a pitched bodily battle, using a hammer to fend off thugs armed with knives, bats and planks of wood. These aspects of the fight are faithfully reproduced in Lee's film, yet the entire set-up is arguably far less plausible in an American setting. Why wouldn't these organised criminals, protecting their lucrative, secret compound, use guns? The Korean gangster film has long been notable for its conspicuous absence of guns, from Kwak Kyung-taek's hugely popular *Friend* (*Chingu*, 2001) and Yu Ha's *A Dirty Carnival* (*Biyeolhan geori*, 2006) to Jang Jin's sardonic *Righteous Ties* (*Georookhan gyeboo*, 2006) which shows the disastrous consequences of a criminal gang acquiring even a single firearm. This is not an invention of the film industry but a social reality of South Korea, where gun control is strict and highly effective (Na 2013). In metropolitan America, the setting of *Oldboy*, the lack of guns in the context of the scene beggars belief; indeed, Lee's more recent film *Chi-Raq* (2015) specifically addresses the devastating social consequences of the America's oversaturation of guns. The only factor keeping guns from appearing in *Oldboy*, above even plausibility and the interests of its director, is a strict fidelity to the showcase scene of the original film.

Another example of incongruent fidelity to the source text is the nature of the incident that triggers Pryce's orchestration of revenge. In both films, once Joe/Daesu have spread tales of sexual promiscuity they have witnessed, the girl in question is shamed and outcast (driven to suicide in Park's film, murdered by her suicidal father in Lee's). Yet while South Korea has an undeniable vein of social conservatism regarding sexually active teenagers, the same kind of social stigma simply doesn't exist in America. The concept of the '*wanggda*' among Korean youth – the individual hated by all and ostracised (Black 2003: 196) – explains why the young woman in Park's film would be driven to suicide. The equivalent sequence of events in Lee's film culminates in Amanda Pryce facing such scorn from her peers that they openly chant the word 'whore' at her in unison. In an odd way, though, this stark and implausible treatment of female sexuality is in keeping with one of Lee's more negative associations: misogyny. Spike Lee has been 'critiqued extensively for his narrow and sexist representations of women', a charge to which the director has readily admitted (Everett 2008: 105), suggesting that his insensitivity to the differing social contexts of Korea and America in this case is a reflection of his personal blindness to gender issues. The larger issue, however, draws this argument back to critical accusations of creative 'auto-pilot' on the part of Lee: aspects of the original film have been transplanted so faithfully as to suggest a lack of care and attention in the remaking process.

CONCLUSION

Long before Spike Lee faced critical backlash for his version of *Oldboy*, the mooted remake by Steven Spielberg, rumoured to star Will Smith, attracted an even more vicious objection before it even entered production. Several critics expressed delight when the project was cancelled (Miller 2009), while another bizarrely declared it was 'worth thanking the heavens' Spielberg wasn't able to direct the film (Suebsaeng 2013). The reason for this elevated negative response can only be the 'brand' that Spielberg and Smith have cultivated as popular, ultra-mainstream entertainers. To the vast majority of critics and audiences in the USA and UK, *Oldboy* – and the 'Asia Extreme' cycle more broadly – is simply the antithesis of populist family entertainment.

Lee's *Oldboy*, therefore, could never have achieved widespread critical support. *Oldboy* being a Hollywood remake of a South Korean film that was celebrated not *in spite of* its transgressive violence but *because of* that content (Lee 2008; Martin 2015), the film's intended audience – and an international community of Western critics – will always view the remake as an inferior product. While Lee's personal promotional campaign to brand his film a 'reinterpretation' was innovative in many ways, and while his film is certainly not without clear signs of an auteur's creative preoccupations, his *Oldboy* failed precisely because the appeal of the South Korean film is, in essence, its Koreanness. Those same 'exotic people' Lee believes American audiences cannot identify with are actually the primary appeal of such films. Had Lee done more to truly transform the material into something closer to his existing authorial canon, the film would have had an alternative selling point (one wonders how a Spike Lee *Oldboy* with a predominantly African-American cast would have fared with critics and audiences).

The case of the reinterpretation of *Oldboy* reveals that the gap between the cinematic cultures of Hollywood and Asia is regarded as vast – that this is far from the reality is a matter for another discussion entirely – and that the differences are simply insurmountable. This critical discourse suggests that the 'extreme' belongs in/to Asia, and is not the province of American filmmakers.

REFERENCES

Acuna, Kirsten (2013), 'Spike Lee's Remake of *Oldboy* Bombs at Theaters – Here's Your Box-Office Roundup', *Business Insider*, 2 December, <http://www.businessin sider.com/oldboy-remake-bombs-2013-12> (last accessed 10 December 2015).
Andrews, Nigel (2013), 'Review: *Oldboy*', *The Financial Times*, 5 December, <http://www.ft.com/cms/s/2/3be8561c-5da9-11e3-b3e8-00144feabdc0.html> (last accessed 10 July 2015).
Black, Art (2003), 'Coming of Age: The South Korean Horror Film', in S. J. Schneider (ed.), *Fear Without Frontiers: Horror Cinema Across the Globe*, Godalming: FAB, pp. 185–203.

Bradshaw, Peter (2013), 'Oldboy', The Guardian, 5 December, <http://www.theguard ian.com/film/2013/dec/05/oldboy-review> (last accessed 10 July 2015).

Brady, Tara (2013), 'Oldboy', The Irish Times, 6 December, <http://www.irishtimes. com/culture/film/oldboy-1.1617845> (last accessed 10 July 2015>.

Chang, Justin (2013), 'Oldboy', Variety, 26 November, <http://variety.com/2013/film/ reviews/oldboy-review-1200848857/> (last accessed 10 July 2015).

Chitwood, Adam (2012), 'Josh Brolin Talks Oldboy Remake and Jason Reitman's Labor Day; Says They Shot Long Improvised Takes for Oldboy Motel Scenes', Collider, 18 December, <http://collider.com/josh-brolin-oldboy-remake-labor-day-interview/> (last accessed 10 July 2015).

Chung, Hye Seung (2013), 'Acacia and Adoption Anxiety in Korean Horror Cinema', in A. Peirse and D. Martin (eds), Korean Horror Cinema, Edinburgh: Edinburgh University Press, pp. 87–100.

Corliss, Richard (2013), 'Spike Lee's Oldboy: Remaking a Sick Classic', Time, 27 November, <http://entertainment.time.com/2013/11/27/spike-lees-oldboy-remaking-a-sick-classic/> (last accessed 10 July 2015).

Everett, Anna (2008), '"Spike, Don't Mess Malcolm Up": Courting Controversy and Control in Malcolm X', in P. Massood (ed.), The Spike Lee Reader, Philadelphia: Temple University Press, pp. 91–114.

Forrest, Jennifer and Leonard R. Koos (2002), 'Reviewing Remakes: An Introduction', in J. Forrest and L. R. Koos (eds), Dead Ringers: The Remake in Theory and Practice, Albany, NY: State University of New York Press, pp. 1–36.

Funnell, Lisa (2014), Warrior Women: Gender, Race, and the Transnational Chinese Action Star, Albany, NY: State University of New York Press.

Hill, Logan (2013), 'Spike Lee, Still Gliding to Success', New York Times, 24 November, p. AR1.

Jancovich, Mark (2002), 'Genre and the Audience: Genre Classifications and Cultural Distinctions in the Mediation of The Silence of the Lambs', in M. Jancovich (ed.), Horror: The Film Reader, London and New York: Routledge, pp. 151–61.

Kastrenakes, Jacob and Bryan Bishop (2013), '"I Wasn't Scared": Spike Lee on Reimagining Oldboy', The Verge, 20 November, <http://www.theverge. com/2013/11/20/5122912/spike-lee-interview-oldboy> (last accessed 10 July 2015).

Kermode, Mark (2013), 'Oldboy', The Observer, 8 December, <http://www.theguard ian.com/film/2013/dec/08/oldboy-review-spike-lee-brolin> (last accessed 10 July 2015).

Lee, Nikki J. Y. (2008), 'Salute to Mr Vengeance!: The Making of a Transnational Auteur Park Chan-wook', in L. Hunt and L. Wing-Fai (eds), East Asian Cinemas: Exploring Transnational Connections on Film, London: I. B. Tauris, pp. 203–19.

Lukas, Scott A. and John Marmysz (2009), 'Horror, Science Fiction, and Fantasy Films Remade', in S. Lukas and J. Marmysz (eds), Fear, Cultural Anxiety, and Transformation: Horror, Science Fiction, and Fantasy Films Remade, Lanham, MD: Lexington Books, pp. 1–20.

Martin, Daniel (2015), Extreme Asia: The Rise of Cult Cinema from the Far East, Edinburgh: Edinburgh University Press.

Massood, Paula J. (2008), 'Introduction: We've Gotta Have It – Spike Lee, African American Film, and Cinema Studies', in P. Massood (ed.), The Spike Lee Reader, Philadelphia: Temple University Press, pp. xv–xxviii.

Mendelson, Scott (2013), 'Box Office Analysis and Review: Oldboy Is, by Default, Spike Lee's Worst Film Ever', Forbes, 27 November, <http://www.forbes.com/ sites/scottmendelson/2013/11/27/review-oldboy-is-by-default-spike-lees-worst-film-ever/#4fc8d0362345> (last accessed 10 July 2015).

Miller, Ross (2009), 'Steven Spielberg & Will Smith Oldboy Remake Dead!', Screen

Rant, 10 November, <http://screenrant.com/oldboy-remake-dead-steven-speilberg-will-smith-out-ross-33910/> (last accessed 12 December 2015).

Na, Jeong-ju (2013), 'US May Learn from Korea's Gun Control', *The Korea Times*, 25 January, <http://www.koreatimes.co.kr/www/news/nation/2013/01/116_129474.html> (last accessed 12 December 2015).

Reid, Mark A. (1993), *Redefining Black Film*, Berkeley: University of California Press.

Robbins, Jonathan (2013), 'Review: *Oldboy*', *Film Comment*, 26 November, <http://www.filmcomment.com/blog/review-old-boy-spike-lee/> (last accessed 10 July 2015).

Roberts, Sheila (2013), 'Spike Lee Talks *Oldboy*, Why He Considers the Film a Reinterpretation, Performances of Josh Brolin and Elizabeth Olsen & His Confidence in Audience Turnout', *Collider*, 17 November, <http://collider.com/spike-lee-oldboy-interview/> (last accessed 10 July 2015).

Rodriguez, Cain (2013), 'New Pics From Spike Lee's *Oldboy*, Josh Brolin Prefers 3-Hour "Director's Cut" Of The Film', *The Playlist*, 7 November, <http://blogs.indiewire.com/theplaylist/new-pics-from-spike-lees-oldboy-josh-brolin-prefers-3-hour-directors-cut-of-the-film-20131107> (last accessed 10 July 2015).

Rosen, Christopher (2013), 'Spike Lee's *Oldboy* Flops', *Huffington Post*, 12 December, <http://www.huffingtonpost.com/2013/12/02/spike-lee-oldboy-flops_n_4371512.html?> (last accessed 10 July 2015).

Savlov, Marc (2013), '*Oldboy*', *The Austin Chronicle*, 29 November, <http://www.austinchronicle.com/calendar/film/2013-11-29/oldboy/> (last accessed 10 July 2015).

Smith, Iain Robert (2013), '*Oldboy* Goes to Bollywood: *Zinda* and the Transnational Appropriation of South Korean "Extreme" Cinema', in A. Peirse and D. Martin (eds), *Korean Horror Cinema*, Edinburgh: Edinburgh University Press, pp. 187–98.

Staunton, Terry (2013), 'Old Boy', *Radio Times*, <http://www.radiotimes.com/film/tp5vh/oldboy> (last accessed 10 July 2015).

Sterritt, David (2013), *Spike Lee's America*, Cambridge: Polity.

Suebsaeng, Asawin (2013), 'Will Spike Lee's Original Three-Hour Cut of *Oldboy* Ever See the Light of Day?', *Mother Jones*, 26 November, <http://www.motherjones.com/mixed-media/2013/11/spike-lee-oldboy-remake-three-hour-version> (last accessed 10 July 2015).

Vance, Kelly (2013), '*Oldboy*', *East Bay Express*, 27 November, <http://www.eastbay-express.com/oakland/oldboy/Content?oid=3772626> (last accessed 10 July 2015).

Verevis, Constantine (2006), *Film Remakes*, Edinburgh: Edinburgh University Press.

Vest, Jason P. (2014), *Spike Lee: Finding the Story and Forcing the Issue*, Santa Barbara: Praeger.

Wright, Anders (2013), '*Oldboy* Gets Disappointing Makeover', *The San Diego Union-Tribune*, 29 November, <http://www.sandiegouniontribune.com/news/2013/nov/29/spike-lee-korean-oldboy-josh-brolin-review/> (last accessed 10 July 2015).

Zacharek, Stepahnie (2013), 'Spike Lee's *Oldboy* is Utterly Unnecessary', *Village Voice*, 27 November, <http://www.villagevoice.com/film/spike-lees-oldboy-is-utterly-unnecessary-6440219> (last accessed 10 July 2015).

13. THE TRANSNATIONAL FILM REMAKE IN THE AMERICAN PRESS

Daniel Herbert

One need not look very hard to find someone denigrating Hollywood remakes of so-called 'foreign' films. In addition to a list of examples on a Wikipedia page, a quick Google search for 'Hollywood remakes of foreign films' will turn up: an article in *Paste* magazine entitled '10 Great Foreign Films with Horrible U.S. Remakes' (Ryan 2014), a piece in *Flavorwire* called '10 Terrible Remakes of Great Foreign Films' (Bailey 2014), and an article on Cheatsheet.com entitled '8 Great Foreign Films Remade Into American Movie Failures' (Arnold 2015). In addition to such clickbait, one can find similar sentiments expressed in any number of film reviews appearing in established print publications. For instance, one critic wrote 'Most Hollywood remakes of foreign films screw things up by dumbing things down', in a review of *Let Me In* (2008), which he praises for being untypical in this regard (Lumenick 2010: 35). Another critic titled his review of *Vanilla Sky* (2001) 'Open to Interpretation: Hollywood Versions of Foreign Films Rarely Live Up to the Originals' (Fine 2001: F16). And lest anyone think this is strictly a contemporary phenomenon, an article from 1936 was entitled 'Many Films from Europe Remade Here: Hollywood Versions Usually Inferior, Declare Critics' (Scheuer 1936: C1). The author lists nearly a dozen examples of such remakes, and says of them, 'Something – charm, lightness, power, what-not – is generally lost in transit' (Scheuer 1936: C1).

Nothing about this discourse should be surprising, especially to those who have studied transnational film remakes with any seriousness. Indeed, some of the scholarship about transnational remakes has aimed, explicitly or otherwise, to move beyond the evaluative and comparatively simplistic discussions of such films that appear in mainstream film reviews. Lucy Mazdon, for instance, begins her extraordinary study of Hollywood remakes of French films by indicating how film critics in England and France have dismissed film remakes in general, and Hollywood remakes of French films in particular, as commercially driven '"pap"', and promises that her book will provide a richer, adequately complex account of the phenomenon (2000: 2). Likewise, in my essay about *Abre los Ojos* (1997) and *Vanilla Sky* I cite a review by critic Kenneth Turan as characteristically dismissive of Hollywood remakes of foreign films. I assert that he and critics like him engage in a discourse 'of quality, artistry, originality, and cultural specificity', which 'assumes a hierarchy of critical taste that tends to nationalize and thereby simplify the transnational relations between' such films (Herbert 2006: 29). Like Mazdon, I then promise to provide a model for understanding transnational remakes which highlights their complexity and mobility and, further, which contributes to the 'problematization' of 'national cinema' paradigms within film studies scholarship more generally (29).

I remain convinced that transnational film remakes require rigorous analysis that illuminates such films' complexities, often through the use of sophisticated theoretical models. But I find that I am dissatisfied with (at least) two elements that have propelled such work, or at least my own work on this topic, and I want to address them in this essay. First, I do not think it is satisfactory that scholarship about transnational remakes should simply try to be more sophisticated than journalistic film reviews. In fact, I have wondered if some scholars have dismissed the writings of popular film critics too hastily, perhaps just as hastily as we have claimed such critics have dismissed transnational remakes. Inspired particularly by Constantine Verevis, who shows that all remakes 'are located in critical practice' (2006: 143), including within 'journalistic reviews of film, video and DVD releases found in mass circulation newspapers' (144), I have grown intrigued by the idea that mainstream criticism might offer forms of thought and terms of analysis that could inform or even improve our academic studies of these films. If we take it that 'culture is ordinary', and that ordinary culture produces important and legitimate knowledge, then we ought to take ordinary film reviews seriously (Williams 1989: 2). Although journalistic film criticism certainly does not represent the sentiments of the general population regarding a film, it can offer a less rarified, comparatively popular response to movies.

My second issue has to do with the function of 'the transnational' in film studies, and more precisely, with the role the remake plays in our understanding of transnational cinema. For more than a decade, a wave of work on 'transnational cinema' has swept the field, plainly represented by edited collections such as *Transnational Cinema: The Film Reader* (Ezra and Rowden

2006) and *World Cinemas, Transnational Perspectives* (Ďurovičová and Newman 2009), the journal *Transnational Cinemas*, which first began publication in 2010, and a great number of individual monographs and articles. Despite the heterogeneity of this scholarship, it largely appears motivated by a desire to disrupt 'national cinema' conceptual paradigms while not succumbing to simplistically conceived notions of 'global cinema', 'the global', or 'globalisation'.

This work has been, on the whole, important and successful in its goals. Yet there have been problems and shortcomings within the discourse on 'transnational cinema' as well. For instance, as Will Higbee and Song Hwee Lim indicate, there has been some fuzziness associated with the very phrase, as they count at least three ways in which the term 'transnational' has been used to define certain films, cinematic practices and movie cultures (2010: 9). In addition to such rhetorical and conceptual inexactitude, Markus Nornes has adroitly asserted that transnational cinema studies has 'put little between its own methodology and that which it critiqued', that is, national cinema studies (2013: 183). Whereas conventional national cinema studies 'searched for and predictably discovered culturally particular deployments of the universalized technology of cinema', which were then 'speciously attributed to a putative national identity', transnational film studies has largely 'searched for and (predictably) discovered traces of transnational flow in cinematic texts' (183–4). From this view, transnational complexity and mobility have been construed all too tidily and firmly. Which raises the question: to what extent has the study of transnational film remakes, my own work included, contributed to this problem?

I cannot solve these problems in this single essay. But, in what follows, I will confront these two issues by examining objects that embody them simultaneously: namely, popular-press reviews of transnational film remakes. Yet we find a telling problem before such an endeavour can even begin, as the very phrases 'transnational film remakes' and 'transnational remakes' *never* appear in journalistic film reviews. Even the academic scholarship on the topic is not uniform in its terminology, as one can find the same corpus of films described, for instance, as 'cross-cultural remakes' (Verevis 2006: 3) or 'international remakes' (Lippit 2012: 149). Of course, these facts do not make the classification suspect or illegitimate. Indeed, as someone who formulated a good part of my intellectual and professional identity around the category 'transnational film remakes', I do bellieve that some remakes are best described as 'transnational' and that, by understanding them as such, we can gain important insights into these films in particular and transnational cinema more generally. But if 'transnational remakes' do not occur as a discursive category among a general population, or even within the more exclusive realm of popular film criticism, then we should question what terms *do* crop up in those discussions that signal something of a more generalised conceptualisation of 'the transnational'. When looking at film reviews published in the USA from the 1930s until the present, we find that although critics typically denigrated Hollywood remakes of foreign films, they also created a rhetorical space for a more nuanced approach to transnational cinema through their use of critical keywords, points of analysis, and methods of evaluation. Specifically, American critics regularly associated both foreign sources and Hollywood remakes with their stars, auteur or genre, in lieu of or in addition to their nation of origin. By appealing to such discursive categories, American film critics (perhaps unwittingly) circumvented the 'limiting imagination of national cinema' (Higson 2000), and thereby point towards ways in which scholars might do likewise as they unravel the complexities of transnational film remakes and transnational cinematic flows more generally. At the minimum, sorting through the ways in which 'the remake' and 'the transnational' operate within mainstream critical discourse might help us reflect on how and why we construct the very corpus of 'transnational film remakes'.

STARS

Historically, one of the oldest and most enduring discursive categories one finds in reviews of Hollywood remakes of foreign films is the 'star'. This fact should not be surprising, given the fact that star discourses arose in the early twentieth century and, from very early on, the Hollywood studios cultivated star personae as part of their marketing strategies. But this should signal to remake scholars the types of transnational flows that appeared more prominently to popular press critics. In fact, some of these reviews fixate on a film's star and never even mention the fact that a film is a remake of a foreign film.

Such is the case in reviews of *Mad Love* (1935), a remake of the German film *Orlac's Hände/The Hands of Orlac* (1924). A review in *Motion Picture Daily*, for instance, does not mention any source for the film, but does note it is '[Peter] Lorre's first American role' ('*Motion Picture Daily*'s Hollywood Preview' 1935: 3). Writing in *Motion Picture Herald* about an early cut of the film, critic Gus McCarthy does not mention *Orlac's Hände* but states that the film 'is adapted from the widely read book' (1935: 50). More importantly, he writes, 'it marks the American screen debut of Peter Lorre. Well known in Europe, his appearances in "M" and "The Man Who Knew Too Much" have made him familiar to American audiences' (50). Here, the critic situates the star-figure of Lorre against the backdrop of national and regional cultural associations. In this characterisation, Lorre was previously associated with Europe and European cinema, and we might infer that American audiences thus situated him as extra-national or foreign, at least according to the logic of this review. Americans are, McCarthy states, 'familiar' with Lorre, or we might say familiar with his foreignness. With this appearance in an 'American' film, however, this critic suggests that Lorre has slipped across some national or regional cultural boundary – the very definition of transnational mobility according to many scholars working on transnational cinema.

The review of *Mad Love* in *Variety* further reinforces the idea that this film is transnational on account of its star rather than its status as a remake. It begins by referring to Lorre as a 'foreign actor', but one who is 'making his first appearance in a Hollywood-milled product' ('Mad Love' 1935: 20, 62). The review mentions the 'French written novel' as the source for the film, but not the German film, thereby indicating something of *Mad Love*'s transnational composition ('Mad Love' 1935: 62). Curiously, the review does indicate that the film is a remake, but cites a 1928 film produced by Aywon, an American independent company, as the precursor text. The review thus characterises the film as composed of a web of influences and sources, but only situates its star performer as transnational, and only implicitly so.

Reviews of the Swedish film *Intermezzo* (1936) and its Hollywood remake (1939) similarly exhibit an interest in the star of both films, Ingrid Bergman, as a figure of transnationality. One story said of the Swedish production: 'Goesta Ekman and Ingrid Bergman put so much sincerity into their acting and enjoy such excellent support that even persons depending on the English titles are likely to be impressed' (Nugent 1937: 10). Here, we see the stars of the film situated as a cultural bridge, one that can overcome the aesthetic and alienating effects of having to read subtitles. The review in *Variety* was both prescient and pointed in its demonstration of a particular cultural politics around the national and the transnational. It states: '"Intermezzo" takes its place among the finest foreign pictures to be shown on American soil this year. It . . . has shown in Ingrid Bergman a talented, beautiful actress. Miss Bergman's star is destined for Hollywood' ('Intermezzo' 1937: 19). In this review, the film remains distinctly non-American, while its star has shown some quality, call it trasnsnationality, that the critic feels would enable her to work 'on American soil'.

A number of reviews of the remake never mention the Swedish version. Those that do situate the remake as distinctly foreign, and at the same time suggest that Bergman functions as a transnationally mobile star-figure. For instance, one story referred to Bergman as 'imported especially from Scandinavia for this production, previously made as a foreign subject against that background' (Schallert 1939: A14). Here, the Swedish film is labelled 'foreign', while Bergman has been 'imported', thus being neither fully American nor Swedish. The review in *Variety* is more detailed regarding the provenance of both the film and its star, stating: '"Intermezzo" is an American remake of a picture turned out three years ago in Sweden . . . with Ingrid Bergman in the femme lead. When David Selznick tabbed Miss Bergman as starring material, he purchased the film rights for a remake, and signed her for her original role' ('Intermezzo' 1939: 12). This passage is interesting for a number of reasons, not the least of which being that it details the legal and financial process by which (official) transnational remakes become possible. While many film scholars might agree that such industrial, contextual information should inform our understanding of relations between the two films, one must wonder how this information would have influenced the typical *Variety* reader of 1939. More importantly, this passage implies that Selznick's primary interest was Bergman and that he remade *Intermezzo* because of her association with it. This star, in this account, provided the mechanism for the generation of a transnational remake.

Of course, not every transnational remake features a star from outside the USA. But the two examples discussed above indicate that some journalistic film reviews treat a film's performer as more important that its source material, and that such reviews confront the transnational mobility of these figures and, on occasion, of the source material as well. Although these reviews are short and not nearly so conceptually sophisticated or rigorously considered as, say, Daisuke Miyao's book-length analysis of Sessue Hayakawa (2007) or any of the essays in the collection *Transnational Stardom: International Celebrity in Film and Popular Culture* (Meeuf and Raphael 2013), they should indicate to scholars working on transnational remakes that stardom is an important, perhaps unavoidable unit of analysis for understanding transnational cinema in general. Given that so many stars have worked in different national contexts, and given the incalculable number of star images that circulate across the world, we would do well to engage more fully with stardom as an element of our analyses of transnational remakes.

Auteurs

In addition to stars, many American reviews of transnational remakes frequently and pointedly discuss the directors of these films. While this might be expected within auteur-based criticism from the 1960s onward, reviews that contend with the artistic capabilities of a remake's director appear before this time. As is the case with references to movie stars, discussions about a film's director often eclipse any discussion about remakes. And, almost as commonly, references to the qualities of a director's work get intermingled with statements about a film's cultural identity. In this respect, directors appear as another, historically durable discursive unit that significantly bears on the popular discussion of transnational film remakes. Nevertheless, this practice presents a new set of problems, particularly as the neo-romantic belief in the auteur as a visionary and singular artist would appear to conflict with a remake's apparent lack of 'originality'.

To take one example, reviews of *Scarlet Street* (1945), a remake of Jean Renoir's *La Chienne* (1931), typically discussed Fritz Lang's directorial impact on the film, but rarely mentioned the previous film or Renoir. *Variety*, for instance, stated 'Fritz Lang's production and direction ably project the sordid tale' ('Scarlet Street' 1946: 8), and the critic for the *Chicago Daily Tribune* wrote, 'Mr. Lang's direction is skillful, with an eye to interesting photographic detail' (Tinée 1946: 24); neither review mentions *La Chienne*. In his negative review of the film, Bosley Crowther acknowledges that it was based on 'a French original, in which it might well have had a stinging and grisly vitality', while also noting, positively, that 'Lang has directed [the film] for dark moods' (1946: 25). Thus this critic conforms to the trend of praising foreign films over their Hollywood remakes, while also finding it worthwhile to note the artistic accomplishments of the director.

Although none of these reviews mentions that Lang had emigrated from Germany, which would explicitly situate him as a transnational auteur, it was hardly necessary to do so. Many of his German-made films played in the USA and were reviewed in American newspapers and, further, many stories in *Variety* and elsewhere detailed his move to the USA and his incorporation within Hollywood. Some critics – for instance, in reviews of the 1951 remake of *M*, directed by Joseph Losey – did mention Lang's cultural background. One review stated:

> Since producers generally and sometimes justifiably have an antipathy toward 'remakes', Seymour Nebenzal should be accorded a kudo or two at the outset for turning again to 'M', that study in crime and abnormal psychology which director Fritz Lang first fashioned in Germany back in 1932. For Mr. Nebenzal, Joseph Losey, the director, and their cast and scenarists again have done justice to a forbidding theme. ('Remake of "M" Opens at the Globe' 1951: 20)

Here, the producer is positioned as the agent that makes a film possible, while the director is presented as one of the creative agents responsible for the 'theme' of the film. More importantly, both Lang and the previous film are associated with Germany, suggesting that Losey did 'justice' with this remake by overcoming, or at least accommodating, national cultural differences. Moreover, the critic suggests that this particular remake overcomes the problems that remakes generally encounter, owing in part to the gifts of its director.

Another review of the remake – this one by Philip K. Scheuer – was also quick to mention the 'memorable German version, filmed 20 years ago by Fritz Lang', and then differentiates the remake from its predecessor in semi-auteurist terms (1951: B8). Scheuer writes:

The writers and director, Joseph Losey, have devised individual scenes and effects with the camera and sound that that are enormously graphic. Some of these might be described as erotic montages, while the choice of the physical backgrounds like the old Bradbury Building is skillful in the extreme. (1951: B8)

Despite these artistic achievements, Scheuer goes on to complain:

As a remake this shocker suffers its severest dislocation by having its setting, its milieu, uprooted from the decadent German city of the original and planted in an American one . . . For the story, complete with gimmick, while provocative and stirring, is somehow not indigenous to this time and place. (1951: B8)

Here we see a strange contradiction, where Scheuer simultaneously praises the film for artfully relocating itself in a transnational fashion and derides it for this same characteristic. In doing so, Scheuer clearly grapples with the transnational migration of the content to a different geographic and cultural context, even if he appears unable to settle on a judgement about this movement. Lang and his film succeed, at least in part, because they are German and appear as German to American audiences. And although Losey has some talent, the film as a whole cannot fully overcome its cultural baggage.

As these reviews accord a significant degree of a film's quality to its director, they situate the director as the agent responsible for making a remake 'work' transnationally. That is to say, even in cases where the director is not overtly designated as a transnational figure in his (or her) own right, these reviews make the director a figure of transnational mobilisation, if not of transnational mobility. This contrasts with the assimilationist way in which film stars had been discussed in other reviews of transnational remakes, where they were seen as benignly 'imported'. And although the semi-auteurist reviews of transnational remakes are typical in evaluating their quality, which in these cases also means commenting on a director's capabilities, such evaluative commentary appears less important than the fact that the film's director is singled out as being at least as important as the source material. This popular discourse does not lead me to suggest that scholars working on transnational remakes need take up auteurism as a theoretical paradigm. But it might prompt us to examine more fully how auteurs, as both industrial and discursive figures, impact, intersect with, or even eclipse the transnational character of these sorts of remakes. Certainly, the relationship between auteurs and remakes has been theorised previously (for example, Verevis 2006: 58–76), and some scholars have theorised the 'transnational auteur' and characterised various film directors as such (Lee 2008: 203–19; D'Lugo 2012: 27–30). But, given that auteurs remain an important element both in the functioning of the commercial film industry and within popular discourses about film culture, scholars studying transnational remakes might attend more closely to the ways in which auteurs do, or do not, affect the transnationality of remakes.

GENRES

If auteurist-minded reviews of transnational remakes were caught up in evaluating the quality of both the films and the abilities of the director, then it was through a discourse about film genres that mainstream film critics found ways of defining a film that were less judgmental aesthetically, but perhaps more so culturally. Of course, 'genre' is an immensely flexible term, and the discourse around genre that appears in reviews of transnational remakes demonstrates a typical slipperiness. Nevertheless, if film genres are, at least in part, a 'contract' between producers and consumers about how a film ought to be defined or understood (Schatz 1981: 16), and if we take it that film reviews provide an important mechanism by which such generic information gets formulated and relayed (Neale 1990: 48–56), then the discourse on genre in reviews of transnational remakes takes on a particular importance for understanding how these films were or were not conceived as 'transnational'. We see that some film reviews were at least as interested in a film's generic definition as they were in its status as remake, and that many discussions about national or cultural identity were situated in this frame. That is to say, film critics didn't so much designate films as transnational because they were remakes as do so by assigning them a hybrid and culturally mixed generic identity.

American reviews of Akira Kurosawa's films, and of the remakes they inspired, clearly demonstrate this point. Critics largely praised *Seven Samurai* (1954), for instance, when it played in the USA. More importantly in this context, these critics almost universally used a discussion of genre to address its cultural identity; specifically, they all characterised the film as a Japanese version of a Hollywood Western genre film. Thus one review stated '"Seven Samurai" is basically a horse opera in Oriental garb' ('First Japanese Film Spectacle Previewed' 1956: B9), and one of Bosley Crowther's two reviews of the film was entitled 'Eastern Western: Kurosawa's "The Magnificent Seven" Follows Format of Cowboy Films' (1956b: 145). In his other review, Crowther actually predicted the transnational remaking of the film, stating that 'although the occurrence of the crisis is set in the sixteenth century in a village in Japan, it could be transposed without surrendering a basic element to the nineteenth century and a town on our own frontier' (1956a: 45). Similarly, in his review of *Yojimbo* (1961), Crowther referred to the film as an 'Oriental Western' (1962: 34), while the critic for the *New Republic* stated, 'Like Kurosawa's *The Seven Samurai* and *The Hidden Fortress* [1958], *Yojimbo* can be compared with a good Western', and he continued, 'There is a rumor that Hollywood is to re-make it as such' (Kauffman 1962: 27). Likewise, a critic writing for *Variety* stated, 'Against a period Japanese backdrop, the tale nevertheless is a natural for transposition to the Yank Western scene, containing some of the ingredients of "High Noon", "Magnificent Seven" itself a remake of a previous Japanese film, and "The Gunfighter"' (Hawk 1961: 6). Reviews such as these situate *Seven Samurai* and *Yojimbo* as transnational through their likeness to, and hence difference from, a Hollywood genre. Moreover, they wrap their discussions of potential Hollywood remakes into this discussion of genre, as though the genre were the mechanism by which the films might become transnational remakes.

Similar views can be found in some reviews of the remakes of these films. A review of *The Magnificent Seven* (Scheuer 1960), for example, stated: 'Its evolution is unique: Bushido to bushwackers, you might say. For "The Magnificent Seven" is a westernization of "The Seven Samurai", a remarkable Japanese film' (Scheuer 1960: B3). In this review, that which had previously been construed as transnational through its generic association with the Western genre is now characterised as 'Japanese', leading the reviewer to situate the *remake* as transitional through its generic transposition. The case of *A Fistful of Dollars* (1964) is complicated by the fact that, as noted by Verevis, it was not a legal remake (2006: 88–9). Thus the reviews that did not mention *Yojimbo* might have done so because it was not officially credited. Nevertheless, even these reviews firmly placed *A Fistful of Dollars* within the Western genre, and often noted its transnationality, for having been directed by an Italian and having been shot in Spain (Terry 1967: A7). Reviewing it for the *Los Angeles Times*, Scheuer (who like many others was highly critical of the film) went so far as to write:

> the only reason I can imagine your taking it in, or vice versa, is to satisfy a possible hankering to study the evolution of a Yanqui western after it has been processed by an Italian director and three co-producing companies – Jolly Film (Rome), Constantin Film (Munich), Ocean Film (Madrid) – employing a heterogeneous but hardly homogenous 'international' cast. (1967: C11)

Here, along with its portrayal of violence, Scheuer disparages the film owing, it seems, to its transnationality, which he relates directly to the film's genre; he never mentions that it is a remake. Finally, Crowther's review in the *New York Times* called the film a 'European-made, English-dubbed, Mexican-localized Western ... which we understand [is based on] "Yojimbo", a Japanese samurai picture by Akira Kurosawa' (1967: 29). Here, the critic indicates that the film is a cross-cultural adaptation, but only as the last item on a list of multiple factors that make the film transnational, including its culturally altered generic identity.

While we should be wary of the kind of essentialist, even nationalist, cultural labels and associations appearing in these reviews, and should be particularly critical of the problematic Orientalist discourse that occurs in relation to *Seven Samurai* and *Yojimbo*, it is nevertheless noteworthy that these critics relied heavily on genre in characterising the cultural identity of both the source films and the remakes. Jason Mittell has argued that genres operate as 'cultural categories', by which he means that, as a label for texts with certain formal or narrative features, a genre only comes into being through the circulation of that label 'within the cultural spheres of audiences, press accounts, and industrial discourses' (2004: 11). While the cases cited above contribute to such an understanding of genre, they also suggest a different notion of genres as 'cultural categories', where a generic label stands in for, or at least becomes entwined with, an assertion about a film's cultural affiliation, be it national, transnational, or otherwise. Thus, although Verevis has analysed the relationship between remakes and genre (2006: 1–2, 84–5, 105–23), these reviews suggest that, in the specific case of transnational remakes, we might attend even more closely to the ways in which a genre gets associated with a cultural identity and, further, to the ways in which a remake's genre contributes to its transnationality. For, it turns out, the 'transnational film remake' is not itself a genre, at least not within the mainstream American press, where instead these films are defined in terms of their stars, directors, and genres more broadly conceived.

Conclusion

In *Film Remakes*, Verevis has previously noted that reviews of remakes, transnational or otherwise, frequently frame their discussions in terms of stars, auteurs and genres (2006: 145–6). In this respect, some comments in this essay may appear unsurprising, but my main point is this: we ought to take these categories seriously in our scholarly analysis of transnational remakes, particularly if we take it that popular film reviews represent a site where important and legitimate knowledge about the cinema is formulated and circulated. This premise leads me to pose three initial questions that future scholarship about transnational remakes might seek to answer. First, how have particular star identities been affected by or interwoven within the production of transnational remakes? I think immediately of Richard Gere, who has appeared in a remarkable number of Hollywood remakes of foreign films, including *Breathless* (1983), *Sommersby* (1993) and *Hachi: A Dog's Tale* (2012), to name a few. Second, how have certain auteurs intersected with the production of transnational remakes? A systematic study along these lines could begin by looking at directors who remade their own films in different national contexts, such as Alfred Hitchcock and Michael Haneke, as well as directors whose own transnational industrial movement coincided with the production of a transnational remake, such as with Christopher Nolan and Walter Salles. Third, in what cases did transnational remakes clearly align with a particular cinematic genre? Although this last question might appear hopelessly broad, there are clear examples of this relationship, such as the cycles of Hollywood remakes of French comedies and of East Asian horror films, analysis of which might provide graspable insights into the larger issue.

Finally, there is a fourth, less concrete but perhaps more foundational question that occurs to me in light of the analysis above. Namely, if the 'transnational remake' is not a category within journalistic film criticism, then what are the stakes for us, as film and media scholars, in formulating such a designation? Scott MacDonald once wrote, 'the job of academe is, at least in part, to maintain the most sophisticated discourse of and about important cultural developments' (2006: 127), and the scholarly discourse on transnational remakes certainly appears to take this as its objective, and rightly so. But, apparently, invoking this phrase does threaten to separate our academic studies of these films from a more popular and generalised discourse. So, to ask the question again, what are the potential benefits and pitfalls of labelling some films 'transnational remakes'?

As an endeavour, transnational film and media studies does not *simply* seek out and describe 'flows' which, it is asserted, disrupt the nation or nation-state as a force that shapes cinematic production, circulation, exhibition and reception. The greater point of such work, it seems to me, is to situate films and cinemas relationally, across a diverse range of geographies of often-divergent scales. The project aims to demonstrate the complex, often-*unpredictable* meanings, identities and cultural affiliations a film may have as it makes its way, historically, through the world. Finding and analysing transnational flows serves this purpose. In this light, the film reviews discussed above provide a richer and broader sense of the different 'flows' that any particular film, remake or otherwise, may follow or exhibit. Even as they do not actually use the term 'transnational', these reviews indicate the multiple factors that make cinema transnational. From my academic perspective, then, they disrupt the nation as a force that shapes cinema and, moreover, disrupt 'the remake' as the primary way in which these films are transnational in the first place. Which leads me to conclude by saying that, for all that it is clear that 'transnational remakes' constitute an important aspect of transnational cinema, we need to attend always to the multiple ways in which any given remake, like any other film or collection of films, is 'transnational'.

REFERENCES

Arnold, Nathanael (2015), '10 Great Foreign Films Remade Into American Movie Failures', *Cheatsheet.com*, 26 May.

Bailey, Jason (2014), '10 Terrible American Remakes of Great Foreign Films', *Flavorwire.com*, 31 October.

Crowther, Bosley (1946), 'The Screen', *New York Times*, 15 February, p. 25.

Crowther, Bosley (1956a), 'Screen: Japanese Import', *New York Times*, 20 November, p. 45.

Crowther, Bosley (1956b), 'Eastern Western: Kurosawa's "The Magnificent Seven" Follows Format of Cowboy Films', *New York Times*, 25 November, p. 145.

Crowther, Bosley (1962), 'Screen: Oriental Western', *New York Times*, 16 October, p. 34.

Crowther, Bosley (1967), 'Screen: "A Fistful of Dollars" Opens', *New York Times*, 2 February, p. 29.

D'Lugo, Marvin (2012), 'The Politics of the Transnational Auteur', in Jo Labanyi and Tatjana Pavlović (eds), *A Companion to Spanish Cinema*, Malden, MA: Wiley-Blackwell, pp. 27–30.

Ďurovičová, Nataša and Kathleen Newman (eds) (2009), *World Cinemas, Transnational Perspectives*, New York: Routledge.

Ezra, Elizabeth and Terry Rowden (eds) (2006), *Transnational Cinema: The Film Reader*, London and New York: Routledge.

Fine, Marshall (2001), 'Open to Interpretation: Hollywood Versions of Foreign Films Rarely Live Up to the Originals', *Los Angeles Times*, 11 November, p. F16.

'First Japanese Film Spectacle Previewed' (1956), *Los Angeles Times*, 29 June, p. B9.

Hawk (1961), 'Yojimbo (The Bodyguard)', *Variety*, 30 August, p. 6.

Herbert, Daniel (2006), '*Sky*'s the Limit: Transnationality and Identity in *Abre los Ojos* and *Vanilla Sky*', *Film Quarterly*, 60: 1, pp. 28–38.

Higbee, Will and Song Hwee Lim (2010), 'Concepts of Transnational Cinema: Towards a Critical Transnationalism in Film Studies', *Transnational Cinemas*, 1: 1, pp. 7–21.

Higson, Andrew (2000), 'The Limiting Imagination of National Cinema', in *Cinema and Nation*, edited by Mette Hjort and Scott Mackenzie, London: Routledge.

'Intermezzo' (1937), *Variety*, 29 December, p. 19.

'Intermezzo' (1939), *Variety*, 4 October, p. 12.

Kauffman, Stanley (1962), 'An Unemployed Samurai', *The New Republic*, 17 September, pp. 27–8.

Lee, Nikki J. Y. (2008), 'Salute to Mr. Vengeance!: The Making of a Transnational Auteur Park Chan-wook', in Leon Hunt and Leung Wing-Fai (eds), *East Asian Cinemas: Exploring Transnational Connections on Film*, London and New York: I. B. Tauris, pp. 203–19.

Lippit, Akira Mizuta (2012), 'Video Cinema Ether (VCE)', in Ming-Yuen S. Ma and Erika Suderburg (eds), *Resolutions 3: Global Networks of Video*, Minneapolis: University of Minnesota Press, pp. 145–58.

Lumenick, Lou (2010), 'Blood & Gutsy – Terrifying Vampire Gives Pal Courage in Bold Horror Movie Remake', *New York Post*, 1 October, p. 35.

MacDonald, Scott (2006), '16mm: Reports of Its Death are Greatly Exaggerated', *Cinema Journal*, 45: 3, pp. 123–30.

'Mad Love' (1935), *Variety*, 7 August, pp. 20, 62.

'The Magnificent Seven' (1960), *Variety*, 5 October, p. 6.

Mazdon, Lucy (2000), *Encore Hollywood: Remaking French Cinema*, London: British Film Institute.

McCarthy, Gus (1935), 'The Cutting Room', *Motion Picture Herald*, 25 May, pp. 50–1.

Meeuf, Russel and Raphael Raphael (eds) (2013), *Transnational Stardom: International Celebrity in Film and Popular Culture*, New York: Palgrave Macmillan.

Mittell, Jason (2004), *Genre and Television: From Cop Shows to Cartoons in American Culture*, New York: Routledge.

Miyao, Daisuke (2007), *Sessue Hayakawa: Silent Cinema and Transnational Stardom*, Durham, NC and London: Duke University Press.

'*Motion Picture Daily*'s Hollywood Preview' (1935), *Motion Picture Daily*, 29 June, pp. 3–4.

Neale, Steve (1990), 'Questions of Genre', *Screen*, 31: 1, Spring, pp. 45–66.

Nornes, Abé Markus (2013), 'The Creation and Construction of Asian Cinema Redux', *Film History*, 25: 1–2, pp. 175–87.

Nugent, Frank (1937), 'The Screen in Review', *New York Times*, 25 December, p. 10.

'Remake of "M" Opens at the Globe' (1951), *New York Times*, 11 June, p. 20.

Ryan, Danielle (2014), '10 Great Foreign Films with Horrible U.S. Remakes', *Pastemagazine.com*, 24 February.

'Scarlet Street' (1946), *Variety*, 2 January, p. 8.

Schallert, Edwin (1939), 'Ingrid Bergman Hailed as New Film Personality', *Los Angeles Times*, 27 September, p. A14.

Schatz, Thomas (1981), *Hollywood Genres: Formulas, Filmmaking, and the Studio System*, Boston: McGraw-Hill.

Scheuer, Philip K. (1951), '"M" Sordid, Powerful Story of Child Killer', *Los Angeles Times*, 26 October, p. B8.

Scheuer, Philip K. (1936), 'Many Films from Europe Remade Here: Hollywood Versions Usually Inferior, Declare Critics', *Los Angeles Times*, 26 July, p. C1.

Scheuer, Philip K. (1967), 'Sadistic "Fistful of Dollars" Bleeds to Death in Killings', *Los Angeles Times*, 19 January, p. C11.

Scheuer, Philip K. (1960), 'Swords of Bushido Become Guns in "Magnificent Seven"', *Los Angeles Times*, 30 October, p. B3.

Terry, Clifford (1967), 'Movie is a "Fistful" of Vapid Violence', *Chicago Tribune*, 30 January, p. A7.

Tinée, May (1946), *Chicago Daily Tribune*, 9 January, p. 24.

Verevis, Constantine (2006), *Film Remakes*, Edinburgh: Edinburgh University Press.

Williams, Raymond (1989), 'Culture is Ordinary', in Robin Gable (ed.), *Resources of Hope: Culture, Democracy, Socialism*, London: Verso, pp. 3–18.

NOTES ON THE CONTRIBUTORS

Carl R. Burgchardt is a Professor in the Department of Communication Studies at Colorado State University, specialising in the history and analysis of US public address, rhetorical theory and criticism, and film studies. He is the editor of *Readings in Rhetorical Criticism* (four editions), and has published articles and book reviews in *Adaptation, Argumentation & Advocacy, Historical Journal of Film, Radio, and Television, Quarterly Journal of Speech,* and *Western Journal of Communication.*

Kenneth Chan is Associate Professor of English at the University of Northern Colorado. He is the author of *Remade in Hollywood: The Global Chinese Presence in Transnational Cinemas* (2009) and *Yonfan's Bugis Street* (2015).

David Desser is Professor Emeritus of Cinema Studies, University of Illinois. He is the author of *The Samurai Films of Akira Kurosawa* (1983) and *Eros Plus Massacre: An Introduction to the Japanese New Wave Cinema* (1988); the editor of *Ozu's Tokyo Story* (1997); and co-editor of *Reframing Japanese Cinema: Authorship, Genre, History* (1992) and *The Cinema of Hong Kong: History, Arts, Identity* (2002), among others. He is a former editor of *Cinema Journal,* and the co-editor of *The Journal of Japanese and Korean Cinema.*

David Scott Diffrient is William E. Morgan Endowed Chair of Liberal Arts and Associate Professor of Film and Media Studies in the Department of

Communication Studies at Colorado State University. His articles have been published in such journals as *Cinema Journal, Historical Journal of Film, Radio, and Television, Journal of Film and Video, Journal of Popular Film and Television, Post Script, Transnational Cinemas*, and *Velvet Light Trap*, as well as in edited collections about film and television topics. His books include *Omnibus Films: Theorizing Transauthorial Cinema* (2014) and *Movie Migrations: Transnational Genre Flows and South Korean Cinema* (2015). He is the co-editor of *Journal of Japanese and Korean Cinema*.

Daniel Herbert is an Associate Professor in Screen Arts and Cultures at the University of Michigan. He is author of *Videoland: Movie Culture at the American Video Store* (2014). His essays appear in *Canadian Journal of Film Studies, Creative Industries Journal, Film Quarterly, Flow, Media Industries, Millennium Film Journal*, and *Quarterly Review of Film and Video*, as well as in several edited collections.

Michael Lawrence is Senior Lecturer in Film Studies at the University of Sussex. He is the author of *Sabu* (2014) and the editor of *Indian Film Stars* (2016). He is the editor, with Laura McMahon, of *Animal Life and the Moving Image* (2015) and, with Karen Lury, of *The Zoo and Screen Media: Images of Exhibition and Encounter* (2016). His articles have appeared in *Screen, Adaptation* and *British Journal of Film and Television*. He is currently working on a study of transnational adaptations and remakes in popular Hindi cinema.

Kathleen Loock is a post-doc. member of the Popular Seriality Research Unit at Freie Universität Berlin. She is author of *Kolumbus in den USA: Vom Nationalhelden zur ethnischen Identifikationsfigur* (2014), co-editor of *Film Remakes, Adaptations, and Fan Productions: Remake | Remodel* (2012) and *Of Body Snatchers and Cyberpunks: Student Essays on American Science Fiction Film* (2011), and editor of a special issue on serial narratives for *LWU: Literatur in Wissenschaft und Unterricht* (2014). She is currently writing a cultural history of Hollywood remaking and preparing, with Frank Krutnik, a special issue on film seriality for the journal *Film Studies* (2017).

Daniel Martin is Associate Professor of Film Studies in the School of Humanities and Social Sciences at the Korea Advanced Institute of Science and Technology (KAIST). His recent research concerns the international circulation of films from South Korea, Japan and Hong Kong. He is the author of *Extreme Asia: The Rise of Cult Cinema from the Far East* (Edinburgh University Press, 2015) and co-editor of *Korean Horror Cinema* (Edinburgh University Press, 2013), and has published articles in *Cinema Journal, The Journal of Film and*

Video, *Continuum*, *Film International*, *Acta Koreana*, *Asian Cinema*, and *The Journal of Korean Studies*.

Lucy Mazdon is Chair in Film Studies at the University of Southampton. She is the author of numerous works on film and television, including *Encore Hollywood: Remaking French Cinema* (2000) and *France on Film: Popular French Cinema* (2001). With Catherine Wheatley she co-edited *Je t'aime, Moi non plus: Franco-British Cinematic Relations* (2010) and co-authored *French Film in Britain: Sex, Art and Cinephilia* (2013).

R. Barton Palmer is the Calhoun Lemon Professor of Literature at Clemson University, where he also directs the World Cinema programme. He is the author, editor, or general editor of more than seven books dealing with various literary and cinematic subjects. His latest monograph is *Shot on Location: Postwar Hollywood and the Exploration of Real Place*, and recent edited collections include: (with Murray Pomerance) *Thinking in the Dark: Cinema, Theory, Practice* (2015); and (with Amanda Ann Klein) *Cycles, Sequels, Spin-Offs, Remakes, and Reboots: Multiplicities in Film and Television* (2016).

Rashna Wadia Richards is Associate Professor and T. K. Young Chair of English at Rhodes College. She is the author of *Cinematic Flashes: Cinephilia and Classical Hollywood* (2013) and co-editor of the collection *For the Love of Cinema: Teaching Our Passion In and Outside the Classroom* (forthcoming).

Iain Robert Smith is Lecturer in Film Studies at King's College London. He is author of *The Hollywood Meme: Transnational Adaptations in World Cinema* (Edinburgh University Press, 2016) and co-editor of *Media Across Borders* (2016). He is co-chair of the SCMS Transnational Cinemas Scholarly Interest Group and co-investigator on the AHRC-funded research network Media Across Borders.

Constantine Verevis is Associate Professor in Film and Screen Studies at Monash University, Melbourne. He is author of *Film Remakes* (Edinburgh University Press, 2006) and co-author of *Australian Film Theory and Criticism, Vol. I: Critical Positions* (2013). His co-edited volumes include: *Second Takes: Critical Approaches to the Film Sequel* (2010), *Film Trilogies: New Critical Approaches* (2012), *Film Remakes, Adaptations and Fan Productions: Remake/Remodel* (2012), *B Is for Bad Cinema: Aesthetics, Politics and Cultural Value* (2014), *US Independent Film After 1989: Possible Films* (Edinburgh University Press, 2015), and *Transnational Television Remakes* (2016).

Andy Willis is a Reader in Film Studies at the University of Salford and Senior Visiting Curator: Film at HOME. He is the co-author of *The Cinema of Alex de la Iglesia* (2007), the editor of *Film Stars: Hollywood and Beyond* (2004), and the co-editor of *Defining Cult Movies: The Cultural Politics of Oppositional Taste* (2003), *Spanish Popular Cinema* (2004), *East Asian Film Stars* (2014), and *Chinese Cinemas, International Perspectives* (2016).

INDEX

References to notes are indicated by n; references to images are in italics.